Your
CREAT*i*VE
BRA*i*N

Seven Steps to Maximize Imagination,
Productivity, and Innovation in Your Life

Shelley Carson, PhD

Harvard Health Publications
HARVARD MEDICAL SCHOOL
Trusted advice for a healthier life

JOSSEY-BASS
A Wiley Imprint
www.josseybass.com

Published by Jossey-Bass
A Wiley Imprint
989 Market Street, San Francisco, CA 94103-1741—www.josseybass.com

Jossey-Bass books and products are available through most bookstores. To contact Jossey-Bass directly call our Customer Care Department within the U.S. at 800-956-7739, outside the U.S. at 317-572-3986, or fax 317-572-4002.

Jossey-Bass also publishes its books in a variety of electronic formats. Some content that appears in print may not be available in electronic books.

Library of Congress Cataloging-in-Publication Data

Carson, Shelley, date
  Your creative brain: seven steps to maximize imagination, productivity, and innovation in your life / Shelley Carson.
      p. cm.
  Includes bibliographical references and index.
  ISBN 978-0-470-54763-2 (hardback); ISBN 978-0-470-65103-2 (ebk);
  ISBN 978-0-470-65142-1 (ebk); ISBN 978-0-470-65143-8 (ebk)
 1. Creative ability. 2. Cognition. 3. Brain. I. Title.
  BF408.C216 2010
  153.3'5—dc22
                                                            2010018175

Printed in the United States of America
FIRST EDITION
HB Printing   10 9 8 7 6 5 4 3 2 1

✴ CONTENTS

iii

✳ PART 3
Putting the CREATES Strategies to Work   257

To Stevie and Nacie—
the creative bookends of my life

✳ PREFACE

This book begins in a small lab room in William James Hall. It is a late fall afternoon, and the shadows are growing long as Professor Bill Milberg removes the specimen from a formalin-filled Tupperware container. As usual, the source of this coveted specimen remains shrouded in mystery, leading to wild speculation among the doctoral students about how Milberg obtained it. He places it in my gloved hands, and I am suddenly transfixed. It is an almost mystical experience. What I am holding is an individual's universe—the sum of one man's knowledge, his dreams, his favorite songs, his memories. I am holding a human brain.

The enormity of the power of this object threatens to overwhelm me (or maybe it is the formalin fumes?) and I think: *How is it possible that the concepts for skyscrapers, interstate highway systems, orchestral symphonies, great works of literature and art, rockets that will take us to the moon and beyond, as well as acts of intense greed and cruelty all have their beginnings in an object similar to the three-pound universe within my hands? How bold—and how creative—is the human brain! How is it possible that the brain, small enough to fit within my curved hands, can conceive and manifest all our human-made marvels? I suddenly* realize that to attempt to answer this question will be an insatiable driving force in my professional life.

Fast-forward to 2010. By now, I've had the privilege of meeting hundreds of creative brains—housed within the skulls of the unique individuals who have taken part in my studies, enrolled in my creativity courses, and consulted me to help them in their creative professions. Many of these individuals have been instrumental in talking me into writing this book. Let me briefly introduce you to three of those creative people.

Corey was a student in my creativity course a few years ago. When it came time to engage in some of the creativity tests we conduct in the class, he declined. He told me that he wasn't creative himself but was only taking the course because his girlfriend was an artist and he wanted to understand her better. (Corey, you get kudos for wanting to understand your girlfriend but you still have to take the tests!) Of course, it turns out that Corey was creative after all; but his pathway to innovative output was different from that of his girlfriend, and he needed to understand how to access his own unique pathway.

Jenna is an interior designer who almost lost the career she loved because she was having trouble coming up with new ideas. Every time she had an idea about a new design, she immediately rejected it because it didn't conform to the outdated standards she had learned in design school decades ago. She contacted me because she was afraid to let herself think innovative thoughts that weren't "tried and true." Jenna needed to get out of the *evaluation* mode before she could take advantage of her innate ability to generate new ideas.

Richard, an independent film producer and director who contacted me for help, had just the opposite problem. Unlike Jenna, he couldn't *stop* his innovative thoughts, and as a result, his latest film was in crisis. Each night he came up with original ideas for plot changes, character nuances, set design changes, and new ways to depict the deep themes within his movie. The next day, he'd stop production to go over these exciting modifications with the cast and crew. Eventually, most of the cast left the project, fed up with the constant changes and delays, and Richard was left with nothing but the great visions in his mind to show for all his time. Richard had to learn how to stop *generating* ideas and focus on the work of *implementing* them.

Perhaps like Corey, you feel that there are creative people and there are uncreative people (and you have placed yourself in the latter category). Perhaps like Jenna, you sense that creative ideas are out there ready to be discovered, but you're afraid to let go of the "safe" mental space that's bounded by what is "tried and true." Or perhaps like Richard, you're full of creative ideas but unable to stop generating them long enough to bring any one idea to fruition. If you identify with any of these, you'll find that I wrote this book for you!

Here is something I've learned in the years of study and experimentation since my first encounter with the human brain in Bill Milberg's class. The differences between the brains of highly effective creative achievers and the brains of the rest of us are far less important than the commonalities. There are certainly genetic differences that influence creativity, and of course, there will always be people who are more creative than others. However, through the study of highly creative brains, we've found that *all* of us have creative brains. We are all—barring serious brain injury—equipped with basically the same brain structures. It is the way we *activate* these structures (our brain activation patterns) and the way we form connections between these structures that appear to affect our ability to think creatively. The exciting part is that new findings indicate we can manipulate these brain activation patterns—and we can form new connections within the brain—with training; in short, we can learn to activate our brains in similar patterns to those of highly creative individuals.

In this book I present a model that describes seven different brain activation patterns. I call this the CREATES brainsets model. It is based on neural activation correlates of what I believe to be the most salient mental aspects of human creativity. These include: openness and cognitive flexibility, mental imagery, divergent or associative thinking, convergent or deliberate thinking, judgmentalism, self-expression, and improvisation or flow. In my model, these aspects of creativity are conceived as *states* (or transient mental activation patterns) rather than as *traits*. Some of these states facilitate the generation of creative ideas, while some of them facilitate the implementation of ideas. The trick is to know which is which and how to get from one to another. That's what this book is about.

Clearly all of these states of creativity have their own underlying brain mechanisms; hence some of the confusion in the research literature about how creativity actually plays out in the human brain. It is my contention that you can enhance your creative output by: (1) understanding which of these various states related to creativity you prefer—I call this preference your "mental comfort zone"—and (2) gradually venturing out from your comfort zone to explore different aspects of creativity by learning to modify your brain activation state.

Although the CREATES model is just that—a model and not proven scientific fact—it is based on the latest neuroscience and research in the field of creative thinking, and the training aspects of the model are based on established psychological methods of behavioral change. Each of the seven brain states described in the CREATES model is accompanied by a set of exercises to help you enter that state. Like most such exercises, these have not been studied in rigorous trials to prove their efficacy, but they've produced positive results for the Coreys, Jennas, and Richards with whom I've had the pleasure of working. I urge you to sample a wide variety of the exercises and decide for yourself which are most effective for you.

My hope is that the contents of this book will aid and inspire you to take your innate creative abilities to the next level. And I invite you to let me know about your results! You can contact me—and explore the additional reader-only content and interactive tools—at http://ShelleyCarson.com. I challenge you now to read further, and then to discover, to perform, to produce, to invent, or to express—in short, to take advantage of—the unique and precious resources that dwell within YOUR CREATIVE BRAIN.

✳ ACKNOWLEDGMENTS

Your Creative Brain is truly the product of many creative brains, most prominently that of wonder woman Julie Silver, my editor at Harvard Health Publications. This book would not exist without her vision, expertise, enthusiasm, and encouragement. It's hard to believe one person can wear so many hats and be so good at them all! Thanks for your guidance and creativity, Dr. Julie! Along with Julie, I'd like to thank Tony Komaroff at HHP, as well as those who provided insightful blind reviews. Speaking of reviewers, I owe a debt of gratitude to mentor and colleague Ellen Langer for her helpful editorial comments.

This book also owes its existence to my literary agent, Linda Konner, who insisted that I write a book and who knew this book would be written before I knew myself. Thanks, Linda—I hope this is the first of many! Thanks also to Betty Anne Crawford, who took my manuscript to the world.

To Alan Rinzler, my editor at Jossey-Bass, thanks for believing in this book and for making the process so easy for me! Thank you also to Nana Twumasi, Susan Geraghty, Donna Cohn, and all the folks at Jossey-Bass and Wiley who helped in the production of this book. And to Richard Sheppard, thank you for your artistic additions!

My lovely daughter, Nacie, who is a writer extraordinaire in her own right, was instrumental in helping me shape academic content into readable prose. Thank you for helping me with the vision and the revision of this work! You are my source of inspiration, and it was so fun to share the process of writing this book with you.

I'd like to thank three scholars who have been instrumental in my career: Jordan Peterson, now at the University of Toronto, who has been my mentor and is now my colleague, friend, and constant wellspring of creative research ideas; Richard McNally, who took me into his lab when I was an orphan grad student and has continued to amaze and inspire me to this day; and Jill Hooley, who first encouraged me to explore the topic of creativity as a worthy academic endeavor.

I want to thank all of the students who have taken my creativity courses over the years and have contributed as much to my knowledge of the subject as I (hopefully) have to theirs. To the many artists, writers, musicians, and film directors and producers who have consulted me concerning their creative difficulties (and triumphs!), please know that you have contributed so much to my knowledge of the creative process (and please don't be upset if you see yourself—identity changed to protect the innocent, of course—in this book!).

Thanks are also due to the scholars, authors, and friends who took the time to read my manuscript and who contributed valuable commentary, including Stephen Kosslyn, Howard Gardner, Tal Ben-Shahar, Teresa Amabile, Dean Keith Simonton, Harrison Pope, Alice Flaherty, Dan Schacter, Bernard Golden, Diane Terman, and Peter Marc Jacobson.

It's hard to imagine how anyone can write a book without extensive support on the home front. My husband, David, has nurtured me throughout the writing process, providing meals, an occasional glass of wine during my marathon nighttime writing sessions, good advice, and hugs when needed. Love always, honey!

Thanks also to my son, David Jr., who also helped provide food and support while he was home for winter break. I owe you a few home-cooked meals, Son!

Finally, I would like to acknowledge Caveman #2 and indeed all the courageous men and women who, from before the dawn of written history, used their creative brains to pave the way for the incredible wealth of art, music, and scientific advances we enjoy today. They gave us the wheel and tools, harnessed fire, and recorded their experiences on the walls of caves. They travelled from continent to continent without the aid of ships or navigation. They endured enormous hardships yet their spirit of exploration and ingenuity endured and allowed us to be here today. We truly stand on the shoulders of unnamed creative giants!

PART 1

Meet Your Creative Brain

❈ 1

Wanted: Your Creative Brain

YOU ARE IN POSSESSION of one of the world's most powerful supercomputers, one that has virtually unlimited potential not only to change your life, but also to change your world.

This supercomputer has the ability to adapt to ever-changing environments, understand subtle patterns, and make connections between seemingly unrelated things. It can design skyscrapers, cure life-threatening illnesses, and send humans into space.

It can make you successful, rich, happy, and fulfilled . . . and it's located right inside your skull.

The supercomputer I am talking about is your brain, that miracle machine that allows you to do everything from brushing your teeth in the morning to presenting complex facts and figures to your boss in the afternoon.

Think about it: our brains have shepherded us through some pretty amazing evolutionary developments in record time. In the past 10,000 years, we've invented the wheel, built the pyramids in Egypt, discovered penicillin, developed the Internet, and sent devices of our own making beyond the outer regions of our solar system.

To put it into perspective, consider the fact that the turtle has been around for roughly 220 million years and has yet to make an innovative lifestyle improvement.

So what separates us from the turtle? The answer is: our creative brain. Our brain allows us to feel, love, think, be, and, most important, create.

You may think that creativity is a gift only certain types of people possess, like the Einsteins, Mozarts, or Shakespeares of the world. However, the latest neuroscience research suggests that creative mental functioning involves a set of specific brain activation patterns that can be amplified through conscious effort and a little practice. These are skills that anyone can master. By learning how and when to turn the volume up or down in certain parts of the brain, you can develop your creative potential to achieve greater success and life fulfillment.

In the following chapters, you'll learn about seven brain activation patterns—the CREATES brainsets. You'll see how each brainset affects the way you experience the world around you and how each contributes to the process of creative problem solving. Through entertaining exercises, you'll learn to use these brainsets to take advantage of your creative potential and enrich your life and the lives of those around you.

But the purpose of enhancing creativity is not only for enrichment; it's a vital resource for meeting the challenges and dangers, as well as the opportunities, of the accelerated-change climate of the twenty-first century.

The information and technology explosion, along with cyber-communication and globalization, is transforming the way we learn, the way we do business, and the way we form relationships with each other. The rule books for virtually *every* aspect of human endeavor and interaction—from corporate life to personal life to dating and even parenting—are being rewritten right in the middle of the game. So if all the old bets are off, how do you survive and thrive? The most important asset you have for negotiating this rapidly changing world is **your creative brain**.

Your creative brain can lead you to discover a new and better way to manage some aspect of your business. It can help you to express your unique life experience in a way that inspires or educates others. You can use it to ensure that the best traditions of the past get incorporated into the future or to add beauty to your environment. Your creative brain can even reshape your vision of retirement so that you continue to grow and prosper throughout the decades ahead. There is truly no limit to the potential of your creative brain. . . .

Regardless of your mission for the future, it is crucial that you develop your creative capacities. By developing your creative brain, you can not only adapt to the changing world, but you can make a contribution to that change. By developing your creative brain, you will also prime your brain to discover, innovate, and produce your original contribution to what is shaping up to be a twenty-first-century Golden Age.

Before we go further, let's define exactly what we mean by that nebulous term *creativity*. Though philosophers and writers have come up with a number of definitions for *creative,* there are two elements to the definition that virtually all of us who study creativity agree need to be present in the creative idea or product. First, the creative idea or product needs to be *novel* or *original,* and second, it has to be *useful* or *adaptive* to at least a segment of the population.[1] Note, for example, that the scribblings of a toddler who has just learned to hold a crayon are *novel* . . . but, as a product, they are not considered *useful* or *adaptive.*

You can take these elements of novel/original and useful/adaptive and apply them to virtually any aspect of your life to increase your productivity and happiness. You can also apply them to the betterment of your community and to the enrichment of society. When you learn to use your creative brain more efficiently, there is no limit to the innovative ideas, products, and new ways of doing things that you can explore.

Your brain is the repository of a unique store of information: it contains autobiographical, factual, and procedural knowledge that no one else on the planet has access to. When you combine pieces of this knowledge in novel and original ways, and then take the resulting combinations and find applications for them, you are using your creative brain as it was built to be used.

Neuroimaging techniques, such as fMRI (functional magnetic resonance imaging), PET (positron emission tomography), and SPECT (single photon emission computed tomography), have allowed scientists to peek into the brains of highly creative people to see how they unconsciously manipulate their brainsets at various stages of the creative process. For example, different brainsets appear to be activated in highly creative people when they're coming up with new uses for a household item than when they're combining information from a variety of sources to find the solution to a unique problem.[2] The brainsets you'll become familiar with in future chapters reflect what we've learned from those studies. You'll learn:

o   Strategies for accessing brainsets associated with creativity
o   When in the creative process to access each of them
o   And finally, how to switch easily between different brainsets to enhance your productivity and reduce creative "block"

If you're still unsure about how these brainsets can really benefit your life, then you're in good company. Two of the most common questions I hear in my seminars are these: "Isn't creativity mainly for artists, writers, and musicians?" And "What if I'm just not a creative person?" Let's address these questions right now.

"Isn't Creativity Mainly for Artists, Writers, and Musicians?"

It's true that when we think of creative individuals, we tend to think of those with careers in the arts and sciences. We think of those who have brought richness to our lives by painting a Sistine Chapel, revealing human nature through the lines of *Hamlet*, uplifting us with an "Ode to Joy," or illuminating our night hours with the electric light. In fact, most of the formal research that's been conducted on creative individuals has concentrated on achievements in the arts and sciences because it is easy to recognize creative accomplishments in these domains of endeavor. The creative aspects of achievement in business, sports, diplomacy, and real-life problem solving are harder to recognize and quantify, but clearly they are just as important.

If you think creativity is just for artists and scientists, then consider these facts:[3]

- Most Fortune 500 companies and many government agencies have hired a creativity consultant within the past year. Creativity has become an important factor in the survival of businesses.
- The number of business schools offering courses in creativity has doubled in the past five years.
- Former U.K. Prime Minister Gordon Brown acknowledged that creativity and innovation are critical to the future of the U.K. economy.
- Forty-three books and 407,000 Web sites are devoted to creative parenting.
- A number of books discuss the importance of creativity in the field of sports, and the theme of the 2009 worldwide conference of the European Network of Academic Sports was "Creativity and Innovation in University Sport."
- Creative athletes, such as Michael Jordan, Roger Bannister, Bill Russell, and—yes—Tiger Woods, often possess personality traits that are found in highly creative individuals in the arts and sciences.

Let's look at a couple of examples of how creativity can serve you in areas of your life that have nothing to do with art, music, or science.

First, in the domain of business, the economic downturn of the past several years has hit small businesses, large corporations, and individual contractors. If your business is going to fight the uphill battle of survival, you need to find creative ways to cut costs while maintaining quality, provide an innovative product or service rather than the same old product that your competitors are providing, and invent ways to create or maintain market share.

If your business has already succumbed to the economic downturn, you need to be creative in reinventing your professional life, whether it's using skills you already possess to market yourself or developing a new set of skills to enter an entirely new business or profession. Reinventing your professional life takes creativity and courage. But it can be one of the most rewarding enterprises of your life.

Second, in the domain of family you may be one of millions of parents who are faced with the dilemma of how to pass on family values to children who live more harried lives than most adults did just a generation ago. How do you communicate with a child who, despite your best efforts, is wired 24/7 to an iPod, Facebook, IM, and Grand Theft Auto? How do you impart a sense of balance to a child who is constantly bombarded by media that equate self-worth with anorexic thinness, pleasing a man in bed, or having the athletic prowess of a superhero? You *can* do it—but as a parent, you need every ounce of creativity you can muster to compete with electronic gadgets and today's sensationalized media agenda for your child's attention and subsequent welfare.

Speaking of which, how do you keep *yourself* balanced when there are so many demands on your time and personal resources? To maintain your energy—and your sanity—you need to find creative ways to manage your time so that you can juggle the demands of modern existence while still ensuring that your hours and days remain rich and meaningful.

In short, creativity is important for artists, writers, musicians, and inventors; but it is also crucial for societies, businesses, and individuals who need to juggle fulfillment with the demands of the rapid-change culture. You not only need to be creative to enhance your life, you also need to be creative to survive.

"What If I'm Just Not a Creative Person?"

We are all creative. Creativity is the hallmark human capacity that has allowed us to survive thus far. Our brains are wired to be creative, and the only thing stopping you from expressing the creativity that is your birthright is your belief that there are creative people and uncreative people and that you fall in that second category.

Think back to the last conversation in which you participated. Think about what you said. Notice how you pulled selected words representing specific objects, situations, or actions from your memory store and combined them in a novel, never-before-spoken order (unless you work from some sort of talking points sheet) to convey meaning to your listener. The fact is that if you've done nothing but speak in this life, you have demonstrated your creativity over and over again. Each time we speak we put words together in a novel and original way that is useful for our purposes—the essence of creativity!

But of course you do more than speak. You are a creative problem solver. Take a minute to think of the last time you solved a minor problem in your life without an instruction manual. I guarantee you've already done such creative problem solving once or twice just today. How about the last time you used a household item for a purpose other than the one for which you bought it? Examples: using a piece of furniture or a box to hold a door open, using a newspaper to cover your head in a sudden rain shower, or using an empty soup can to water flowers. Finding alternate uses for items is indeed a creative act.

If you've planted a garden, arranged the furniture in your living room or office, deviated from a recipe, driven a new route to the shopping mall, or figured out how to calm a crying child, you've demonstrated your creativity. The truth is that *every day* you perform *hundreds* of creative acts. Take a moment to think of what you did yesterday and count how many acts were unscripted improvisations, how many problems you encountered and solved (including picking out your clothes, deciding what to eat, how to put out work-related or family-related fires); don't compare yourself to others, just think about your own creative acts . . . and revel in the wonder of your creative brain.

Creativity is *not* an elite activity. And it doesn't matter if you don't gravitate toward traditionally creative professions or activities; you can bring creativity to any endeavor and make it more successful. You *are* creative!

Here's one final incentive to exercise your creative brain: being creative makes you more attractive to the opposite sex (really).

According to evolutionary psychologist Geoffrey Miller, individuals who can use their creative talents successfully to form new adaptive ways of doing things are more likely to survive. As such, creativity is a "fitness indicator" and will, therefore, be attractive to potential sexual mates. Miller suggests that certain human-specific creative endeavors, such as music production, artistic creations, and humor, may have evolved partially to advertise creative fitness to potential mates similar to the way that the peacocks evolved elaborate tail displays or that bowerbirds build colorful nests.[4]

Intuitively, it does seem that we find individuals who sing, write novels or poetry, or who create art or build inventions to be sexually attractive (how else do you explain the female attraction to Mick Jagger?). This intuition is actually backed up with some empirical evidence. Evolutionary psychologists David Buss and Michael Barnes studied mate selection preferences in both married couples and unmarried college undergrads.[5] For the married couples, *artistic-intelligent* was the third most sought-after trait in a long-term mate (after *kind* and *socially exciting*). For both male and female undergraduates, creativity ranked in the top 10 desirable characteristics for a long-term mate (less important than *physically attractive* but more important than *good earning capacity*).

So far, here's what we've established:

o   Using your creative brain is crucial for adapting to the fast-changing climate of the twenty-first century.

o   Creativity is not just for artists, poets, and musicians.

    °   *You* are creative.

    °   Creative behavior is sexy.

In the next chapter, you'll be introduced to the CREATES brain-sets, and you'll take a fun quiz to determine which brainset defines your personal Mental Comfort Zone. Your creative brain has the capacity to make you successful, however you gauge success. By using the brainsets in the following chapters, you'll optimize this capacity.

※ 2

Your Mental Comfort Zone

SCENARIO: YOU'VE BEEN CHARGED with coming up with a theme for a fund-raising event for your community organization. Take a moment to determine which of the following strategies will be most helpful for you as you choose an appropriate yet compelling and novel theme:

a. You scan newspapers and magazines for events to determine which themes have been used by other organizations.

b. You think of the qualities and characteristics of your organization and consciously, through trial and error, focus in turn on how each of those qualities might be used in a theme.

c. You absorb information about local events, you go to a party store and look around, you look through some historical documents about your organization; then you let all of that information congeal in your brain while you think about what you want for dinner.

d. You send out a message asking for ideas from your colleagues, and then you judge each of the ideas that are submitted.

e.   You pick a common theme and then allow your mind to dance with the idea as you come up with ways to enhance, change, and embellish the common theme.

Which did you choose?   a   b   c   d   e

The truth is that any one of those strategies may lead you to pick an adequate theme for your fund-raiser. But if you could use all those strategies effectively . . . and use them in the right order . . . your chances of coming up with a great theme that will make your fund-raiser a unique experience are multiplied exponentially!

You can use your creative brain to generate and execute creative ideas in any area of your life, whether it involves your business, social, personal, family, or artistic activities. Whether your task is to write a symphony, find ways to bring in new clients to your firm, or rearrange the living room furniture, you will be more successful if you take advantage of the best "state of brain" for the task.

In order to identify such brain states, I've combined findings from neuroimaging studies, brain injury cases, neuropsychological investigations, interviews with hundreds of creative achievers, extensive testing of additional hundreds of individuals in my research at Harvard, and information from the biographies of the world's most prominent creative luminaries. The result is the CREATES brainsets model, a set of seven brain activation states (or "brainsets") that have relevance to the creative process. I've dubbed them "brainsets" because these brain activation patterns are the biological equivalents of "mindsets"; just as your *mindset* determines your mental attitude and interpretation of events, your *brainset* influences how you think, approach problems, and perceive the world.

The CREATES model for improving creativity and productivity is based on three findings that have substantial scientific support:

○   First, creatively productive individuals are able to access specific brain states that others may find more difficult or more uncomfortable to access (note that this ability to access brain states may be due to genetic or environmental factors or a combination of both).

○ Second, creatively productive individuals are able to switch among different brainsets depending upon the task at hand.

○ Third, it is possible to train yourself to access these creative brainsets and to switch flexibly among them, even if this does not come naturally to you at first.[1]

As you read about the brainsets in the CREATES model, you'll notice that there is a certain amount of overlap in both brain activation and brain function among them; they are not wholly discrete states. This is because most parts of the brain perform several different functions depending upon which other parts of the brain are simultaneously activated or deactivated. The interactions and interconnections among brain structures are enormously complex (as we would expect in an organ that has conceived such diverse concepts as the CERN particle accelerator and the *American Idol* reality show). We are only beginning to fully understand this complexity.

I don't want to mislead you into thinking that the CREATES model—or the neuroscience research presented in this book—is the final answer in the description of the creative brain. The CREATES brainsets are hypothetical constructs based on our current knowledge of human psychology and how the brain works. As our knowledge of the wonderful human brain expands, so will our understanding of the CREATES model. This current set of brain activation patterns will no doubt be amended, and additional brainsets that can benefit us in our creative endeavors will be described. We will also find more efficient methods of accessing these brainsets. With these caveats in mind, let's take a brief look at the brainsets that comprise the CREATES model:

Connect
Reason
Envision
Absorb
Transform
Evaluate
Stream

The *Connect* Brainset

When you access the *connect* brainset, you enter a defocused state of attention that allows you to see the connections between objects or concepts that are quite disparate in nature. You are able to generate multiple solutions to a given problem rather than focusing on a single solution. The ability to generate multiple solutions is combined with an upswing in positive emotion that also provides incentive and motivation to keep you interested in your creative project. I've based the *connect* brainset on research that examines a type of cognition called *divergent thinking*, as well as on research into how we make mental associations, and a condition known as synaesthesia. You'll learn about divergent thinking, synaesthesia, and the *connect* brainset in Chapter Seven.

The *Reason* Brainset

When you access the *reason* brainset, you consciously manipulate information in your working memory to solve a problem. This is the state of purposeful planning that comprises much of our daily consciously directed mental activity. When you say that you're "thinking" about something, you are generally referring to this brainset. The *reason* brainset is derived from neuroimaging research that has examined consciously directed aspects of cognition, including establishing goals, abstract reasoning, and decision making. You'll learn about these aspects of cognition, which are sometimes referred to as "executive functions," and the *reason* brainset in Chapter Eight.

The *Envision* Brainset

When you access the *envision* brainset, you think visually rather than verbally. You are able to see and manipulate objects in your mind's eye. You see patterns emerge. In this brainset you tend to think metaphorically as you "see" the similarities between disparate concepts. This is the brainset of imagination. I've based the *envision* brainset primarily on research that examines mental imagery and imagination. You'll learn about mental imagery, visualization, imagination, and the *envision* brainset in Chapter Six.

The *Absorb* Brainset

When you access the *absorb* brainset, you open your mind to new experiences and ideas. You uncritically view your world and take in knowledge. Everything fascinates you and attracts your attention. This state is helpful during the knowledge-gathering and incubation stages of the creative process (you'll learn more about the creative process in Chapter Four). The *absorb* brainset is based primarily on research that examines mindfulness, the personality trait of openness to experience, and investigations into how we respond to unusual or novel events. You'll learn about openness, novelty, and the *absorb* brainset in Chapter Five.

The *Transform* Brainset

When you access the *transform* brainset, you find yourself in a self-conscious and dissatisfied—or even distressed—state of mind. You can use this state to *transform* negative energy into works of art and great performances. In this state you are painfully vulnerable; but you are also motivated to express (in creative form) the pain, the anxieties, and the hopes that we all share as part of the human experience. I've based the *transform* brainset on research that examines the relationship between mood and creativity. Historians, biographers, and scientists have long noted an association between creativity and certain types of mental illness, such as depression. Does such an association exist? You'll learn about this relationship and the·*transform* brainset in Chapter Ten.

The *Evaluate* Brainset

When you access the *evaluate* brainset, you consciously judge the value of ideas, concepts, products, behaviors, or individuals.

This is the "critical eye" of mental activity. This brainset allows you to evaluate your creative ideas and products to ensure that they meet your criteria for usefulness and appropriateness. The construction of the *evaluate* brainset stems from research conducted on how we make judgments and eliminate options. The neural architecture that allows us to make rapid and accurate judgments appears to be dependent not only on turning up the activation in certain parts of the brain, but also on turning *down* the activation in other parts. You'll learn about judgments and the *evaluate* brainset in Chapter Nine.

The *Stream* Brainset

When you access the *stream* brainset, your thoughts and actions begin to flow in a steady harmonious sequence, almost as if they were orchestrated by outside forces. The *stream* brainset is associated with the production of creative material, such as jazz improvisation, narrative writing (as in novels or short stories), sculpting or painting, and the step-by-step revelation of scientific discovery. This state is important in the elaboration stage of the creative process. The *stream* brainset comes from research conducted on improvisation in music, theater, and speech, and on a mental state described by psychologist Mihaly Csikszentmihalyi as *flow*.[2] This state has also been called being "in the zone" or "in the groove." You'll learn about improvisation, flow, and the *stream* brainset in Chapter Eleven.

You will likely find that some brainsets feel more comfortable to you than others. These brainsets comprise your mental comfort zone, and you need to identify them before you can expand your creative horizons. You can get an idea of your personal mental comfort zone by completing the questions and exercises on the following pages. This is not a scientifically validated test, and there are no right or wrong answers; rather, the questions and exercises are indicators of your personal preference.

Which Brainset Do You Prefer?

Cluster One Questions are multiple choice. You can complete them in only a few minutes to get an idea of your preferred brainset. **Cluster Two Questions** are "hands-on" exercises that will take longer but will give you a richer understanding of your mental comfort zone. Again, the test is not scientifically validated; however, the individual questions and exercises have been based on findings from the areas of research that form the basis of each of the seven brainsets. The students and creative groups that I work with have found this assessment to be informative as well as fun. You will find the material in Part Two of this book more personally relevant if you have an idea of your own mental comfort zone. You can choose to do Cluster One now and save Cluster Two for later or you can complete both at the same time.

Cluster One Questions

Please circle the answer that applies to you most of the time. Remember that there are no wrong answers.

1. When you read a magazine article, do you tend to skim the article looking for the main points or do you tend to read the article from the beginning word for word?

   a. skim   b. word for word

2. When someone proposes a new project, are you able to immediately see what might go wrong?

   a. yes   b. no

3. Do you tend to prefer to multitask or do you tend to work on one project at a time?

   a. multitask   b. one project at a time

4. Do you have a good sense of time or do you find that you often lose track of time?

   a. good sense of time   b. often lose track of time

5. Is it easy for you to think up new ideas?

   a. yes   b. no

6. Are you particularly good at spelling?

   a. yes   b. no

7. Do you find it hard to get hooked into the story of a movie or novel?

   a. yes   b. no

8. Do you often have vivid dreams?

   a. yes   b. no

9. Are you good at solving crossword puzzles?

   a. yes   b. no

10. Do you consider the following statement to be true or false: "Everything is connected to everything else."

    a. true   b. false

11. When you go on vacation, do you prefer to have a set itinerary or do you prefer to have a freeform vacation?

    a. set itinerary   b. freeform

12. Do you prefer to eat dinner at the same time each night or do you prefer to eat whenever you get hungry?

    a. set time   b. when I get hungry

13. When deciding how to get from point A to point B, do you prefer to have written or verbal instructions, or do you prefer to look at a map?

   a. written instructions   b. map

14. Do you believe you may be psychic?

   a. yes   b. no

15. Do you tend to think more in pictures or in words?

   a. pictures   b. words

16. Point A is your starting point and Point B is your destination. Which of the two paths below reflects your preferred journey?

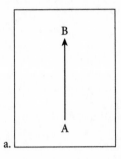 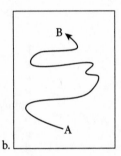

   a. path a   b. path b

17. Do you think you would make a good movie critic?

   a. yes   b. no

18. How do you typically respond if someone criticizes one of your ideas?

   a. try to get something constructive out of the criticism that can help you

   b. become irritated with the critic

   c. feel humiliated and shamed

19. Do you tend to spend a lot of time daydreaming?

    a. yes   b. no

20. When you walk into a room, can you quickly notice if something is out of place?

    a. yes   b. no

21. Do you enjoy cleaning out your car, or do you find it to be a necessary chore?

    a. enjoy   b. chore

22. Does it feel like others just don't move fast enough for you?

    a. yes   b. no

```
    P            P
    P            P
    P            P
    P            P
    PPPPPPPPPP
    P            P
    P            P
    P            P
    P            P
```

23. When you looked at the above diagram, which letter did you notice first?

    a. P   b. H

24. You've consented to host a fundraiser for a local charity at your home. Which of the tasks below describes the part you would like to play in this event?

    a. I have a vision for the theme of this event, and I'd like to tell others my vision and let them handle the details.

    b. I'd like to be directly involved in details such as planning the menu, the decorations, the entertainment, and the publicity.

   c. I'd like to be involved in as few details as possible. Just tell me when to show up for the party.

   d. I only consented to be the host because I felt guilty about not doing enough for my community.

25. Do you have days where you just don't want to get out of bed?

   a. yes   b. not really

26. Do you get excited to start a new project but have trouble finishing it?

   a. yes   b. no

27. Do you have trouble filtering out distracting noises?

   a. yes   b. no

28. Would others describe you as a "go-getter"?

   a. yes   b. no

29. Do you often have periods where ideas chase each other in your head so fast you can hardly keep track of them?

   a. occasionally   b. often   c. never

30. Do you often go on spending sprees?

   a. occasionally   b. often   c. never

31. Which of the following best describes how you would like to spend an evening with a friend?

   a. go to a movie and dinner

   b. go someplace quiet to talk about your problems

32. Do you think other people would consider you to be upbeat or sort of a drag?

   a. upbeat   b. a drag

The scoresheet for the Cluster One Questions is located in Appendix One. You can either fill out the scoresheet now or complete the Cluster Two Exercises beginning on the next page.

Cluster Two Exercises

The **Cluster One Questions** make up a "self-report" assessment. That is, the responses are based on the responder's *opinion* of the appropriate answer. Even though people try to be honest, their answers to self-report questions can still be biased. For instance, they may unconsciously select the answer they think is most socially desirable. Or, if they don't like the assessment, they may unconsciously try to sabotage the results.

Researchers, therefore, try to give additional assessments that measure behavior rather than personal opinion when possible. That's why the Cluster Two Questions are included (besides, they're fun!). Though the Cluster Two exercises as a whole have not been empirically validated, each of the exercises has been used separately to evaluate some aspect of psychological or brain functioning related to the seven brainsets. The best evaluation of your mental comfort zone will come from combining the results of both the Cluster One Questions and the Cluster Two Exercises.

For this part of the assessment you will need a stopwatch or timer, several pieces of blank paper, a pen or pencil, a ruler with metric measurements, and about 25 minutes of uninterrupted time. Before you begin, cut a blank piece of paper to the size of this page. Do not look at the exercises until you're ready to begin.

EXERCISE #1

Read these directions and then set the timer for three minutes. Find and count all the words in the passage on the next page that have both the letter s *and the letter* t *in the same word. The letters do not need to be next to each other. When your timer goes off, stop reading and record the number of words you found that contained both* s *and* t.

Much of the work your brain completes is done below the level of your conscious awareness. You don't even know it's happening . . . and it's amazing stuff. Neuroscientists refer to this unconscious brain work as *implicit* processing. Since much of the process of creativity is implicit, it's important that you know and trust what's going on in there.

Let's take a very simplified look at implicit processing. For example, what processes occur when you recognize a familiar face? First, you take in information through your eyes. Now your eyes don't "recognize" a face—they just pass on information coming in from the environment about color, shape, and movement. Color, shape, and movement are all processed by different parts of the vision system located in the back of the brain (in the occipital lobes). Once each of these streams of information has been processed, they are assembled in an association area of the occipital lobes. If the assembled picture looks like a face, this information is then delivered to a brain structure deep in the temporal lobe called the fusiform gyrus, where it is checked against patterns of familiar faces. Simultaneously, the information is sent to other parts of the limbic system (located primarily in those subcortical structures deep inside the temporal lobe) that determine whether the face is friend or foe. In other words, should you approach or run from this face? And still other parts of the brain associate the face with additional visual and sound information (such as posture, the way the person walks, the sound of her voice), as well as with other information known about this person. Only then does the lightbulb of recognition illuminate, and you realize *Hey, that person in the produce aisle is my old high school teacher!*

1. Number of words you found that contained both *s* and *t*:

   _____

2. Did you finish the passage in the allotted time?

   a. yes   b. no

3. Did you find that you read the content of the passage, or were you able to concentrate on finding the letters *s* and *t*?

   a. read the content   b. concentrated on the letters

4. Without looking back, what part of the brain recognizes familiar faces?

   a. amygdala   b. hippocampus   c. fusiform gyrus

EXERCISE #2   PART 1

Set your timer for thirty seconds. Now, look carefully at the dot on the opposite page until the timer goes off. Then turn the page and proceed to Exercise #3.

EXERCISE #3

Read these directions and then set the timer for three minutes.

Your friend Ron sits at the desk in the cubicle next to you. Ron really likes to talk to you and often bothers you while you're phoning clients, and many times you don't finish your work because he is bothering you.

Think of as many ways as you can to solve this problem and write them on a blank sheet of paper. Stop writing when the timer goes off.

EXERCISE #4

Time how long it takes you to complete the following exercise in your head (don't write anything on paper while you're trying to solve it). There is no time limit.

Find a common English three-letter word, knowing that

- L O G has no common letter with it.
- T O G has one common letter, not at the correct place.
- S I T has one common letter, at the correct place.
- GOB has one common letter, not at the correct place.
- A I L has one common letter, not at the correct place.[3]

1. The three-letter word is _____
2. How long did the exercise take? _____

EXERCISE #5

Time how long it takes you to find the solution to the mental rotation puzzles below.[4] For each problem, decide which of the comparison shapes on the right is identical to the standard shape on the left. There is no time limit.

	Standard	Comparison A	Comparison B	Comparison C
1				
2				

How long did it take to solve both problems? _____

EXERCISE #6

Set the timer for five minutes. On a separate sheet of paper, finish the following story. Stop writing when the timer goes off.

It was a dark and stormy night. I was driving west on I-90 when the lighting on my dashboard began to go dim and the car began to lose speed. I pulled over onto the shoulder just as the car died completely. I flicked on the hazard lights and pulled out my cell phone. Why hadn't I remembered to charge the phone battery before I left? I crossed my fingers that I had enough juice to make one call. That's when I realized . . .

EXERCISE #7

On a separate sheet of paper, describe what you see in the following pic-ture.[5] Describe your first impression. Then look at it again and see if you see something different. Describe what you see.

EXERCISE #8

Set the timer for three minutes. Find and count the proofreading errors in this passage. Stop when the timer goes off.

If you're tempted to skip the mini neuro-anatomy lesson in the next chapter, don't! Late, when you're practicing the brainsets, you'll need to know which parts of the brain your amping up or down. By visualizig your brain, you will be better able to enter each each brainset.

A number of artists and writers doesn't want to know what's going on in their brains for fear of shattering the mystical process called *inspiration* or *illumination*. Inspiration is the magical moment when an idea springs seemingly fully-formed from nowhere into conscious awareness. While some researcher have indeed tried to remove the mystique from the creative process, that is definitely *not* the purpose of theses book. In fact, the more you learn about how your brain takes perceptual infrmation from the environment and transform it into ideas that lead to skyscrapers and symphonies, the more you'll stand in awe of the process of creative inspiration. Just as knowing that men landed on the moon and brought back moon rocks doesn't shatter the mystique of the moon, the fact that we can now see inside the living human brain does not shatter the mystique of that marvelous courteous.

1. How many errors did you find? _____
2. Were you distracted by the content of the passage or were you able to concentrate on the errors?

   a. distracted by content

   b. able to concentrate on errors

EXERCISE #9

Set the timer for five minutes. On a separate sheet of paper, write down all the small things you can think of that give you pleasure. The list should include activities that can be completed in your own home and without the participation of other people.

Some examples:

- Listening to a favorite musical piece (name the music)
- Taking a hot shower
- Drinking a cold glass of water
- Drinking a favorite hot beverage (such as coffee or herbal tea)
- Looking at a favorite photograph
- Reading a favorite poem
- Remembering a happy event

Make your list specific, so that you describe the memory or the favorite music. Keep writing until the timer goes off.

Note: you will be using this Small Pleasures list in later chapters, so you might want to rewrite or type it on a clean sheet of paper.

EXERCISE #10

Set the timer for five minutes. In this exercise you are presented with three words and asked to find a fourth word that is related to all three.[6] *Here's an example:*

Paint   Doll   Cat   _____

The answer in this case is *"house"*: *House paint, doll house,* and *house cat.*

Try to answer all five of the following word combinations before the timer sounds.

Luck	Rock	Times	_____
Stop	Pocket	Tower	_____
Share	Fish	Money	_____
Horse	Dive	Chair	_____
Leaves	Free	Water	_____

EXERCISE #2   PART 2

Take the piece of paper you cut that is the size of this page and, without looking back, draw a dot on the page in the exact location that you remember seeing the dot in the first part of Exercise 2.

Now go back to that page and place your paper over the page. Place your ruler so that it is parallel to the binding of the book and measure how far off your dot is vertically from the original dot. Next place your ruler perpendicular to the binding and measure how far off your dot is horizontally from the original dot. Add the vertical difference and horizontal difference together.

a.   The difference is less than three centimeters
b.   The difference is greater than or equal to three centimeters

You can score your exercises and interpret the results using the guidelines in Appendix One.

Now that you know which brainset you prefer, it's time to think about leaving your mental comfort zone. Just as an athlete works on the mechanics of his or her sport that don't come naturally in order to improve or excel, you need to broaden the mechanics of your mental comfort zone to improve your creative thinking skills. This means that you may have to venture into mental territory that feels strange or unfamiliar to your creative brain. But don't worry, I think you'll find that rewards are worth the effort!

Before you start training your brain, however, you need to know your way around it. In the next chapter, you'll begin your journey into the vast fertile territory of your own creative brain. That journey will prepare you to process and appreciate more of the stimuli you encounter every day, to organize it, and to use it creatively.

❋ 3

Tour Your Creative Brain

YOUR BRAIN IS A novelty-seeking machine. It contains mechanisms that promote exploring the environment, learning new information, and synthesizing that new material into original ideas. There is no doubt about it: your brain is built for creativity.

Of course, that's not *all* your brain is built for. Besides being a factory of creative ideas, your brain is charged with other tasks, such as keeping you alive. Your brain must monitor both the external environment (the world) and the internal environment (your body) for signs of threat and then respond appropriately when threat is detected. That involves interpreting the intentions of other people, recalling scenarios from your past to see if something that's happening out there right now might follow a pattern that didn't work out so well for you before, and figuring out what excuse you're going to give your spouse this time for not getting the trash out soon enough for the weekly pickup. (However, note that this last aspect of insuring your survival—like so many others—also requires *creativity*.)

So when it's not preoccupied with your survival, your brain can devote more of its resources to being creative. The way the brain is connected to itself is crucial to creativity. We've known for decades that some of the most creative ideas come from making associations between remote or seemingly disconnected ideas or concepts.[1] Newer

39

research is indicating that connections between disparate areas of the brain are also associated with measures of creative thinking.[2] Indeed, creativity is all about making associations. But how does your brain make associations? To understand this, we first have to understand how parts of the brain communicate with each other.

How the Brain Communicates with Itself

Your brain contains around 10 billion nerve cells, called neurons, each of which can form up to 10,000 connections with other neurons, making a total of 100 trillion connections.[3] That's the storage capacity of your brain—and it is tremendous. To fully understand how to enhance your creativity, let's take a closer look at neurons and the other building blocks of the brain.

Each neuron is composed of a cell body, a set of arms called dendrites that receive information from other neurons, and an axon that transmits information to other neurons (see below). Axons are protected by a fatty sheath called myelin. This sheath acts as insulation in

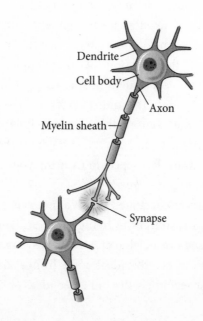

the same way a plastic coating insulates an electrical wire. And, like other types of electrical insulation, myelin allows electrical signals in your brain to travel more rapidly and keeps the signal traveling on target down the length of the axon.

Neurons communicate with each other chemically via a small space, called a *synapse*, between the axon of the sending neuron and a dendrite of the receiving neuron. When the sending neuron has been activated or "turned on," it releases chemicals called neurotransmitters from small vesicles at the end of its axon. These chemicals enter the synapse and then latch onto openings called receptors on the dendrite of the receiving neuron like keys in a lock. If enough receptors are keyed, the receiving neuron will fire . . . which triggers another neuron . . . which triggers another neuron in a domino effect. Now your brain is communicating with itself! Depending upon which network of neurons is firing, that communication may be sending signals to your arm to pick up the telephone; it may be amplifying the aroma of fresh-brewed coffee in the morning; or it may be retrieving the memory of a moonlit night in Aruba.

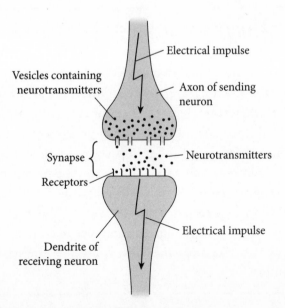

The Synapse Between Neurons Is Where Cell Communication Occurs

When you learn something new or form a new memory, new connections are made between neurons. The act of learning can actually create new dendrites and new connections. In other words, learning literally changes your brain! The more you learn, the richer and denser your "neural forest" will become. If you revisit those memories or bits of learning, you'll increase the speed and strength of these connections. It's like building highways between cities.

The more people need to get from New York to Boston, the more highways will get built and the wider they'll become. Likewise in the brain; if you connect two pieces of information, your neurons will build a road. If you use that road often, your brain will turn it into a superhighway. In addition to helping with learning and memory, these mental superhighways can significantly aid the process of creative thought, which is after all our ultimate goal. Now that we know the building blocks of the brain, let's take a tour around the parts of your brain that are most important to the process of thinking and acting in novel and creative ways.

WHERE MEMORIES ARE STORED

A memory is not stored in one specific location in the brain. Parts of the memory are stored in different locations; for instance, when you remember a summer evening from your childhood, the smell of fresh-mown grass is stored in one location, the feel of grass beneath your feet in another, the sight of fireflies dancing in another, and the memory of joy in yet another location. Because all of these pieces of the memory are connected by a network of neurons, when one piece of the memory is called up, the connections for the whole memory will fire and you will experience the gestalt of the memory.[4]

Geography of the Brain

Just to orient ourselves, we'll take a quick look at some basic brain geography. Let's lay the foundation for our understanding of the brain by looking at the various hemispheres and lobes.

The Right and Left Hemispheres

The brain is divided into two halves—the right and left hemispheres—which are connected by a large tract of neurons called the corpus callosum that allows communication between the two halves. Neurologists have long known that each hemisphere controls the opposite side of the body (so if you want to raise your right hand, it is your left hemisphere that sends the order); however, it was not until the middle of the last century that we learned the hemispheres are actually two complete brains, each with its own personality, likes and dislikes, and skills.

In the 1960s, Nobel Prize winner Roger Sperry and his associate Michael Gazzaniga conducted a set of experiments on several patients who had split brains. Their corpus callosa had been surgically severed in an effort to control life-threatening epileptic seizures. These patients were left with two brains that often had conflicting ideas. For example, the left brain of one patient named Paul wanted

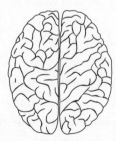

Left Hemisphere	**Right Hemisphere**
letters, words, language	geometric patterns
verbal memory	face recognition
speech, reading, writing	environmental sounds
arithmetic	melodies, musical chords
objective processing	nonverbal memory
systematic problem solving	sense of direction
abstract thinking	mental rotation of shapes
sequential processing	avoidance emotions
analysis	concrete thinking
logical problem solving	parallel processing
approach emotions	holistic picture versus details

to be a draftsman, while the right brain wanted to be a race car driver. Another patient caught himself trying to hit his wife in rage with the right hand (controlled by the left hemisphere) while the left hand tried to protect her.[5]

These split-brain patients were not merely curiosities; they provided a great volume of information on the specialties of each half of the brain. You've no doubt read in the popular press that the right brain is specialized for creativity. Well, that isn't exactly true. Both halves of the brain are necessary for truly creative work. However, thanks to Drs. Sperry and Gazzaniga and others who have studied split-brain patients, we now know much more about the contributions of each hemisphere to the creative process. We'll talk more about the right and left hemispheres in later chapters.

The Lobes of the Cerebral Cortex[6]

Each hemisphere of the brain is covered with a thin layer (about the depth of three dimes stacked on top of each other) of neuron cell bodies. This thin layer is called the *cortex*. The cortex of the human brain is wrinkled to provide more surface area. The bulge part of the wrinkle is called a gyrus, and the creased part is called a sulcus. Surprisingly, most of us have wrinkles in basically the same locations in our brains. In fact, the major wrinkles are so predictable that scientists have named them and use them as landmarks in the brain.

The cerebral cortex is divided into four different regions called *lobes*. Lobes in the more rearward parts of the brain (the temporal, parietal, and occipital lobes) are primarily devoted to processing sensory information coming in from our five senses and storing long-term memories. The frontal lobe is divided functionally into two parts: part of it directs motor movement, and another part—the prefrontal cortex (PFC)—is the center of higher-order thinking processes, such as conscious decision making, planning for the future, and self-awareness.

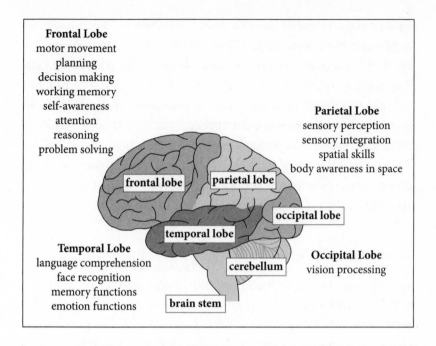

Frontal Lobe
motor movement
planning
decision making
working memory
self-awareness
attention
reasoning
problem solving

Parietal Lobe
sensory perception
sensory integration
spatial skills
body awareness in space

frontal lobe   parietal lobe

occipital lobe

temporal lobe

Temporal Lobe
language comprehension
face recognition
memory functions
emotion functions

cerebellum

brain stem

Occipital Lobe
vision processing

The neuron cell bodies of the cortex have a grayish appearance. These are the "little gray cells" made popular by Agatha Christie's famous sleuth Hercule Poirot. Beneath the thin cortical layer are the axons that connect the neurons to each other. Because they're coated in the fatty myelin sheath, they have a lighter appearance (and are, therefore, referred to as "white cells" or "white matter"). Nestled in the white matter deep in the brain are some additional groupings of neuron cell bodies. These groupings are often referred to as "subcortical structures," and they are important for processing information from our senses, our emotions, and for forming memories.

Let's get a little more specific now and look at a few areas that are important for creative thought and behavior. There is, of course, no "creativity" center in the brain. This is because creative cognition is a complex mental phenomenon that involves multiple sequential acts that utilize widespread circuits throughout the brain. In fact, many complex mental functions do not appear to reside in a specific location but are instead spread among richly connected constellations of neurons located across the brain.[7] Although we are still learning about these networks of neurons and the mental functions for which they are responsible, we can with some certainty identify a number of brain regions that are important to the various stages of creative thought. (You'll learn more about those stages in the next chapter.) Here, then, are some brain landmarks that appear to be "hot spots" for the networks associated with creative thinking. Remember, however, that no area of the brain works alone but is dependent upon other areas with which it is connected.

The Executive Center

The first stop on our tour is the executive center, which is composed of the anterior and lateral (front and side) regions of the prefrontal cortex and some highly interconnected regions of the medial prefrontal cortex, including the orbitofrontal cortex (OFC) and the anterior cingulate cortex (ACC).[8] This executive part of the brain is in charge of planning, abstract reasoning, and conscious decision making. As in corporate structure, this is the "boss" of the brain. Other regions report either directly or indirectly to the executive. However, like all busy executives, it does not receive "raw" information but rather summaries of what's going on. Most of what reaches the executive center has already been reviewed and edited by "middle management" regions. Lots of information gets weeded out downstream and never makes it to the executive's desk. Therefore, though the executive has final say over decisions, these decisions may be based on summaries of information that are incomplete, erroneous, or biased.

Your *working memory* is controlled by the executive center. Sometimes called short-term memory, working memory is the ability to hold in mind several different pieces of information for a limited time (such as the phone number you just looked up or the stops you need to make on the way home from work) and to manipulate that information to solve problems.[9]

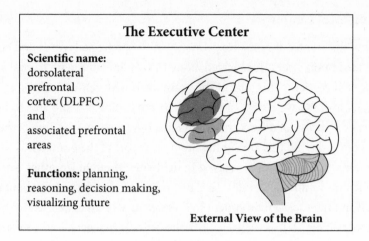

The executive center is important for virtually all aspects of creativity.

o   It's crucial to "problem finding," in which you determine new areas of venture that are ripe for change.

o   It's necessary for "thinking through" these problems to come up with appropriate solutions.

o   It's also crucial for being able to break away from one way of looking at a problem in order to see it from a different perspective. The ability to take different perspectives is, as we will see in later chapters, one of the most important skills for creative thinking.

o   Finally—and this is really important for your creative growth— the executive center decides when to step out of the way and let lower-order areas of the brain have center stage to present their ideas. If you have an executive that finds it necessary to micromanage the rest of the brain, you'll compromise your ability to come up with creative ideas. An effective executive is open to ideas from lower-level management. Likewise, an effective executive center can confidently delegate responsibility to other parts of the brain.

The "Me" Center

The "me" center also resides primarily in the prefrontal cortex and consists of brain structures located along the midline of the prefrontal and parietal cortices. This part of the brain deals with self-awareness, emotions, and the awareness of what others are feeling.[10] Being able to take the perspective of others and to imagine how they may be seeing you is accomplished in this area of the brain. This part of the brain tends to be active when you're not involved in deliberate thought (in other words, when your mind is "at rest"). The "me" center sends information about the self and the social environment to the executive brain to be used in decision making, and, as such, is one of the "middle management" centers.

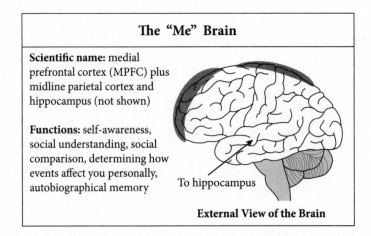

The "Me" Brain

Scientific name: medial prefrontal cortex (MPFC) plus midline parietal cortex and hippocampus (not shown)

Functions: self-awareness, social understanding, social comparison, determining how events affect you personally, autobiographical memory

To hippocampus

External View of the Brain

The "me" brain is important for creativity in the following ways:

○ It mediates your self-expression.
○ It allows you to take another person's perspective, which may be important in writing, art, interpersonal, and business creativity.
○ It's active when you're daydreaming or fantasizing, both of which are helpful to creativity.[11]

Self-awareness can, however, interfere with other aspects of creativity. Therefore, there are times when you'll want to turn the volume on this "me" center down.

The Judgment Center

Our final stop in the frontal lobe is the judgment center of the brain. Judgment is actually a circuit between the executive center and several other structures in the prefrontal cortex, including the *orbitofrontal cortex* or OFC and *anterior cingulate cortex* or ACC.[12] This part of the brain compares our actions to internalized standards of behavior and sends out alarm messages when we're out of line. Scientists first learned about the function of this part of the brain through the strange case of Phineas Gage, a New Hampshire railroad worker. One day in 1848, Gage was tamping a charge of dynamite into a hole with a large iron rod. The dynamite exploded driving the iron tamping rod through the side of his face, destroying an area of his frontal lobe. He survived the accident, made an excellent recovery, and lived another thirteen years. However, personality changes were marked, including a tendency toward profanity and an inability to control his "animal tendencies."[13] In other words, his ability to make good judgments was impaired. Scientists have since identified a "disinhibition" syndrome associated with damage to the orbitofrontal cortex (the area of the brain just above your eyes) that includes poor judgment, inappropriate speech, emotions, and sexual advances.[14]

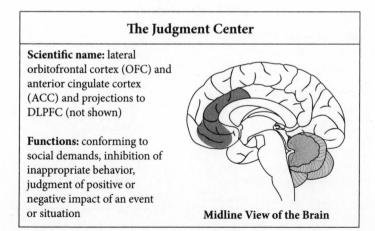

The Judgment Center

Scientific name: lateral orbitofrontal cortex (OFC) and anterior cingulate cortex (ACC) and projections to DLPFC (not shown)

Functions: conforming to social demands, inhibition of inappropriate behavior, judgment of positive or negative impact of an event or situation

Midline View of the Brain

The judgment center is also important in determining whether an event or situation will have a positive or negative impact for you. It is part of middle management, sending filtered information about appropriateness to the executive center.

The judgment center is important for the evaluative aspects of creativity. Once you've come up with a creative idea, you need to determine whether the idea is appropriate. You also need to evaluate a creative project on an ongoing basis as you bring your creative idea to fruition. However, because the judgment center acts as a filter, there are stages in your creative process when you need to turn down its volume and allow more ideas—even those that will later be determined to be bad ideas—to feed forward into conscious awareness.

The Reward Center

The reward center of the brain includes neural projections to a small cluster of subcortical neurons called the nucleus accumbens.[15] When this center is turned on, your self-confidence soars and you feel euphoric. Animal studies show that given a choice between stimulating this reward center or eating, mice will choose to turn on the reward center (they will actually starve to death in order to get this stimulation).[16]

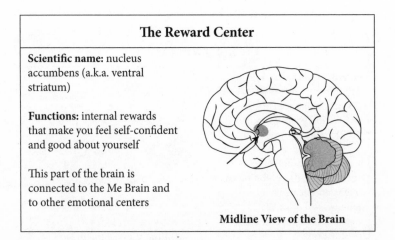

The Reward Center

Scientific name: nucleus accumbens (a.k.a. ventral striatum)

Functions: internal rewards that make you feel self-confident and good about yourself

This part of the brain is connected to the Me Brain and to other emotional centers

Midline View of the Brain

The reward center is important for creative motivation. Research on motivation is unequivocal in finding that creative activity that is linked to internal or "intrinsic" rewards is of higher quality than that motivated by external rewards.[17] The reward center also affects the filtering mechanisms of the brain. Activation of this center allows more ideas and information to feed forward from the association centers in the rear of the brain (see below).

The Fear Center

Here's how fear basically works. First your senses take in information about the environment. This information is sent to a small subcortical almond-shaped structure called the amygdala (Greek for almond). The amygdala determines whether there's a potential threat and, if it detects threat, it sends a message to your body that releases adrenalin, prepares you for fight or flight, and leaves you feeling anxious or fearful, depending upon the degree of danger. The same information is also sent to the executive center, which can turn off the alarm if the threat is perceived to be false.[18] Fear is important for survival; so when the amygdala is active, your thought processes are emotionally hijacked and your ability to think creatively is diminished.[19]

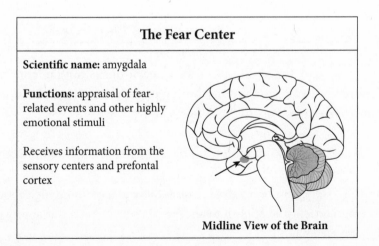

The Fear Center

Scientific name: amygdala

Functions: appraisal of fear-related events and other highly emotional stimuli

Receives information from the sensory centers and prefontal cortex

Midline View of the Brain

Although fear and anxiety are necessary for survival, they are detrimental to creativity, so learning to control the fear center of the brain is important to enhancing your level of creativity.

The Association Centers

The association centers in the rear of the brain (temporal, parietal, and occipital lobes) pull together information that is called for by the executive center or that is brought up spontaneously during unplanned or unstructured thought. They integrate sight, sound, smell, and touch to form meaningful experience. These centers have direct connections to the executive center in the prefrontal lobe.[20]

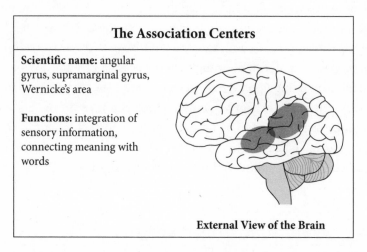

The Association Centers

Scientific name: angular gyrus, supramarginal gyrus, Wernicke's area

Functions: integration of sensory information, connecting meaning with words

External View of the Brain

Of course, the ability to make associations is fundamental to creativity; therefore, the functioning of the association centers is important to creativity in the following ways:

○ They allow information from distant parts of the brain to come together.
○ They appear to be involved in our ability to take knowledge about one concept and apply it to another (in other words, our ability to use metaphors).[21]

○ They act as an internal research-and-development department that produces both novel and mundane combinations of stored and perceived material.

It is of interest that when researchers examined Einstein's brain (certainly one of the most creative brains ever to inhabit a human body), the biggest difference found between his brain and so-called normal brains was in the area of parietal association (one of our association centers).[22]

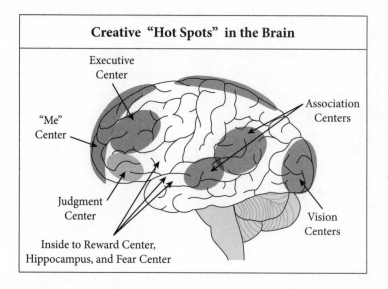

Creative "Hot Spots" in the Brain

Executive Center

Association Centers

"Me" Center

Judgment Center

Vision Centers

Inside to Reward Center, Hippocampus, and Fear Center

The brain centers that we've just discussed are "hot spots" for creative thought and activity. Many of them are highly interconnected. Also, each of these brain centers may participate in multiple brain networks. Just as you may at any given time participate on several teams (say, a project team at work, a committee for your community charity, as well as a tennis team at your local health club), these brain centers may participate in multiple neural networks that perform different functions, such as feeling emotion, learning new information, visualizing the future, or coming up with creative ideas.

When you activate different brain centers, you change the way you access information both from the environment and from your own personal memory stores. Here's an example. Say you're in Rome standing in the Piazza della Rotonda. If your fear center is activated, you may look toward the Pantheon and see a structure that can protect you from danger. If your reward center is activated, you'll likely look at the Pantheon, bring up all the information you've learned about its past, and see it as an architectural and historical marvel. Your perspective is different depending upon what parts of the brain are firing. Brain activation patterns are, likewise, instrumental in how you formulate creative thoughts and how likely you are to implement your creative ideas.

Now that you're armed with relevant knowledge about the brain, it's time to learn how to use different brain activation patterns—the CREATES brainsets—to increase your creative ideas and productivity. So let's get creative . . .

✳ 4

Brainsets and the Creative Process

SEVERAL YEARS AGO, Dr. Richard Wiseman of the University of Hertford-shire collaborated with the British Association for the Advancement of Science to run an experiment called LaughLab. People from all over the world sent in jokes and also rated how funny they found other people's jokes.[1] The following joke was rated the second funniest:

> Sherlock Holmes and Dr. Watson go on a camping trip. After a good dinner and a bottle of wine, they retire for the night, and go to sleep.
>
> Some hours later, Holmes wakes up and nudges his faithful friend. "Watson, look up at the sky and tell me what you see."
>
> "I see millions and millions of stars, Holmes," replies Watson.
>
> "And what do you deduce from that?"
>
> Watson ponders for a minute.
>
> "Well, astronomically, it tells me that there are millions of galaxies and potentially billions of planets. Astrologically, I observe that Saturn is in Leo. Horologically, I deduce that the time is approximately a quarter past three. Meteorologically, I suspect that

we will have a beautiful day tomorrow. Theologically, I can see that God is all powerful, and that we are a small and insignificant part of the universe. What does it tell you, Holmes?"

Holmes is silent for a moment. "Watson, you idiot!" he says. "Someone has stolen our tent!"

Now where did the learned Dr. Watson go wrong here?

The answer is "overthink." When asked to "tell me what you see," Watson did a conscious search of his mind for appropriate solutions to Holmes's question. He came up with a number of plausible answers, all with some relevance to the question at hand. But the most salient answer escaped him. Not that the salient answer in this case was particularly creative in nature, but it serves as an example of how overthinking can keep you from seeing solutions that are right before your eyes. Sometimes your executive center has to quit consciously overdirecting your thought processes. Sometimes you have to quit thinking so hard about the answer to a conundrum and allow the research-and-development team in the rear portions of your brain to do the work and send the answer forward.

Notice that I used the word *sometimes*. That's because there are indeed many situations in which you will come up with novel and useful ideas by conscious deliberation and step-by-step thought. Neuroscientist Arne Dietrich has named this the *deliberate* pathway to creativity.[2] In this pathway, you *deliberately* and consciously walk toward a creative solution step by step. You feel, as you approach a creative insight, that you're getting "warmer"—closer and closer to the solution.

However, a second pathway to creative thought, the *spontaneous* pathway, allows creative solutions to be generated at an information processing level *below* conscious awareness. These solutions, when they appear to meet a certain level of appropriateness, will push forward into consciousness as an "aha!" moment. You feel, as you walk down this pathway, that you are wandering through the woods, until "voilà!" the trees part before you to reveal the creative insight in all its glory. There is no sense of getting "warmer" or closer to a solution until the insight bursts forth.[3]

The *Deliberate* and *Spontaneous* Pathways to Creativity

The main difference between these two pathways in terms of neuroscience is that the executive center in the prefrontal cortex—especially the executive center in the dominant left hemisphere of your brain—remains steadfastly in control of the creative process in the *deliberate* pathway. The executive center directs what you think about and what you call up from your memory bank as you attempt to work creatively. Bach, for example, in the creation of the elegant Brandenburg Concertos, employed mathematical constructs, purposeful inversions of basic themes, and counterpoint that were carefully thought-out and arranged.[4] He constructed the concertos step-by-step using the executive center of his brain to manage the process. In the Brandenburg Concertos, we have a collection of creative products that were representative of the deliberate pathway.

In contrast, in the *spontaneous* pathway, the executive center (purposely or due to fatigue) relinquishes some control of the contents of conscious thought. This allows more ideas from association centers in the temporal and parietal lobes that would ordinarily be blocked from awareness to manifest themselves in consciousness. There is evidence that the *spontaneous* process also allows more integration from the nondominant hemisphere of the brain (that would be the right hemisphere for right-handed people and even many left-handers). The result is that a creative idea may suddenly spring into consciousness when you're least expecting it.

Mozart purportedly described this pathway in an 1815 letter (the authenticity of which has been challenged):

> When I am, as it were, completely myself, entirely alone, and of good cheer—say, travelling in a carriage, or walking after a good meal, or during the night when I cannot sleep: it is on such occasions that my ideas flow best and most abundantly. **Whence** and how they come, I know not; nor can I force them.[5]

Although scholars dispute whether this letter attributed to Mozart is bogus,[6] we see similar descriptions of the spontaneous pathway in letters and accounts given by other composers, poets, and artists beginning in the Romantic period of the arts and continuing to today. Jay Greenberg, for example, a child prodigy who has recently been praised as the greatest musical genius since Mozart by his Julliard professors, says "he doesn't know where the music comes from, but it comes fully written—playing like an orchestra in his head." He hears all the parts of a composition simultaneously. By the age of 12, he had already written five symphonies that were highly regarded by professional composers and conductors—symphonies composed via the *spontaneous* pathway.[7]

How is it possible that a whole symphony could present itself in the brain of a musician? No wonder composer Robert Schumann (who also apparently employed the *spontaneous* pathway) believed that he wasn't actually writing some of his musical compositions; he believed that they were being dictated to him by Beethoven and Mendelssohn "from their tombs."[8] This experience of sudden creative insight feels foreign to the mind because the person has no memory of having done the work necessary to come up with the creative idea. It feels almost like what psychopathologists call "thought insertion"—a delusional sense that someone or something has put thoughts directly into your brain without your consent.

An interesting example of this is described by Sylvia Nasar in her superb biography of Nobel Prize–winning mathematician John Forbes Nash, *A Beautiful Mind*. (The book was the basis for the 2001 movie, which won four Academy Awards.) Nash, who had been diagnosed with paranoid schizophrenia, was asked why he believed that aliens from outer space had recruited him to save the world. He responded, "because the ideas I had about supernatural beings came to me the same way that my mathematical ideas did. So I took them seriously."[9] Nash's mathematical ideas *and* his delusions arrived as sudden insights (which goes to show that all insights are not necessarily appropriate).

Recently, researchers from Northwestern University identified a region of the brain that lights up just at the moment of insight.[10] This region, in the temporal lobe of the right hemisphere, seems to be associated with the pulling together of broad concepts that are being processed below the level of conscious awareness. These researchers found that not only does this region of the brain activate at the moment of insight, but the brain also produces a high-frequency brain wave called a gamma signal in this same area during the moment of insight. This burst of electricity may allow the brain to direct its attention to the newly formed concept as it suddenly appears in consciousness.

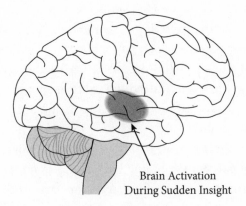

Brain Activation
During Sudden Insight

SOURCE: Adapted from Jung-Beeman et al. (2004).

Deliberate and *Spontaneous* Networks in the Brain

Early functional brain imaging studies were focused on locating brain areas that are active during *deliberate* thought processes (such as purposefully solving problems, retrieving knowledge, and making plans—the so-called *higher-order* thinking skills). Studies identified the *lateral* areas of the prefrontal cortex as the main part of the brain that becomes activated during *deliberate* thought relative to a resting state (during which subjects were instructed not to think about anything). Other parts of the brain lit up as well, depending upon the nature of the deliberate task subjects were asked to perform in the brain scanner.

Researchers also noted that attention was highly focused during *deliberate* processing.[11]

It wasn't until the mid-1990s that researchers began to pay attention to the so-called "resting state" that had heretofore been considered only as a comparison to *deliberate* thought. It turns out that the brain isn't actually resting at all during such times. In fact, certain parts of the brain are quite active when we aren't controlling our thoughts deliberately. These parts form a network—now called the "default" network—that appears to be associated with *spontaneous* (or undirected) thought. The default network consists of areas of the medial (middle) prefrontal cortex and other midline areas in the frontal and parietal lobes, as well as the association areas in the rear of the brain. When you are resting from *deliberate* thought (such as when you're daydreaming or performing an automatic task that doesn't take too much focused attention), this default network lights up. The value of this default network, and indeed the value of spontaneous thought itself, is now recognized as important to imagination, reverie, and envisioning the future.[12]

In essence, the *deliberate* pathway appears to activate more frontal and lateral parts of the brain, whereas the *spontaneous* pathway appears to activate more midline and rear parts of the brain. The benefit of the *deliberate* pathway is transparency, and control. You know the step-by-step process you went through to come up with your idea *and* you retain conscious control of the process. The benefit of the *spontaneous* pathway is the possibility of more novel and more abundant ideas. When you think consciously and deliberately, your attention is focused and you can only process one thought at a time; however, spontaneous thoughts appear to originate below the level of conscious awareness where processing occurs in parallel, meaning that multiple ideas using a wider database can be processed at the same time.[13]

You probably have a preferred pathway—just as you have preferred brainsets in which you spend most of your waking time. If you completed the quiz in Chapter Two, you already know which pathway you prefer. Remember that neither pathway is "wrong." And, as a creative person, you will want to learn to take advantage of *both* pathways. But perhaps you're wondering: How do I find these pathways? Where does the pathway—either pathway!—to creativity begin?

When you create, you do something that no one has ever done before. Because it's never been done, there are no rule books or rubrics for how to proceed. Right? You have to forge ahead, blazing new ground, stepping onto the edge of chaos and looking over the cliff to infinity.

Well, sort of. But it's not exactly true that there are no guidelines for how to proceed.

Luckily for us, written accounts of the creative process have been noted since the days of the early Greeks, when the mathematician Archimedes first reportedly ran naked through the streets of Syracuse shouting "Eureka!" Archimedes, you will remember, had been tasked by Syracuse's King Hiero with determining the volume of gold in an intricate royal crown (the suspicious king suspected that his jewelers were replacing some of the valuable gold with a lesser metal). Archimedes worked on this problem for some time; he was taking a break from this work when he went to the local communal baths and observed that water splashed out of the tub as he submerged himself. Hmmm . . . that's interesting; the volume of an irregularly shaped object can be calculated, he realizes, by noting the amount of water the object displaces when it is submerged. Archimedes couldn't wait to take this discovery back home and apply it to his crown problem (hence the yelling and running-naked-through-the-streets part of the process).[14]

Since the time of Archimedes, many other creative luminaries have described the elements of their creative process in essays, letters, diaries, and journals.[15] Thus, we have a pretty good repertoire of anecdotal reports of the creative process. Fortunately, most of the more modern accounts do not include running naked through the streets (although, as we'll see in the later chapter on the *absorb* brainset, running—suitably attired—may in fact induce a mental state that facilitates creative insight).

The Creative Process

Graham Wallas, in his classic work *The Art of Thought*, presented one of the first models for the creative process based on his knowledge of the accounts written by artistic and scientific luminaries. Wallas described creativity as including the following stages: *preparation* (gathering background information and exploring and focusing on the problem to be solved); *incubation* (internalizing the problem and then taking a break from actively thinking about it); *illumination* (a moment of insight in which a creative solution to the problem pops into conscious awareness); and *verification* (judging the appropriateness of the solution or idea, elaborating on it, and actually applying it to the original problem).[16]

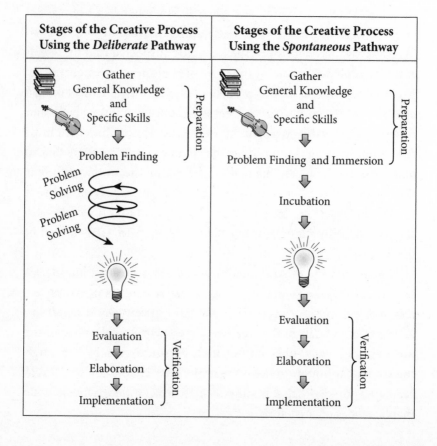

These stages can serve as a road map to the creative process regardless of whether you want to work creatively in the field of art, science, music, business, sports, or your personal life. Let's unpackage the stages in more detail, adding some variations on the model presented by Wallas.

Preparation

Louis Pasteur's famous quote "le hasard favorise l'ésprit preparé" ("chance favors the prepared mind")[17] can be applied to virtually all endeavors that require creativity. Before you can generate creative ideas, you need to be prepared. The preparation stage of the creative process includes four main components: (1) gathering general knowledge, (2) acquiring specific skills and information, (3) problem finding, and (4) problem immersion.

Since the basic premise of creative ideas is that they are original and useful combinations and recombinations of disparate bits of information (see Chapter One), then it stands to reason that the more bits of information you have stored in your brain, the more raw material you'll have to combine into original ideas.

Your brain is home to an immense repository of information, including semantic knowledge (gleaned from school, books, and other sources of information), autobiographical memories (your moment-by-moment experience of the world), and physical skills (how to ride a bike, play the oboe, hit an eight-iron, or fly an F-16). This collection of information is *unique to you*. No one else has this particular mental library. That's why **there is no doubt that *you can* create novel and original ideas**—because nobody else has your unique database.

In one way, you've been preparing to solve problems creatively since your first moments of life; *everything* you have learned, from how to hold a spoon to your understanding of the intricacies of quantum theory, is fair game for creative recombination. The broader your range of interests and the broader your quest for knowledge, the greater the chance that you will be able to combine information in creative ways that are both original and useful. Intellectual curiosity and the quest for knowledge are the first fruitful steps in your mission to become more creative and innovative.

The second part of the preparation process consists of acquiring the skills and information that are specific to your particular area of desired creative endeavor. If you wish to be a more creative painter, you need to know the basics about paints, colors, brushes, how to spread the paint on the canvas, how to use color to represent shadows, and how to draw using perspective. In addition, you need to know what's happening in the domain of art currently so that you can use the techniques developed by others to aid your creative quest (and also so that you don't spend your time rediscovering techniques and innovations that someone else has already developed). Experts call this aspect of preparation "learning the domain." Since creativity is thinking or doing something that hasn't been done before, it helps to know what *has* been done before in order to take the game to the next level. Learning as much as you can about your specific area of creative endeavor not only generates interest in that area, it also helps you with the next component of the preparation stage: problem finding.

Problem finding is the search for—and definition of—a problem or dilemma that can be solved with a creative idea. A creative problem or dilemma can be basically any situation that presents a challenge or opportunity for change or improvement. Problem finding does not mean that you go out looking for troublesome aspects of your life or work to criticize—we have bosses and mothers-in-law to do that job; it's more like exploring new ways that things could be done or could be done *differently*.

So Georges Seurat says in essence "what if I try to paint with tiny dots of color instead of lines?" and theoretical physicists now known as string theorists start asking "how can we combine the evidence for quantum mechanics and general relativity in a way that accounts for more of the scientific data?" Or the automobile designer asks "how can I sculpt this car door to show off the lines of this new model more effectively?"

Of course, problem finding is not always necessary. Many times your profession or your avocation or life itself may have already defined a creative problem for you. You don't have to formulate problems such as "how can I combine a career with raising children?" or "how can we make a dent in curing cancer?" Many dilemmas such as these are already defined and are out there waiting for your creative solutions.

The final aspect of the preparation process consists of immersing yourself in the problem or dilemma that needs a creative solution. You consider the problem from many aspects, you turn it over in your head, and you attempt to generate potential solutions. You marry yourself, however briefly, to the problem. You become temporarily obsessed with it.

Incubation

Then you let it go. You rest. You turn your attention elsewhere. This stage of the process is called *incubation* because, just as you can look at a chicken egg each day for several weeks without being aware that a baby chick is developing inside, you can send your creative dilemma to the back burner of your brain for a period of time without being aware that it too is developing out of sight (or in this case, out of "mind").

This is the point at which the *deliberate* and the *spontaneous* pathways to creative ideas diverge. If you're *deliberately* trying to solve the problem (like Dr. Watson and the case of the missing tent) you will resist the incubation period and you'll continue to consciously search for a solution to the problem. Your executive center will continue to call up information from the rear storage areas of the brain and you'll manipulate that information in your prefrontal lobes until you come up with a solution or insight.

If you're taking the *spontaneous* route, you'll notice that taking a break from your creative problem can allow several beneficial things to happen in the brain.[18]

First, the break gives you a chance to recover from mental fatigue. Because the preparation stage of creativity is such hard work, a forced break may allow you to recharge your mental batteries, so to speak, so that you can later return to thinking about your problem refreshed.

Second, you may have noticed that if you're trying to think of a specific word (say the name of a large Indonesian ape) and the wrong word comes to mind (baboon), you will find it harder to image the correct word (orangutan) because the baboon answer keeps popping up every time you think of large apes. Often, one potential but unhelpful solution may block your ability to think up other solutions while the unhelpful one is still fresh in your mind. The incubation period, however, allows you time to forget inappropriate solutions upon which you may have become fixated.

Third, the incubation period allows you to attend to other matters while you continue to work on the problem at a level below conscious awareness. Once you've posed the problem, your creative brain continues to ponder and generate solutions even when your attention is directed elsewhere.

Finally, the incubation period allows you to focus on things in your environment that are not related to your problem. The unrelated environmental information you perceive could act as a clue to a possible creative solution. Just as Archimedes noticed the water overflowing when he sank into the bathtub so many centuries ago, something you see in the world around you could stimulate a connection between bits of information in your associational centers that will lead to a "eureka!" moment.

Illumination

If you're *spontaneously* solving the problem, your executive center will delegate the work and a solution may suddenly spring into consciousness when you're least expecting it. Although Wallas called this stage of the process *illumination*, it is more often called "insight" or "inspiration" (from the Greek notion that the gods breathed into—or inspired—mortals with their godlike ideas). Rudyard Kipling called it summoning his daemon; others call it contacting their muse.

All describe feeling as though the creative idea were coming from somewhere outside themselves because they did not consciously think up the idea; it was just suddenly there.

Many people believe that illumination is the province of so-called creative geniuses. However, one of the premises of this book is that all of us can achieve creative illumination in many different areas of our lives by learning to access different brainsets. Illumination is a skill that can be learned!

Verification

Once the potentially creative solution has arrived via illumination, the real work begins. The verification stage includes three steps: evaluation, elaboration, and implementation.

Not all creative ideas are *good* solutions to your problem. When an idea comes to mind, you need to determine whether it's worth pursuing. You need to look at the strengths and weaknesses of the idea and judge it for appropriateness. This is the *evaluation* stage. If you decide the idea is a keeper, you take it to the next step. If you decide the idea is not worth further investment of your time, you toss it out and either renew your immersion in your problem or wait for another solution to emerge.

Let's say you like your idea. In the next step, *elaboration*, you flesh out the idea. If you're writing a short story and you have a creative idea for a plot, then you fill in the story's details in this step. If, like Mozart, you had an idea for a symphony, you write down the notes for each instrument and make whatever adjustments are necessary. At the end of the elaboration phase, you should have a finished product.

Now for the final phase of the process: *implementation*. Your work is no good unless it reaches your intended audience. The implementation process may include selling your idea or product to a manufacturer, or a recording company, or a newspaper, or the bank that's going to loan you the money to start up your business. The implementation step is getting your work out there. It's closing the deal—so that your wonderful idea or product doesn't languish in the bottom drawer of your dresser or in a hidden file on your computer.

Great! Now we've followed the creative process from the time you first held a spoon till the moment when you sign your big contract with Sony. Of course, the process isn't always a straight line through these steps. You often have to go back and repeat several steps more than once before you can complete the process.

There are specific brainsets that will aid you in maximizing creativity at each stage of the creative process. You'll be revisiting the stages of the creative process as you learn about each brainset. Remember that both the *deliberate* and the *spontaneous* pathways can lead to novel and original concepts, ideas, and products. As you gain knowledge of the CREATES brainsets, you'll learn more about which brainsets and which pathway will be most productive for your current situation.

Mapping the brainsets onto the appropriate stage of the process and learning to switch between brainsets is going to give you a big creative edge. These skills are not only going to give you an advantage in business, they will lead you to greater self-actualization, enjoyment, and a richer inner and outer life as well.

One of the techniques we'll be using to train these creativity skills is called the "token economy" system. The token economy incentive has been shown to lead to behavior change in a variety of clinical settings, including drug and alcohol addiction centers and Weight Watchers International.[19] If this incentive is powerful enough to change drug and eating behaviors, you may want to consider using it to learn how to access different brainsets.

The token economy system works like this: each chapter that follows includes fun and interesting exercises to help you access a particular brain state. If you complete the exercise, you are awarded a token or tokens depending upon the difficulty of the exercise. (If you go to http://ShelleyCarson.com, you can print out a set of color-ful tokens. However, you can also just check off the tokens as described in Appendix Two of this book.) When you earn twenty tokens, you can exchange them for a reward that you establish for yourself. You will also get access to bonus information about creativity on the http://ShelleyCarson.com Web site. If you decide you would like to use the evidence-based token economy system, just go to Appendix Two and follow the directions before you continue reading.

A second technique that I suggest you use as you read this book is to keep a creativity journal. As you become more adept at entering the brainsets described in the chapters ahead, you'll find that more and more ideas appear to you. These ideas may be fleeting. By writing down both creative problems (that is, any situation that can be approached creatively) and creative solutions, you'll be sure to have an ongoing supply of creative material on which to focus. Another advantage of keeping a creativity journal is that you can record what time of day and what you were doing when creative ideas occurred to you, as well as when you were most productive. This will help you to recognize patterns about your own access to different brainsets.

It is time to start investigating the seven brainsets in detail. The good news is that you've already had some experience with all of the brainsets that follow. You will now begin to develop and apply them. To start your journey down the pathway to creativity, just turn the page! As Sherlock Holmes would say to Dr. Watson, "The game is afoot!"

PART 2

Training Your Creative Brain

5

Opening the Mind:
Accessing the Absorb
Brainset

*Genius in truth means little more than the faculty of
perceiving in an unhabitual way.*

—WILLIAM JAMES, 1890[1]

So Easy a Caveman Could Do It

TWO CAVEMAN MEN have escaped a landslide and are watching from atop a safe outcropping of basalt as trees, earth, and rocks of all sizes careen down the hill beside them.

"Ugh—whew!" says Caveman #1 (translation: "Thank our lucky bright spots in the sky! We've cheated death again—let's get out of here!").

"Ugh—wow!" Caveman #2 responds (translation: "No, wait. Do you notice that the rounder rocks are moving down the hill more quickly and smoothly than the jagged rocks? That's really interesting!").

Which caveman is accessing the *absorb* brainset?

❑   Caveman #1
❑   Caveman #2

The first and arguably most important strategy for thinking and acting creatively is to develop your ability to absorb information nonjudgmentally. This ability is facilitated by what I will describe in this chapter as the *absorb* brainset. One result of accessing the *absorb* brainset is that you notice new things. You become quite curious about the world around you, and you take in all kinds of new information without judgment. Because creativity and innovation require a broad knowledge base from which to synthesize new ideas, spending time in the *absorb* mode allows you to gather assorted knowledge that may be

"It looks novel and original all right. I just don't see how it's going to be useful."

useful in solving later problems. Caveman #2 was able to use the knowledge he gathered on the day of the landslide for future innovation.

A second result of accessing the *absorb* brainset is that you are more receptive to seeing associations between things in the environment and problems you're trying to solve. Creativity researchers call this "opportunistic association." Joe Lawson, the originator of the wildly successful caveman ad campaign for GEICO Insurance, says that the idea for the caveman campaign "just sort of popped out one day" (a common *spontaneous*-pathway occurrence). He and other members of the ad team were thinking about a new campaign that would highlight how easy it is to use the GEICO Web site. "We were just sort of fed up with how politically correct the culture had become and how difficult that made it to do our jobs well. So we insulted cavemen, just to get it out of our system."[2] When you think about combining the "insulted cavemen" theme with the "easy Web site" theme, the campaign's now-famous premise seems obvious. In fact, it seems *so easy a caveman could do it*. But, of course, it's only obvious if you're in an *absorb* brainset that allows you to "see" this concept without prematurely judging it as silly.

The third result of the *absorb* brainset is that you remain receptive to ideas originating in your unconscious. Just as Joe Lawson's caveman idea " . . . popped out one day," other innovators, as we saw in the last chapter, report that their ideas occur to them when they're not even thinking about solutions to a problem. During these times, they are relaxing, resting their minds, or even dozing. Mozart, as you'll recall, describes the arrival of insight while he was riding in a carriage after a good meal. A popular songwriter, whom I was interviewing for one of my research studies on creativity, described the following when asked about her creative process.

> I don't actually write the songs—angels write them. Sometimes when my antenna is up I can pull the songs in from the air. When that happens I quickly write down the lyrics and melody so I can get it to my agent before someone else pulls in the same song . . .

I don't seem to be able to put up my antenna at will; it just happens sometimes.[3]

Like Mozart and my songwriter, the memoirs of creative individuals are filled with descriptions of ideas "popping into their heads" unbidden. Sounds easy, doesn't it? Stick up your antenna, and presto, innovative ideas appear!

So easy a caveman could do it? Maybe not.

If you tend to be a *deliberate* thinker (see Chapter Four), your ability to be creative is probably being held captive in the metaphorical back rooms of your brain. Like overinvolved parents, the executive and judgment centers of your authoritarian prefrontal lobes may be keeping your best ideas and insights away from you. They do this for two reasons (also like authoritarian parents): first, if you open the doors to those back rooms of the brain—the antechambers of consciousness—to let creative ideas in, then other unfiltered thoughts, perceptions, memories, and visions will come rushing in as well. That could lead to confusion at best and mental chaos at worst. Second, your executive and judgment centers don't want to relinquish control. For many people, the executive center in the prefrontal lobes (especially in the dominant left hemisphere) is a control freak (after all, the decisions *it* makes are ultimately responsible for your behavior). So your creative potential is stuck back there like a rebellious teenager who's been grounded.

To let the creative potential out, you have to wait till the authoritarian prefrontal lobes are distracted with other tasks. Or—better yet—teach them to take short power naps so you can enter the *absorb* brainset. You *need* to spend time in this brainset in order to unleash the inventive powers of your brain.

Defining the Absorb Brainset

The *absorb* brainset is basically a receptive state of the brain, in which you are open to information generated in the external environment (the world) as well as from the internal environment (the mind). The state is well known to hypnotists, Buddhist monks, yoga enthusiasts, and creative luminaries. It's associated with such words as autohypnosis, trance, alpha state, absorption, mindfulness, primary process thinking, openness to experience, dissociation, and transliminality. To some of you this may sound reminiscent of New Age crystals and pyramids. But here's the deal. The benefits of a receptive state of brain are backed by a great deal of scientific research, and unless you're willing to access this state you'll find it difficult to be innovative and creative. You'll be stuck trying to solve problems using *deliberate* processes that, while often effective, are more tiring and time-consuming. Simply put, you'll be opting for Edison's 99% perspiration instead of the 1% inspiration pathway to creativity and innovation.

Three principal factors define the *absorb* brainset: attraction to novelty, delayed judgment, and mental or cognitive disinhibition.[4] Let's look at each component separately.

Attraction to Novelty

How do you know but ev'ry Bird that cuts the airy way,
Is an immense world of delight, clos'd by your senses five?

—WILLIAM BLAKE[5]

Artists, scientists, and innovators of all professions tend to spend a great deal of time in an open and receptive brainset, allowing them to perceive the "immense worlds" that may be "clos'd," as Blake intimates, to others. Perceiving what others do not see in the world around you—and associating these perceptions with already-attained knowledge or skill—allows you to make innovative leaps, whether in art, science, business, or your personal life. You can see what is not seen by others because your attention system is attracted to novelty. There are several well-known examples of this phenomenon:

Isaac Newton conceived the notion of gravitation as he sat in a contemplative mood and witnessed an apple fall from a tree.[6]

Vincent van Gogh revolutionized art by seeing the sublime in everyday objects. He wrote to his brother Theo: "The figure of a labourer—some furrows in a ploughed field—a bit of sand, sea, and sky—are serious subjects, so difficult but at the same time so beautiful, that it is indeed worthwhile to devote one's life to the task of expressing the poetry hidden in them."[7]

Alexander Fleming discovered penicillin after *noticing* that bacteria failed to grow in an area of a laboratory dish that had been accidentally contaminated with a peculiar mold.[8]

Some years back my friend, the painter and writer Angel Fernandez, offered to drive me from the Notre Dame campus to O'Hare Airport to catch a flight. We were driving at breakneck speed on the Dan Ryan Expressway when he jammed on the brakes and demanded that I look at an overpass. I looked, but all I saw was dirty snow piled up on the side of the road. Nothing would do but that we get off at the next exit, retrace our route heading south, then get back on the northbound road, to see . . . an overpass in the snow. This time he drove slowly so that I could appreciate the angle that the snow bank made against the arch of the overpass, so that I (who by the way was definitely "clos'd by my senses five" and utterly furious about probably missing my flight) could share in this "immense world of delight." Now I'm certainly not recommending that you become so taken with everyday items that you cause havoc on the expressways, but you can see that the brain that is captured by the novelty of everyday objects is more likely to "see" the environment in innovative and creative ways. (For practice in noticing new aspects of everyday surroundings, see *Absorb* Exercise #1.)

Delayed Judgment

When you're in the *absorb* brainset, you're not judging ideas, objects, situations, other people, or (perhaps most important) yourself. You don't need to categorize things or situations as right-wrong, good-bad, or should-shouldn't. Your inner authoritarian parent is taking a vacation, and you're free to explore. Perceptions of the outer world, memories, and ideas float across the wide screen of your mind, and you find them intensely interesting without the need to censor them. Yes, you might get into some mental mischief, but it will be worth it.

One aspect of this state of suspended judgment is what nineteenth-century poet Samuel Taylor Coleridge called the "willing suspension of disbelief."[9] In exchange for entry into new and fantastic worlds of fiction, you agree to accept the premises on which those worlds are built. For instance, when we read or watch the work of J.R.R. Tolkien, we agree to believe that the world is populated by hobbits, sorcerers, elves, and orcs rather than Asians, Africans, Americans, and accountants. (I have a neighbor who can't watch *Law and Order* because he's unwilling to suspend disbelief. "They could never get a case to trial that quickly so how can I believe anything else that happens on that show?") He's an accountant. This is not to say that all accountants are unable to suspend disbelief. *My* tax accountant not only suspends disbelief, he actually thinks he's Jimmy Buffet. Walking into his office is like submerging onto a coral reef off Key West, replete with brightly colored fish, talking parrots, and 1970s Margaritaville music . . . now if only he would serve me a Margarita to soften the blow of what I owe Uncle Sam this year!

Another aspect of delayed judgment is the willingness to take an idea to its logical or illogical conclusions without prematurely nixing it. For instance, German officials must have been accessing an *absorb* brainset when the representatives of the company Solar Lifestyle presented their idea for solar-powered talking trashcans on the streets of Berlin. Instead of categorizing the idea as "rubbish" (pardon the trash pun), city officials funded a number of the trash cans that say *"vielen danke,"* *"merci,"* or "thank you" (Berlin being an international city) when citizens toss in their refuse. (Note also the willing suspension of disbelief of the many passersby who respond to the talking cans with *"bitte schön"* ["you're welcome"].)[10]

My colleague Ellen Langer, the innovative social psychologist and artist from Harvard, formulated the cognitive theory of "mindfulness" more than twenty years ago. Mindfulness is a flexible frame of mind that results from drawing novel distinctions about the situation and the environment. Her theory of mindfulness has much in common with the personality trait of openness; however, unlike personality theorists, Langer views mindfulness as a state of mind rather than a stable trait. Her research has indicated over and over again that this state can be cultivated and learned. In contrast to mindfulness, the state of mind*less*ness is characterized by pigeonholing experiences, ideas, and people into rigid categories. Langer calls this tendency to judge or categorize without reflection "premature cognitive commitment."[11] For instance, identify the object below:

If you identified it as a chair, you've made a premature cognitive commitment to see it as a piece of furniture on which one sits. By doing so, you've reduced the probability that you'll be able to see its myriad other realities. It could also be a table, a weapon, firewood, a stepping stool, or a work of art. Turned on its side it could be a barricade or a fence. By absorbing this object in an open manner—by suspending judgment or categorization—you can see a world of possibilities that disappear when you label it a "chair."

Of course, it would be impossible to navigate through even a single day without categorizing and judging our environment to some extent. Indeed, our brains are wired to concoct schemas (judgments of "how the world is") to describe the situations, objects, and people around us. If, for example, your brain did not judge the flat surface below your bed to be a "floor" (a platform that can be walked upon), and instead thought of it as planks from a tree that could be used as weapons, firewood, or building materials, you might not set foot outside the safety of that plush, resilient square thing in which you sleep! When I say that your judgment is suspended or delayed in the *absorb* brainset, I don't mean that it renders you incapable of judging or categorizing altogether, but rather that judgments and categories become somewhat more loosely defined, so that you're capable of seeing objects, situations, and people from multiple perspectives; in other words, you are in the biological equivalent of Langer's *mindful* state. (For practice in delaying judgment, see *Absorb* Exercise #2.)

Cognitive Disinhibition

Hand-in-hand with the suspension of judgment is a phenomenon called *cognitive disinhibition*.[12] This is somewhat different from *behavioral disinhibition* (which can cause you to dance on a table with a lamp shade on your head at the office holiday party). Cognitive disinhibition is the failure to gate out information from your conscious awareness that is irrelevant to your current goals or to your survival. This is good news, of course, if you are failing to gate out creative ideas that arise in your unconscious thought processes. It means that more information originating in the metaphorical back rooms of your brain is making it into your conscious mind. The authoritarian prefrontal parents we talked about earlier are power napping and letting your creative self into the front parlor. Let's look at disinhibition more closely.

As you accomplish the many tasks that comprise your daily life, you are not consciously aware of most of what your "senses five" perceive or the multitude of decisions your brain is making on your behalf. If you *were* aware of all of these perceptions and decisions, you'd be overwhelmed with information and you'd find it difficult to complete even the simplest task. Imagine, for example, trying to brush your teeth in the morning with conscious awareness of the following:

Sound of clock ticking in bedroom
Level of light inside bathroom
Distinguish toothbrush from other objects on counter by size, shape, color, angles
Estimate distance of toothbrush from shoulder
Level of light reaching eyes—adjust pupil dilation

These are only a few of the sensory-motor inputs going on at any given instant. The complete list would include several hundred items.

Luckily, our brains have built-in filtering systems that limit the contents of our conscious awareness to information from the environment that's relevant to either our current goals (for example, brushing teeth, getting a shower, or getting dressed) or our survival (bright flashes of light, loud noises, strong odors, and pain will always be allowed into conscious awareness because they have been associated throughout evolution with potential danger). These automatic filters occur at a number of points during information processing and are collectively referred to as *cognitive inhibitory systems* or *cognitive inhibition*. They act by evaluating each bit of information that enters through our five senses and determining whether it's important or unimportant to our current plans. Information that's categorized as unimportant is blocked from attention and we never become consciously aware of it. Likewise, stimuli from our senses about the *external* world are constantly evoking memories, mental images, and thoughts (such as "what are the chances that car will change lanes right in front of me?"). Most of these *internally* generated stimuli are also blocked out by our cognitive inhibitory systems and we are not consciously aware of them either. (For instance, imagine the mental confusion that would ensue if you were trying to locate your car in a busy parking lot, and the memory of every place you had ever parked a car flowed into your conscious awareness!)[13]

After we've performed a task (such as brushing our teeth, driving to work, writing a report, or preparing a meal) a few times, we are able to cognitively inhibit even more stimuli associated with the task, and the bulk of the information processing needed to perform the task becomes automatic. Most of us have become very good cognitive inhibitors. We are so efficient at traversing our daily lives that we automatically precategorize the information around us as irrelevant and we never notice it. Cognitive inhibition increases our task efficiency. The downside of efficiency is that this wealth of rich information (from both external and internal sources) is automatically and quite simply closed off to us. The more "automatic" your thoughts and actions become, the more information is removed from possible attention. You can easily see how this might affect your ability to be creative. You can't make novel and original combinations out of information of which you're not even aware.

The goal of the *absorb* brainset is to turn down the efficiency of your cognitive filters and let more information into your conscious awareness. This will increase the probability that you can make novel and original connections between unrelated stimuli—the essence of innovation. (Cognitive filters are relaxed, for example, during dreaming sleep. For practice in cognitive disinhibition, see *Absorb* Exercises #5 and #6.)

Neuroscience of the *Absorb* Brainset

Exactly what does your brain look like when you access the *absorb* brainset? Remember that we said the *absorb* mode is characterized by delayed judgment, disinhibition, and novelty seeking. Well, the brain activation patterns of people when they're experiencing these characteristics are reflected in the *absorb* brainset. Specific neurotransmitters in the areas of the prefrontal lobes that control judgment and inhibition (including the executive and judgment centers described in Chapter Three) are less active than they would be if you were consciously thinking about something using *deliberate* processing (like how you're going to get to the dry cleaners, the pharmacy, and the post office during your lunch hour).[14] Meanwhile areas further back in the brain—the temporal, occipital, and parietal lobes (which neuroscientist

Arne Dietrich jointly refers to as TOP)[15]—are more active. Finally, neuroimaging studies reveal that there is relatively more activation in the right hemisphere of the brain when people are in the reflective *absorb* state than when they are deliberately thinking or solving problems.[16]

The *Absorb* Brainset and Alpha Activity

The brain is an electrochemical organ. Neurons communicate with each other by generating a mild electrical impulse. Although the electrical activity in the brain is relatively weak, some researchers believe that a fully functioning brain may generate enough electricity to power a flashlight bulb. Ordinarily, when you're alert and thinking, the prefrontal lobes are dominated by electrical activity of high frequency (13–30 Hz) and low amplitude called *beta* waves. *Beta* activity is associated with a high level of cognitive activation. When you enter the *absorb* brainset, *beta* activity is reduced and brain waves exhibit slower frequency (5–12 Hz) and higher amplitude, called *alpha* and *theta* waves. *Alpha* and *theta* activity are associated with a more relaxed and receptive mental state. The late Colin Martindale and his colleagues at the University of Maine have done extensive research on the brain wave patterns of highly creative versus less creative groups. Martindale's work indicates that highly creative people slip into low-frequency brain states more readily than less creative people.[17]

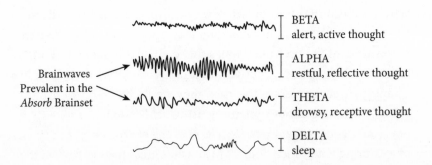

This state of quieting the activity of the thinking/planning/judging prefrontal lobes allows more information from the perceptual processing centers and the associational centers further back in the brain to feed forward into conscious awareness. Martindale also found that creative people intuitively switch to this state of alpha activity in the frontal regions of the brain when they're solving problems creatively, whereas less creative individuals rev up their beta activity when trying to be creative.[18] (For practice at enhancing alpha activity in the brain, see *Absorb* Exercises #3 and #4.)

Cognitive Disinhibition and the Open Brainset

My colleague Jordan Peterson and I found that openness, the personality trait associated with easy access to the *absorb* brainset, is related to a deficit in one aspect of the cognitive filtering system called *latent inhibition*.[19] Reductions in this filter are associated with a mild increase of the neurotransmitter dopamine in a certain region of the brain called the *mesolimbic pathway*.[20] It is interesting to note that alcohol has an effect on this dopamine pathway, which might explain why many artists and musicians have used alcohol to "summon their muse." (For practice in cognitive disinhibition, see *Absorb* Exercises # 5 and #6.)

ALCOHOL AND THE MUSE

The state of cognitive disinhibition and receptivity that we are calling the *absorb* brainset is so important to the creative process that people from all creative walks of life seek it out through a number of methods. One such method that has been especially popular with writers and musicians is entering the *absorb* state through the influence of alcohol or drugs. Over two thousand

(continued)

ALCOHOL AND THE MUSE (*continued*)

years ago, the Roman poet Horace wrote "No poems can please for long or live that are written by water drinkers."[21] In more modern times William Styron, the late American novelist, wrote in his memoir *Darkness Visible*:

> Like a great many American writers, . . . I used alcohol as the magical conduit to fantasy and euphoria . . . as a means to let my mind conceive visions that the unaltered sober brain has no access to.[22]

Other writers have reported that alcohol promotes the "period of incubation and the development of ideas." And indeed, a set of experiments conducted by Scandinavian researchers Torsten Norlander and Roland Gustafson demonstrated that a mild dose of alcohol used at the incubation/insight stages of the creative process actually led to higher scores on a measure of creativity.[23] Unfortunately, using alcohol or drugs to access the *absorb* state or summon the muse seems to have a larger downside than benefit. Although alcohol and certain drugs have been shown to induce a state of cognitive disinhibition[24] they also induce a state of behavioral disinhibition—leading to such negative outcomes as unplanned sexual encounters and the aforementioned dancing on tabletops wearing a lamp shade. Further, if you start using substances to summon your muse, you run the risk of conditioning yourself to associate creativity with inebriation. You may feel that you can only be creative when you've imbibed. You may also run the risk of addiction or alcoholism. As Tom Dardis notes in his book *The Thirsty Muse*, American writers have had a love-hate relationship with alcohol, and five of the eight American winners of the Nobel Prize for literature have been alcoholics.[25]

Attraction to Novelty and the *Absorb* Brainset

Dopamine in the mesolimbic pathway is also linked to novelty seeking, another aspect of the *absorb* brainset.[26] Dopamine is the primary brain chemical linked to our internal reward circuit.[27] In the *absorb* brainset, you are actually being internally rewarded for attending to novel aspects of both your external and internal environment. When you engage in certain prosurvival behaviors (eating when you're hungry, drinking when you're thirsty, and mating with an appropriate sex object), you get a shot of dopamine to a specific area of the brain called the *nucleus accumbens*.[28] This, in turn, produces a feeling of mild euphoria, which makes it more likely that you'll repeat those behaviors—Mother Nature's way of encouraging us to survive as individuals and as a species. When in the *absorb* brainset, you're also rewarded with dopamine for paying attention to novel aspects of your external and internal environment. This enhances your chances of coming up with novel ideas—perhaps Mother Nature's way of making sure we survive by creatively adapting to our ever-changing environment. (You can practice noticing novelty in your environment by practicing *Absorb* Exercise #1 at the end of this chapter. When you reward yourself with a token for completing the exercise, you are training yourself to associate reward with attention to novelty.)

When to Access the *Absorb* Brainset

It's ideal to get into the *absorb* brainset at the following times during your creative process.

The Preparation Stage

First, use the *absorb* set when you're *gathering information* of a general type. The more knowledge of all sorts that you acquire, the more likely you are to have materials to combine in novel and original ways to solve problems and come up with innovative ideas. Creative people tend to have a multitude of varied interests across a broad spectrum of topics. When you access the *absorb* brainset, you become attracted to the novel aspects of things around you. You "amp up" your intellectual curiosity. You become motivated to explore new worlds of knowledge; you let your curious state of brain lead you from one area of inquiry to another in somewhat the same way that surfing the net leads you from one Web page to another. Research suggests that when you're exposed to information in an absorbing, nonjudgmental way, you encode it more broadly in your long-term memory. You make more connections to the information, creating multiple pathways for retrieval.[29]

Second, use the *absorb* brainset when you're *problem finding*. Creative, innovative people are always coming up with ideas of how to improve their worlds. They see how things could be as well as how things are. Here's an example in the realm of what is called "everyday creativity." Anita, another of my highly creative subjects, had only a high school education. Because she had a young son, she could only work part-time "mother's hours." Her first job was as a waitress at a small family-owned breakfast joint near the ocean. After several weeks on the job, Anita started thinking of changes she would make if she owned the restaurant. In the evenings after her son was in bed, she played around with designing a new, more attractive menu that included drawings of seashells to promote the ocean theme. She spent her evening hours learning how to draw different types of shells that she copied from pictures on the Internet. She then took her ideas to the owners of the restaurant. For a small amount of money they had the new menus printed and also allowed Anita to paint seashells on the plain walls of the restaurant. Anita next found some inexpensive vinyl fabric with a shell motif and—again with only a little money—made new tablecloths for the restaurant. She suggested that the owners serve a Sunday brunch buffet, and she decorated the buffet table with shells that she and her son had gathered from the beach. In just a few short months, Anita, even with no education or training in creative arts, had made a very big difference in her work environment.

By accessing the *absorb* brainset and noticing new things in your environment, whether in your business, your home, your civic organization, or the sports team you coach, you can—like Anita—"see" opportunities to make changes that can improve and enrich your surroundings.

The Incubation/Insight Stage

The concept of the brain state represented in the *absorb* brainset is anything but new. Philosophers, scientists, and poets have long described a state in which they are more aware and receptive not only to the environment but to new ideas that arise through spontaneous processing in the "antechambers of consciousness."[30] Sometimes this absorbing and receptive state is accessed when the person is dozing or extremely relaxed, as we saw earlier in this chapter. Sometimes it is accessed because the individual is genetically predisposed to accessing disinhibited brain states. At other times, it may be purposefully entered through meditation or training protocols such as you find at the end of this chapter.[31] The state of openness and disinhibition that characterizes the *absorb* brainset sets the stage for novel associations and combinations of memories, sensory experiences, and mental images that are generated in the rear parts of the brain to make their way into conscious awareness, often in a sudden and meaningful burst of neural excitement.[32] This "lightbulb" or "aha!" experience is the central feature in the *spontaneous* pathway to creative ideas. Though you don't have to spend the entire incubation period of the creative process in the *absorb* mode, you need to access it before insight or illumination can occur. Neuroimaging studies clearly indicate that people are in this open and receptive state immediately before the moment of insight.[33]

Cavemen, Take Heart

"First you invented the wheel; now you invented the graphic novel. There're no good ideas left for the rest of us!"

Accessing the *absorb* brainset is an integral part of the creative process. In the *absorb* brainset, your intellectual curiosity and ability to notice new things in the environment are enhanced. This will aid you in *problem finding* ("seeing" problems or situations that can then be creatively addressed). In the *absorb* brainset, your need to evaluate or judge objects, persons, events, or situations is suspended. And more information from the senses and the unconscious mind are allowed into your conscious awareness.

Although there are genetic differences in the tendency to access the *absorb* brainset,[34] it's also a skill that *can* be learned. But like any skill, it can only be acquired with regular practice. If you don't see results immediately, keep practicing. All of the exercises in this chapter (and additional exercises located on the Web site http://ShelleyCarson .com) will enhance your ability to access the open and receptive state of the *absorb* brainset.

Accessing the *absorb* brainset is only one step toward training your creative brain. In the next chapter you'll enhance your power of imagination using the *envision* brainset. The *absorb* and *envision* brainsets have some neural underpinnings in common. In fact, you can use the *absorb* brainset as a gateway to enter the *envision* brainset. However, just as the *absorb* brainset allows you to *passively* access information in a nonjudgmental manner, the *envision* brainset allows you to deliberately and *actively* manipulate that information to generate creative ideas. Read on to rev up your imaginative powers . . . and continue to practice the *absorb* exercises. As you practice, it will become progressively easier for you to access the *absorb* brainset at will.

You may find that it's *so easy that a caveman could do it.*

Exercises: The *Absorb* Brainset

Absorb Exercise #1: Attraction to Novelty: Noticing New Aspects

Aim of exercise: To open your conscious awareness to sensory stimuli and enhance your ability to "see" the world around you. You will need a stopwatch or a kitchen timer. This exercise will take you five minutes. Try to do it twice a day for several weeks until it becomes second nature.

Procedure: Set the stopwatch or timer for five minutes, and don't look at the time during this exercise. Now take in the environment around you right this minute, and try to view it with curiosity but *without* judgment. You may be reading this book in a comfortable chair by the fire, in a crowded airport, or in a sparse San Quentin prison cell. No matter where you are, your environment is infinitely interesting. In order to notice new aspects of your environment, begin with what you see.

○ Look for colors and notice how subtly or drastically the colors change where there are shadows or where sunlight or artificial light strikes the walls, floors, and ceiling. Look closely and see how the color of fabrics or paint may vary where it has faded.

○ Look for angles and notice the variety of angles in your environment. Look at the angle of the door frame to the ceiling. Notice the angles made by furnishings in your environment. Also notice the angles of incidental items in the environment, say a newspaper tossed on a table, a jacket draped over a chair, or a piece of trash left in the corner of a subway car. If you can see out a window, notice the angles made by objects outside, the angle of a tree or a bush to the window sill, of the angle of rain falling.

○ Notice movement in your environment. Is there a fire flickering in a fireplace? Are curtains moving gently in the breeze? Is a fly flitting around the room? Are people in motion around you? If so, notice the patterns of their movement. If you are in a vehicle, notice the movement of the landscape streaming by the window (of course, do *not* perform this exercise while you are actually driving).

Now pay attention to what you can hear.

○ First, listen to the foreground noises in your environment. Is there a television or radio turned on? Are other people talking? Rather than listening to words that are spoken, listen to the tonal qualities and the modulation of the voices. Do the voices remind you of angry thunder, or of a babbling brook?

○ Can you hear music? If so, listen to its qualities. Is the rhythm fast or slow? Constant or varied? Is the music a major or minor scale? Can you hear more than one instrument? Are the different instruments playing different melodies and harmonies?

○ Can you hear a dog barking, water running, a toilet flushing, someone coughing? Listen to the variations in all of these sounds. Listen for other outside noises, the buzz of traffic, a lawn mower, a distant siren.

○ Listen for background noises. Notice the hum of an air conditioner, a furnace, or a refrigerator. If you hear rain, listen carefully for variations in its sound. Rain makes a different noise when it hits the lawn, the road, trees, or a metal roof.

Next, pay attention to what you can feel.

○ Become aware of the air around you. Is it moist or dry? Warm or cool? Can you feel movement in the air, like a gentle breeze? Be perfectly still for a moment and see if you can detect variations in the temperature of the air.

Next, pay attention to the odors and fragrances in your environment.

o   Can you detect any food smells? Any floral smells? Resist the temptation to judge what you smell . . . just notice the different odors and fragrances of this place.

Continue to notice new aspects of your environment without judging them until your stopwatch or timer signals that the five minutes are up. Immediately give yourself a reward from the Small Pleasures list you made during Exercise #9 in Chapter Two. The purpose of this is to condition yourself (yes, just like Pavlov's dogs!) to be attracted to novel things in your environment. If you are using the token economy incentive, award yourself one *absorb* token each time you complete the exercise. Soon your brain will associate noticing new things with reward, and you'll develop the habit of experiencing the "immense worlds" that, as Blake wrote, are "clos'd" to others.

Absorb Exercise #2: Delayed Judgment: The *Absorb* Brainset and Food

Aim of exercise: To suspend judgment and increase appreciation for the novelty of perceptual experiences through the sense of taste. You'll need a recipe book and ingredients. The perceptual part of this exercise should take you about 10 minutes. Try to do it once a week until it becomes second nature.

Procedure: Try one new food dish each week. This should be a dish that you haven't tried before, or haven't tried in the past year.

o   Find a new recipe in a cookbook, magazine, or online. It should contain at least one ingredient with which you're not familiar. This could be a spice or seasoning, a fruit, vegetable, or meat.
o   Prepare the dish at a time when you're not rushed.
o   Spend 10 minutes exploring the taste of the new dish. Make sure *not* to judge the food ahead of time or during the tasting.

- ○ Notice the aroma of the food. Spend an entire minute just experiencing the uniqueness of the aroma. Do you notice a blend of aromas?
- ○ Taste the food with an effort to notice the basic aspects of taste. Is it spicy? Sweet? Pungent? Bitter? Dry? Salty?
- ○ Now notice the blending of flavors. Can you discern several different tastes?
- ○ Do the new ingredients you're trying remind you of other ingredients with which you're familiar? If so, consider the similarities, and consider the contrasts. Remember not to make judgmental contrasts (such as "This tastes like teriyaki but not as good"). Instead, make objective contrasts ("This tastes something like teriyaki, but I detect a ginger aftertaste").
- ○ Notice how your new dish interacts with other food in the meal. Are there harmonies among these foods, or point-counterpoint complexities?

When you're finished with your meal, praise yourself for trying the new dish. Even if you really didn't like the food, think about how interesting it was to try it. Continue to try at least one new recipe a week, and use positive self-statements to anticipate this food ritual ("I really look forward to trying a new food each week" or "I'm excited about the recipe I'm going to try this week"). Some of my creative subjects turn this exercise into a social event. They meet with friends and do the exercise together in a congenial atmosphere. (Note that it is possible to do the exercise in a restaurant by ordering a dish that you have not tasted before.) Whether you do the exercise with others or alone, make the meal a positive experience.

If you're using the token economy incentive, award yourself one *absorb* token each time you complete the exercise. Soon your brain will associate new perceptual experiences with reward, and you'll decrease your need to pass judgment and increase your positive response to novelty, both of which are principle components of the *absorb* brainset.

Absorb Exercise #3: Enhance Alpha and Theta Activity: Aerobic Activity Recovery

Aim of exercise: To increase *alpha* wave activity in your prefrontal lobes and increase creative potential. Research indicates that during the two-hour period following aerobic exercise, *alpha* and *theta* wave activity are increased in the prefrontal cortex.[35] During this period, you'll find it easier to access the receptive absorb brainset.

Procedure: Check with your doctor to make sure you are fit enough to engage in aerobic exercise.

o   Think about an open-ended problem that you'd like to solve or a creative dilemma that you'd like to address. This could include anything from finding a topic for an upcoming talk or paper, to developing a new product, to planning a children's birthday party.

o   Complete a 30-minute session of moderate aerobic activity. Exercise can include running, jogging, fast walking, cycling, spinning, swimming, or stair climbing. To complete moderate aerobic exercise, work out a pace that allows your pulse rate to remain somewhere between 60 and 80% of your maximum heart rate. You can determine this rate by subtracting your age from 220. Then multiply the result by .6 and .8 to find your target pulse rate range.

o   Use the two-hour period after your exercise session to reflect on your creative dilemma. During this period, you will be more creative and open to new ideas and solutions.

If you're using the token economy system, award yourself one *absorb* token each time you complete the exercise.

Absorb Exercise #4: Enhance Alpha and Theta Activity: Openness Meditation

Aim of exercise: To increase *alpha* and *theta* wave activity in your prefrontal lobes. Research indicates that as you gain more skill with meditation, you will find it easier to access a receptive brainset as indicated by *alpha* and *theta* activity.[36] You'll also find that you pay more attention to novel stimuli in your environment. Note that there are many different categories of meditation, and studies indicate that each type has different effects on brain activation patterns. This very simple exercise is intended for the novice meditator. It should take you about 10 minutes. Try to do it at least once a day. You should experience additional benefits from this exercise, such as decreased heart rate and blood pressure and a reduction in stress.

Procedure: When first beginning to do openness meditation, choose a quiet, comfortable location where you will not be disturbed.

o   Close your eyes and focus on your breathing. Breathe in with your abdomen rather than your chest. To practice this, place one hand on your abdomen. As you inhale, your hand should move forward (away from your spine). As you exhale your hand should move inward. This takes some practice, so don't get frustrated if you don't get it right off the bat.

o   Gradually slow your breathing, holding the inhalation for a few seconds before you release it. Breathe in and out, slowly and rhythmically. With each breath, feel yourself relaxing.

o   As thoughts flit across your mind, notice them and then gently push them aside. If important issues come to mind, again, notice them but do not dwell on them; gently push them aside, knowing you can focus on them at a later time.

o   Continue breathing, focusing on your breath, giving yourself permission to just be.

o   Remain in this openness meditation, focusing on your breathing and the present moment, for about 10 minutes.

o   At the end of this time, open your eyes, smile, stretch for a moment if you feel like it, and continue with your day.

Note that smiling at the end of the meditation period acts as an internal reward. Smiling not only reflects a positive mood but actually acts to promote positive feelings. The purpose of this is to condition yourself to associate *alpha* and *theta* activity in your prefrontal lobes with pleasant feelings. This will make it more likely that you'll slip into an *alpha*-rich receptive brainset when you're not busily engaged in other activities.

If you're using the token economy system, award yourself one *absorb* token each time you complete the exercise.

Absorb Exercise #5: Disinhibition: The *Absorb* Brainset and REM Sleep

Aim of exercise: To access a state of disinhibition that allows information to feed forward from the unconscious into conscious awareness. Alan Hobson and Robert Stickgold, from the Harvard Medical School, have extensively researched the relationship between creativity and the sleep-wake cycle. They've found that associative information formed in the unconscious mind is more likely to be accessed by conscious awareness during the period immediately following awakening from REM sleep, the sleep state associated with dreams.[37] In this exercise, you will attempt to access this fertile post-REM period. You will need an alarm clock and a tape recorder or pad and pen for writing. This exercise will take you 15 minutes.

Procedure: The drowsy periods that precede and follow sleep are well known as doors through which the unconscious mind can be accessed. Because there are individual differences in sleep patterns you may have to experiment with your wake-time before catching yourself in REM sleep.

- Think about an open-ended problem that you'd like to solve or a creative dilemma that you'd like to address.
- Set your alarm clock for 30 minutes earlier than you normally wake up. Because early morning sleep cycles contain longer periods of REM sleep than the nighttime sleep hours, your chances of

waking yourself during a dream (REM cycle) are more likely in the early morning. (Note that you can also try this alternate strategy: Allow yourself to "sleep in" by waking at your normal time and then setting your alarm for an additional 30 minutes.)

o When the alarm clock wakes you, immediately begin to record your thoughts on the recorder or the paper. During this period, you will be more creative and open to new ideas and solutions.

If you're using the token economy system, award yourself one *absorb* token each time you complete the exercise.

Absorb Exercise #6: Induce Mild Disinhibition: Dialogue with Your TOP

Aim of exercise: To increase your access to the *absorb* brainset and loosen the cognitive filter that prevents novel ideas from making it into conscious awareness. This exercise should take you under five minutes. Try to do it twice a day until it becomes second nature.

Procedure: TOP stands for **T**emporal, **O**ccipital, and **P**arietal lobes (in other words, the back of the brain). The TOP functions below the level of conscious awareness so you are not aware of what goes on back there. However, the TOP is the seat of much of the association centers and much of the associational work that goes on in the brain. When an idea pops into your head, it is actually feeding forward from the TOP regions of the brain to the prefrontal lobes. In this exercise, you will "talk" to your TOP to encourage conscious awareness of new ideas.

o First, you may want to give your TOP a name. It is your *muse* after all, the small voice that whispers insights to you. You may want to name it after a mentor or a person who has been an inspiration to you. You may want to name it after a fictitious character. Or you may want to give it a fanciful name that has a pleasant ring for you. One of my writer subjects simply named his "Muse." If you want to think of the TOP as being a conduit to a source outside of yourself (such as the songwriter who felt she had an antenna to the angels), that's fine. But whether you picture your source of inspiration as residing outside or inside your head, remember that you need the cooperation of your TOP to access your novel ideas (so it probably isn't a good idea to name it something like Shithead or Numbskull).

○   Open the conversation with small talk. "So how's it going back there?" "Are you getting enough glucose?" "Is the temperature okay?"

○   Discuss any creative problems you may be having. "I'd like to figure out how to stage the battle scene in Act II," "I'd like to find a substance to use a filament in my bulb," "I'd like to find a way to prove this mathematical equation," "I know there's a way to present this ad campaign; I'd like to figure out what to do with it."

○   Listen carefully for an answer. Note that you will likely *not* detect any answers at this time.

○   Vow to keep the communications lines open. "Notify me if you get an idea." "Any time day or night, just send me a message and I'll get it."

○   Thank your TOP for listening and envision either an open gate or an open door between your prefrontal cortex and your TOP.

Now if this exercise sounds silly to you (and it may well sound silly if you're a steadfast *deliberate* thinker), guess what: you're being *judgmental*. See the *Absorb* Exercise #2 for practice in suspending premature judgment.

If you're using the token economy system, award yourself one *absorb* token each time you complete the exercise. If you're not using the token economy incentive, reward yourself with an item from the Small Pleasures list you created in Exercise #9 in Chapter Two. The purpose of this is to condition yourself to be open to novel combinations and solutions arising from the associational cortices in TOP. Reward yourself each time you do the exercise for the first two weeks. After that, continue to do the exercise daily but only reward yourself occasionally. Soon your brain will associate opening up to unusual ideas with reward, and you'll develop the habit of allowing more unconscious material to feed forward.

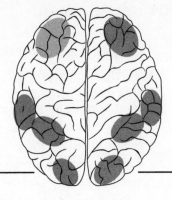

Imagining the Possibilities: Accessing the *Envision Brainset*

Imagination is more important than knowledge.

—ALBERT EINSTEIN[1]

CAVEMAN #2 (you met him in the last chapter) is standing on a cliff at the edge of a deep canyon.

He sees the birds soaring overhead, and, like people of all epochs, he imagines what it would be like to glide through the sky like a bird. He is able, thanks to his recently evolved prefrontal cortex, to envision himself soaring above the canyon.

He can actually "see" the canyon from an aerial view in his mind's eye even though he has never flown.

He can feel the wind rushing in his face (because he has felt wind before and he understands that air would rush by if he were flying), and he can even feel the sun on his back as he swoops above the canyon walls.

However, thanks again to his new prefrontal cortex, he is able to determine that leaping off the cliff to soar like a bird might not be a great idea.

He remembers when Caveman #1 threw a pumpkin over this same cliff a couple of weeks ago. In his mind, he sees what happened to that pumpkin. He feels the shape of his own head and realizes that in many ways his body type resembles a pumpkin more than a bird. He uses that information to speculate and visualize what might happen if he steps off the cliff into the void. He "sees" his own body—now pumpkin-like pulp—at the foot of the canyon.

Sadder but wiser, Caveman #2 walks away from the precipice, the image of his mangled body now stored in memory to be recalled if the urge to fly like a bird arises again in the future.

Much of the same brain circuitry that is used to encode and retrieve real memories can be used to encode and retrieve hypothetical events that are oh-so-helpful in keeping us on terra firma.[2] Our Caveman (who is himself a product of the *envision* brainset) has just displayed one of the reasons that humans have survived these many millennia. We can "see" what is likely to happen if we choose a course of action without actually having to experience the consequences of that action. Thanks to the relatively recent neurological developments in our prefrontal cortex and our memory encoding machinery (an area of the brain called the hippocampus),[3] we do not have to leap off cliffs like lemmings. We can foresee our imagined fate and avoid it if we so choose.

From Memory to Imagination

In order to understand how our brains "do" creativity, we need to reach way back in evolutionary history—back to an era preceding that of our Caveman #2. As we discussed in Chapter Three, the last part of the human brain to develop was the prefrontal cortex. This is also the last part of your brain to develop as you mature. In fact, evidence suggests that the prefrontal lobes are not entirely developed until around age 25.

(Now here's an unsettling thought: Professor Timothy Salthouse of the University of Virginia recently completed a seven-year study that indicated our brains—starting with the prefrontal cortex—begin to decline around the age of 27.[4] If Salthouse is correct, we have *two years* or so of peak prefrontal brain power! But don't worry; thanks to neuroplasticity—the remarkable power of our brain to repair, regenerate, and reorganize itself throughout adulthood[5]—we have many decades of creative productivity ahead of us!)

The prefrontal cortex (PFC), as you'll also remember from Chapter Two, is the home of the executive center. The amazing things that the PFC allows us to do include planning (to fly like a bird), abstract thinking (to envision what would happen if we try to fly like a bird), and conscious decision making (walk away from the cliff without trying to fly). The PFC has connections to areas of the brain where the contents of memory are encoded and stored. When the circuits that connect these areas are activated, we are able to "remember" a future that hasn't happened yet and make better survival decisions.

The same brain circuitry that developed to help ensure our survival has a serendipitous side effect: it also allows us to generate nonsurvival-related creative ideas. We can use this important brain circuitry to imagine rearranging our living room furniture, make up a character for a new novel, devise an original plan for robbing a bank, or a conceive a design for powering a winged aircraft. Thus, the ability to purposefully evoke memories and mental images is the precursor to both imagination and the ability to consciously form creative ideas[6]— the essence of the *envision* brainset.

Defining the Envision Brainset

You learned about how to access a receptive and nonjudgmental brainset in the last chapter on the *absorb* brainset. That ability to enter the *absorb* brainset will set you up to observe new things in your environment, to see potential connections between things in your environment and problems you wish to solve creatively, and also to be receptive to creative ideas that may originate in parts of your brain outside of conscious awareness. Now you'll learn how to use your innate brain circuitry to *deliberately* imagine novel solutions to problems using mental imagery. The *envision* brainset is the brain activation state that facilitates imagination. The *envision* brainset also provides a link between the *deliberate* and the *spontaneous* pathways to creativity by allowing you to retain purposeful and deliberate control of the contents of conscious awareness while accessing information and ideas that are developed at more spontaneous and disinhibited levels of cognitive processing.[7]

The *envision* state is well known to many children, actors, and daydreamers. It is the creator of your so-called "inner world." But if your mental comfort zone is the *reason* or *evaluate* brainset, you may either find it hard to activate this brainset or you may consider it childish or foolish to attempt to do so. Yet the benefits of the *envision* brainset are far-reaching and extend beyond the ability to develop creative ideas.

We have already discussed how you can use the *envision* brainset to make decisions that can have an impact on your safety and your future. However, this brainset also provides the neural basis for how you form a coherent picture of the world (your world schema) and how you form a coherent picture of yourself (your personal identity).[8] A coherent worldview and a sense of identity are both crucial to high mental functioning and good mental health. Further, the ability to envision is gaining rapid acceptance as one of the most sought-after qualities in business managers and corporate executives. The ability to envision also has implications for health. Several studies suggest that mental imagery can aid the healing process.[9] Finally, the ability to use mental imagery to practice athletic skills has shown benefits in sports such as basketball and golf.[10] Many coaches incorporate visualization into their practice routines. Musicians, surgeons, and even high-voltage power line inspectors report using mental imagery to practice their skills.[11] So the bottom line is that even those of you who are skeptical of the value of this brainset will benefit from developing your ability to use it frequently and fully.

The *envision* brainset shares some features with the *absorb* brainset, including the preference for novelty and a mild state of mental disinhibition. However, the most important factors in the *envision* brainset are the generation of mental imagery and the use of hypothetical thinking. In this chapter, you'll learn techniques for increasing both the vividness of mental imagery and the frequency of imaginal or hypothetical thinking.

Mental Imagery

Mental imagery, or "thinking without words," is a type of cognition that employs the perceptual parts of the brain ordinarily used for processing the sensory information of sight, hearing, smell, taste, and touch. Mental imagery is quasi perceptual, meaning that the perceptions are occurring without sensory input from the outside world. But no, they're not hallucinations! (Although many creative individuals report semi-hallucinatory experiences, such as seeing the shapes of objects in clouds or shadows, or hearing the sound of music or voices in the rustling of wind in trees.[12]) There are differences between psychotic hallucinations and creative mental images: first, when mental images related to creative problems are formed—even when they appear in the mind *spontaneously*—they are not mistaken for reality. Second, when you evoke mental images, you are consciously controlling the imagery material, whereas hallucinations generally occur outside of one's conscious direction.

Scientists, such as Einstein and Stephen Hawking, as well as artists, writers, Web designers, engineers, and musicians, have written about the importance of mental imagery in their creative process.[13] Highly creative people appear to be able to form vivid mental images and manipulate those images both to envision creative dilemmas and to come up with creative solutions to problems.

Most of us can "image" music, including the background instruments and voices of a favorite recording, and we may unconsciously keep time to the auditory image by tapping a foot or moving our head. Most of us will smile when asked to summon the image of a loved one's face. Most of us will curl our lip when asked to imagine biting into a lemon, indicating that we are able to form sensory images of objects that aren't actually there so vividly that they can affect our behavior. Though there are individual differences in how vividly you can imagine sights or sounds that are not there, you can learn to improve your ability to vividly image.[14]

Harvard Professor Stephen Kosslyn is one of the world's leading investigators in the field of mental imagery. He and others have discovered that imaging activates the same parts of the brain that are activated by actual sensory input. This means that, as you've probably heard before, these parts of the brain can't tell the difference between the real object and the imagined object. Further, when you visualize an object, neurons in the occipital cortex (the seeing center of the brain) fire in a map that is spatially arranged just like the object you're imagining. The intensity of the firing of these neurons correlates with the vividness of the imagery.[15]

One way to increase your creative capacity is to improve your ability to mentally image, and research indicates that this is definitely possible.[16] Mental imagery includes not only your capacity to see images that are not in the outside environment; it also includes the capacity to hear, smell, feel, and taste that which is not there. (The best way to increase the vividness of mental imagery is to practice imaging. To increase your ability to mentally image, practice *Envision* Exercises #1 and #2.)

Although you will want to enhance your ability to image across all senses, you may find that it is easier for you to begin by manipulating the visual modality of mental imagery. We can divide visual imagery into two basic types. The first type is "pictorial," in which you visualize a replica of an object or scene as it appears in real life or as you might capture it with a camera. Exercise #1 is an example of pictorial imaging. If you have difficulty visualizing pictorially, it may help to physically "trace" the object before trying to visualize it. This tactic, used by artists for over a hundred years, will evoke muscle memory as well as visual memory of the object.[17]

The second type of visual image is "diagrammatic," in which the image is seen as a symbol or diagram of a real object or scene, such as a map or a blueprint. Such diagrams can be very useful if you're trying to locate an object or build anything from a child's table to a skyscraper. As an example, close your eyes and image the East Coast of the United States. There are fourteen states that touch the Atlantic Ocean. Can you name them? Diagrammatic images involve an extra step of mental processing. In addition to imaging an object, you have to transform that object to a symbolic representation before visualizing it. Diagrammatic images allow you to see relationships between objects or between parts of the same object rather than focusing on realistic details. They activate a part of the brain referred to as the "where" visual stream. (This is separate from the "what" visual stream that is involved in visualizing objects rather than locations.)[18]

There are also different sets of neurons in the visual cortex that govern the shape, color, and movement of objects and scenery. Therefore, when you "see" a static image in your mind, you are using a different part of the brain than when you try to rotate or manipulate the object or scene in some way. In order to enhance your ability to use mental imagery in a creative manner, it's important to practice both seeing and manipulating objects. *Envision* Exercises 1–5 comprise a fun set of visualization exercises.

Another way to practice manipulating mental images is through guided sequential visualizations. In one of my creativity courses, we practice a sequential visualization called the secret garden. In the garden sequence, students begin by imagining that they're being transported to a secret garden. Throughout the course, students return to this garden. In between sessions, they consider what types of flora they would like to have in their gardens—from aromatic pines to exotic and colorful blossoms. As the course progresses, even students who had trouble visualizing a tree on their first attempt find that they can now enjoy the fragrances, sights, and sounds of their own unique garden. You can download an audio version of the secret garden sequence from the Web site http://ShelleyCarson.com.

The ability to use mental imagery alone would not be creative. However, when the ability to form and manipulate mental images is combined with hypothetical thinking, the possibilities of what can be conceived are truly astounding!

Hypothetical Thinking

Hypothetical thinking is the foundation of your imagination. When you employ hypothetical or conjectural thinking, you are mentally imaging something that is not manifest in the world of reality (reality being the state of things as they objectively exist, not as we would have them exist). Your conjecture is not "true," or at least it has not been shown to be true. You are thinking in "What ifs."

We've already discussed how "What if?" thinking can help you make decisions (such as whether to jump off a cliff and try to fly). However, hypothetical thinking is not limited by the constraints of current reality. You can use "What if?" or hypothetical thinking to speculate on situations that are not probable in the real world, as well as those that might actually be possible. What if people had three arms instead of two? What if you use red instead of green for the color of the grass in a watercolor painting? What if you replace the cinnamon in Aunt Millie's pumpkin pie recipe with cayenne pepper? What if light is both a particle and a wave? What if Darth Vader turns out to be related to Luke Skywalker? What if you switch the melody from a major key to a minor key? What if you let the killer escape from the asylum in Chapter Twenty-Three? What if Chicago were overrun with Martians? What if I take the next exit and drive to Ohio instead of Florida?

There is an endless array of "What if?" scenarios we could visualize in just a single day. We have this elegant hardware that allows us to imagine, but how often do we use it? We have this sophisticated video game right inside our skull, there to be played at any hour of the day or night. How often do you play with it? Creative people play with mental imagery and hypothetical thinking a lot . . . and the results are not inconsequential. Einstein claims to have used this power of hypothetical mental imaging to form his theory of relativity. He described his creative process as seeing "more or less clear images which can be 'voluntarily' reproduced and combined . . . this combinatory play seems to be the essential feature in productive thought."[19] This is a good description of working within the *envision* brainset.

All right. I'm getting a mental image of those of you who prefer the evaluative brainset rolling your eyes. You may see the "What if?" games as silly or as a self-indulgent waste of time. *But*, as we've discussed, the ability to imagine is a survival tool. It has allowed us to adapt to and eventually control our surroundings by ima gining new and novel resources for ourselves. By forming mental images of highly unlikely scenarios, you are training your brain to think outside the proverbial box. The more you practice "what if-ing," the more easily you will be able to visualize unusual scenarios and the more likely you are to come up with ideas when you need to generate a novel solution to a problem.

Neuroscience of the *Envision* Brainset

What does your brain look like when you access the *envision* brainset? The answer depends upon whether you're deliberately or spontaneously experiencing mental images and on whether you're generating mental imagery or manipulating it (making it move or altering it in some way). Let's look at this more closely.

Spontaneous Generation of Mental Imagery

If you decide to use mental imagery to help you solve a practical problem, the executive center in the prefrontal cortex is activated in the effort to call forth an image, maintain it, and decide how to manipulate it.

The relative activation of the executive center determines your ability to control mental imagery.

Many creative individuals report having extremely strong spontaneous mental images when they are in a defocused state such as the *absorb* brainset or when they are taking a walk or nodding off to sleep. At such times the executive center is taking a break and relinquishing some control of the cognitive processes, allowing images generated spontaneously in the TOP (the temporal, parietal, and occipital lobes of the brain) to more or less take on a life of their own. Charles Dickens is reported to have fended off imaginary urchins from his novels with his umbrella as he walked the early morning streets of London. Nikola Tesla, credited with inventing alternating electrical current, writes that he was walking silently with a friend one evening when a mental image of the idea for the AC generator came to him. "The images I saw were wonderfully sharp and clear and had the solidity of metal and stone."[20]

The most bizarre and uncontrolled mental imagery takes place during REM sleep, when dreams are most prominent. The executive center is relatively deactivated during REM sleep, while the vision areas and the association centers located in the rear areas of the brain are activated. This allows images and sensations, evoked by the firing of random neurons and uninhibited by the sleeping executive center, to take center stage in the mind.[21] (Note that along with randomly generated images, some dream material is nonrandom and appears to relate to recent memory fragments. The reason that we dream and that both random and recent event material populates our dreams is still debated by scientists; however, one theory is that dreaming allows the integration of unassociated information in the creative problem-solving process.[22])

It's interesting that some control over the content of dreams—or at least awareness that one is dreaming—can occur during a state referred to as "lucid dreaming." Lucid dreaming can be primed by presleep suggestions and also by certain forms of training. It appears that the executive center, which is normally at rest during dreaming, is partially reactivated during lucid dreaming and thus commands some control over the content of the mental imagery.[23]

The presence of mental imagery, then, can be deliberately or spontaneously generated in the brain, depending upon the activation level of the executive center in the prefrontal cortex.[24] Likewise, mental imagery can be deliberately or spontaneously manipulated. Some of the most creative insights have arisen from the spontaneous generation of mental images during the illumination stage of the creative process and then consciously and deliberately manipulated after their arrival.

You can attempt to regulate the amount of deliberate or spontaneous control you have over mental images by regulating the activation of the executive center. The chapter on the *absorb* brainset provides exercises that mildly deactivate the prefrontal areas of the executive center. Other traditional (but not necessarily recommended) methods of regulation include dreaming, sleep deprivation, alcohol or drug consumption, meditation, repetitive or rhythmic exercise (such as long-distance running or trance dancing). One of the goals of this book is to teach you to modulate the activation of your executive center at will so that you can enter specific brainsets to facilitate creative thought and productivity. *Envision* Exercise #7 mimics the experiences described by many creative individuals. It combines the use of mental imagery with a state of physical relaxation.

Generating Versus Manipulating Mental Images

When you generate mental imagery, you use virtually the same systems of the brain that you use to process sensory information that comes in from the environment through your sensory organs (eyes, ears, nose, skin, or taste buds). When you generate visual mental imagery, there is evidence that associational centers and the visual center of the brain are activated primarily in the left hemisphere of the brain. When you rotate or manipulate the images, these same areas may be more preferentially activated in the right hemisphere.[25]

But what happens in the brain when you deliberately attempt to conceive of a novel object (combining the generation of a mental image with hypothetical thinking)? Japanese researchers, led by Yasuyuki Kowatari of the University of Tsukuba, investigated this question by asking both formally trained design experts and novices to mentally design a new pen while their brains were scanned using fMRI. They found that the most creative designs were correlated with relatively greater activation of the right prefrontal cortex and the left superior parietal cortex (corresponding to our right executive center and left association center), while deactivating the right parietal cortex. This finding is in keeping with other research that indicates the right prefrontal cortex is involved in the *deliberate* generating of novel and creative material.[26]

The main pattern of activation, then, for the *envision* brainset is a network connecting the executive centers (particularly in the right hemisphere) to left association centers and to areas in the parietal, temporal, and occipital lobes that are dedicated to processing information from your senses.

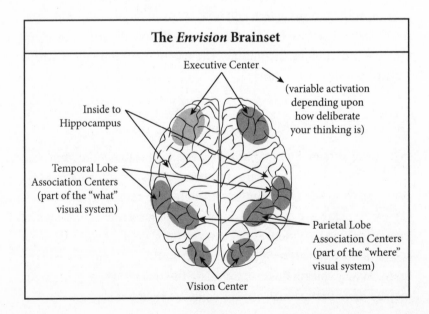

The *Envision* Brainset

Executive Center

(variable activation depending upon how deliberate your thinking is)

Inside to Hippocampus

Temporal Lobe Association Centers (part of the "what" visual system)

Parietal Lobe Association Centers (part of the "where" visual system)

Vision Center

In this chapter, you've seen how you can evoke the activation pattern of the *envision* brainset to enhance mental imagery and increase hypothetical thinking. You've seen that you can use mental imagery to your advantage through both the *deliberate* and the *spontaneous* pathways to creativity. You've seen that the *envision* and *absorb* brainsets can be used in complementary ways. The more you practice the *envision* brainset, the easier it will be for you to envision creative solutions to problems. The *envision* brainset involves creative thinking using internally generated sensory information. But what if you tend to think in words? In the next chapter, you'll add a strategy that is based in verbal or word-based thinking. With the *connect* brainset, you'll learn techniques to increase the fluency of creative ideas in ways that will motivate you to greater innovation and productivity.

As for Caveman #2, his dreams of flying like the birds were not in vain. His ability to hold a mental image of his aspirations, along with the ability and determination of those who came after him, eventually led to flight . . .

Exercises: The Envision Brainset

Envision Exercise #1: Visual Mental Imagery: Your Bedroom

Aim of exercise: To increase the ability to evoke vivid internally generated images. This exercise will take you around five minutes. Try to practice a version of this exercise once a day for a week.

Procedure: Begin by closing your eyes and imagining that you are standing in the doorway to your bedroom. (Note: if you are doing the exercise while in your bedroom, visualize a different room of your house or apartment.)

- Now in your mind's eye, look to your left and see the wall adjacent to the doorway. If there is furniture against the wall, see it. See any pictures, windows, or drapes that may be on this wall. If the open door is against the wall, see it as well.
- Now see the wall of your bedroom to your left that is at a 90-degree angle to the door. Visualize what is on the wall—windows, doors, curtains, furniture, pictures.
- Then move to the wall opposite where you are standing, and vividly see what is on that wall—windows, doors, curtains, furniture, pictures.
- Move to the wall that is at a 90-degree angle to the right of the wall where you are standing. Visualize what is on that wall—windows, doors, curtains, furniture, pictures.
- Finally, see the wall adjacent to the doorway to your right. And vividly notice whatever is there.
- Look around the room once again. Is the bed made? Are there clothes lying on the bed or the floor?
- Is there an odor in the room? Smelly gym socks or a scented candle? Take a moment to sniff.
- Now open your eyes. Try to imagine the four walls of your bedroom vividly with your eyes open. Move from wall to wall and try to see things in as much detail as you did with your eyes closed,

superimposing the mental image on the actual space in front of you.

When you have finished the tour of your room, think about whether it was more difficult to image the room with your eyes open. Practice this exercise once a day for a week, using other rooms, your office, or a closet as the focus of your visualization. As you improve your ability to visualize with your eyes open, try this exercise when you're in a setting that is crowded or noisy. With practice, you can learn to *envision* productively in any setting.

If you're using the token economy system, award yourself one *envision* token each time you complete the exercise.

Envision Exercise #2: Generating Multi-Modal Mental Imagery: Mental Holiday

Aim of exercise: To increase your ability to form vivid mental imagery, including visual, auditory, tactile, and olfactory (smell) images. This exercise is also widely used to decrease anxiety and focus attention inward. You can read through the exercise and then complete the visualization, or you can download an audio recording of the visualization from http://ShelleyCarson.com. This exercise will take you five minutes. Try to practice it at least once a day for several weeks, adding more vividness and detail to your vacation each time you practice.

Procedure: Close your eyes and take three deep cleansing breaths. Now imagine that you are in a place where you have found relaxation and serenity in the past. This could be a quiet beach . . . or a mountain meadow . . . or a redwood forest. Imagine your place of serenity now.

○ What do you see around you? Turn slowly so that you can see in every direction. See the scenery as vividly as possible.

○ What are you hearing? Bird song, the crying of gulls? The sound of the surf? A distant waterfall? Imagine the sounds of your serene place as vividly as possible.

- What are you feeling? The warm sun on your shoulders? A cool breeze against your face? Refreshing sea mist on your face? Cool, smooth grass beneath your feet? Imagine the feel of your serene place as vividly as possible.

- What are you smelling? Fragrant flowers? The salty sea? The smell of pine? Imagine the fragrances of your serene place as vividly as possible.

Now . . . just enjoy your serene place for a few moments . . . as you continue to see, hear, smell, and feel all that is around you. When you feel refreshed, take another deep breath and open your eyes.

If you continue to practice this exercise once a day for several weeks, you'll notice an increase in the vividness of your mental imagery. You will also probably notice that the exercise has a calming influence on you and helps you to "turn off" the stream of verbal thoughts (which psychologists call "self-talk") that constantly runs through your mind.

If you're using the token economy system, award yourself one *envision* token each time you complete the exercise.

Envision Exercise #3: Visual Mental Imagery: Muscle Memory

Aim of exercise: To increase your ability to visualize objects pictorially using mental imagery. This exercise will take you five minutes. You will need a pencil.

Procedure: Stand several feet away from an object in your environment for which you would like to creative a vivid mental picture. Hold the pencil far out from your body and "trace" the object in the air with the pencil. Go over the outside edge of the object first, then trace the interior divisions or lines. When you have spent about two minutes examining and tracing the object in the air, close your eyes and try to envision the object. It may help to try to trace it in the air again with your eyes closed.

If this technique is helpful to you, try to do the exercise daily with progressively more complex objects. If you're using the token economy system, award yourself one *envision* token each time you complete the exercise.

Envision Exercise #4: Mental Imagery: Floor Plan

Aim of exercise: To increase your ability to visualize objects diagrammatically using mental imagery. This exercise will take you under five minutes.

Procedure: Close your eyes and mentally visualize a floor plan of your house or apartment. If your house has more than one floor, visualize how the floor plan of the second level fits on top of the first. Which rooms are on top of each other? If you live in an apartment, try to visualize different levels of the apartment building. Is the lobby floor laid out differently from the upper levels? Spend several minutes in this visualization until you feel that you have the relationship between rooms and floors in their correct location.

You can complete this exercise with other buildings and spaces that are familiar to you.

For instance, you can practice by laying out a mental diagram of your front yard, your backyard, your street, your office building, or the local mall.

If you're using the token economy system, award yourself one *envision* token each time you complete the exercise.

Envision Exercise #5: Manipulating Mental Imagery: Your Car

Aim of exercise: To increase your ability to manipulate mental imagery. This exercise will take you five minutes. You will need a stopwatch or timer and a car, preferably one with which you're familiar. If possible, park the car in a spot where you can walk around it at will.

Procedure: Stand about five feet away from the middle of the left side of the car. Take a look at the car, set the timer for one minute, and close your eyes.

o   Now form a mental image of the car, imagining as much detail as possible. With your eyes closed, move your vision over the mental image from front to back, noting the lines and details of the car. When the timer sounds, open your eyes and look at the car, noting where your mental image was accurate and where it was inaccurate or vague.

o   Now, without moving your position, set the timer for one minute again and close your eyes. This time, form a mental image of how the car would look if you were standing five feet directly in front of it. Try to see the edges of the car in perspective against the backdrop (whether it's the garage or an open space) and move your vision across the image from the passenger side to the driver's side of the car. When the timer sounds, move to the front of the car and see how accurate your image was. People are often surprised at how distorted the car actually looks from the front relative to their image.

o   Once again set the timer for one minute and close your eyes. This time form a mental image of how the car would look if you were standing five feet away and at a 45-degree angle from the back passenger side tail light. Try to see the perspective formed by the edges of the car against the backdrop. With your eyes closed, visualize as much detail of the car from this angle as possible. When the timer sounds, open your eyes and move to the position from which you were forming your vision. Are you surprised by what you see or was your mental image pretty accurate?

Try to practice visualizing a familiar object from different angles each day. The more often you this, the better you will get at manipulating visual images in your mind.

If you're using the token economy system, award yourself one *envision* token each time you complete the exercise.

Envision Exercise #6: Hypothetical Thinking: "What If?"

Aim of exercise: To combine elements of hypothetical thinking and mental imagery to improve imagination. You will need a stopwatch or clock. The exercise will take five minutes.

Procedure: Set the stopwatch for five minutes. Now visualize this scenario: We know that dolphins are intelligent and have large brains. Imagine that a deep sea race of dolphins have developed opposable thumbs and have been able to fashion a machine that allows them to live on dry land and communicate with humans. What changes do you see occurring economically? Socially? Professionally? How would you personally be affected? Allow your imagination to visualize the scenario and stay with it until the stopwatch sounds.

In order to fine-tune your imaginative abilities, practice a "What If?" exercise daily. To come up with your own scenarios, you can take stories out of the local newspaper and change one element of the story. For instance, what if the National Endowment for the Arts provided $200,000 to barbers and hairdressers to exhibit sculptures made of hair clippings? What if environmental groups proposed legislation that made it illegal to kill cockroaches? Make up one scenario each day and spend five minutes visualizing the consequences of your scenario. Don't let reality or propriety constrain your vision.

If you're using the token economy system, award yourself one *envision* token each time you complete the exercise.

Envision Exercise #7: Mental Imagery: Modulation of Executive Control

Aim of exercise: To modulate prefrontal cortical arousal while using mental imagery to improve creative thinking. The exercise will take 15 minutes. Perform this exercise when you are physically exhausted. You may, for instance, try it after aerobic exercise or at the end of a long day. You will need to have an active creative dilemma in mind. You will also need paper and pencil.

Procedure: When you are physically exhausted, form a mental image of your creative dilemma.

o   When you have a firm image of the dilemma as well as an idea of the kind of solution that would work for you (for instance, say your dilemma is that you need to come up with an idea for a new advertising campaign; you know your client's product and you know that the client wants to portray elegance rather than humor or affordability), just relax. You may either: (a) lie down and close your eyes, or (b) sit in a rocking chair, close your eyes and rhythmically rock.

o   As you rest with your eyes closed, observe what happens to your image. If you feel yourself starting to nod off, give yourself the suggestion to dream about your image.

o   After 10 or 15 minutes (or when you wake), immediately write down what has been going through your mind, even if it had nothing to do with your creative dilemma or your image. Note: It's important to write down any thoughts that you have while dreaming or dozing. Because the executive center (which you'll remember controls your working memory) is deactivated during these times, memories of your thoughts will be fleeting. That's why it's very difficult to remember dreams unless you try to recreate them immediately upon waking.

Try to do this exercise several times per week. The more you practice the more likely you are to keep the mental image of your dilemma in mind while you rest. In such cases it will be under less executive control and may mix with other spontaneous images in a way that could be useful to solving your problem.

If you're using the token economy system, award yourself one *envision* token each time you complete the exercise.

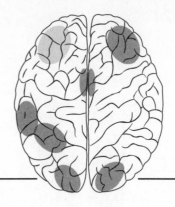

Thinking Divergently: Accessing the Connect Brainset

Ideas rose in crowds; I felt them collide until pairs interlocked, so to speak, making a stable combination . . .

—HENRI POINCARÉ[1]

WHILE THE *ENVISION* BRAINSET allows you to play out ideas, all within the safety of your mind, the *connect* brainset allows you to generate multiple ideas without concern about how they will play out. When you access the *connect* brainset, one idea leads to another and another.[2] Your brain becomes an idea-generating machine.

Defining the *Connect* Brainset

You'll notice several things happening as you learn to access the *connect* brainset. First, you'll start thinking *divergently* rather than *convergently*. Divergent thinking is a type of cognition in which you

123

"How does he come up with all those ideas?"

see many possible answers to questions and problems. In fact, you will risk becoming overwhelmed with possibilities for creative innovation! Second, you will make connections between disparate objects and concepts; these unusual associations will lead to more novel and original ideas. The result? You will find yourself becoming energized and excited about working on your creative problem.[3]

In addition to the qualities of divergent thinking, making unusual associations, and intrinsic motivation, the *connect* brainset shares three important characteristics with both the *absorb* and the *envision* brainsets. As with *absorb* and *envision*, when you access the *connect* brainset the censor in your brain gets to take a break; this allows more ideas to make it through the automatic filtering system into conscious awareness (what we called "cognitive disinhibition" in Chapter Five). You are attracted to novelty and complexity; just as you receive an internal reward for noticing new or novel aspects of things in the *absorb* brainset, you get excited about interfacing with previously unexplored and novel ideas in the *connect* brainset. Finally, as with the *absorb* and *envision* brainsets, you suspend judgment in the *connect* state, especially judgment of your own ideas; thus, when an idea makes it into conscious awareness, you don't direct your attention toward evaluating it. Instead, you direct your attention toward the generation of the next idea, resulting in an array of possible solutions to your creative problems.[4]

Divergent Thinking

Divergent thinking is one of the hallmarks of the creative mind. Many researchers who study creativity refer to the propensity to think divergently as a measure of *trait* creativity or potential creativity.[5] It is sometimes described as the "other" way of thinking. But if *divergent* thought is the "other" way, what is the so-called "normal" way of thinking? That would be what researchers call *convergent* thinking. Let's look at the difference between divergent and convergent thought processes.

Convergent thinking[6] is the type of thinking you do when you access the contents stored in your brain (including knowledge and memories) to come up with the one correct answer to a well-defined problem. You are already familiar with convergent thinking, as it is the form of thought needed to solve questions on standardized tests such as the SAT Reasoning Test. Convergent thinking is also the basis for most questions on high school and college exams. Consider the following sample question from an SAT test in which you are asked to fill in the blanks with the appropriate words:

They were not _____ misfortune, having endured more than their fair share of _____ .

a) cognizant of . . . calamity

b) superstitious about . . . prosperity

c) jealous of . . . success

d) oblivious to . . . happiness

e) unacquainted with . . . adversity[7]

Now if you think convergently, and if you have a decent vocabulary, you fill in (e) and go on your way because (e) is the "right" answer. Being able to think convergently is an important skill; and it is also important in the creative process, as we'll discuss at length in Chapter Eight. However, *convergent* thinking limits your thought processes by assuming that there is one right answer to a problem. Rather than exploring multiple options, the convergent thinker will search for the one salient and correct solution.

Divergent thinking, in contrast, is the propensity to generate multiple solutions to a single problem or dilemma.[8] You think in terms of possibilities rather than absolutes. Whenever you find that you're facing an open-ended problem that does not have one absolute right answer, you will find your divergent thinking skills to be invaluable. Of course, people who tend to be divergent thinkers often view *all* problems as open-ended and consequently generate multiple solutions even when the rest of the world is seeing the problem through *convergent* eyes.

As an example, let's return to our test question.

Convergent Thinking	Divergent Thinking
Directing all of one's knowledge toward a problem that has a singular and specific solution	Using the contents of memory to generate multiple solutions to a problem in an open-ended manner

They were not _____ misfortune, having endured more than their fair share of _____.

 a.   cognizant of . . . calamity

 b.   superstitious about . . . prosperity

 c.   jealous of . . . success

 d.   oblivious to . . . happiness

 e.   unacquainted with . . . adversity

We already noted that (e) is the correct answer (convergently). However, if you tend to think divergently, answer (e) does not jump out at you. Indeed, as a divergent thinker, you will approach the problem differently. Here's the thinking process described by one of my very bright divergent-thinking students:

> At first I thought, (e) looks like a good answer, but (a) could also be correct; some people who have experienced calamities aren't really cognizant of their misfortune because they're in denial. And then again (b) could be the answer because prosperity might make some people less superstitious about misfortune since they haven't really experienced true misfortune and would therefore not be developing superstitions to ward it off. Or (d) could be the answer; happiness could in some cases be considered a misfortune because when you're happy you may become too content and then you might miss out on opportunities because you're not looking for them, or you may not see adversity coming at you.[9]

In other words, what is very clear-cut to the person who tends to think *convergently*, is anything but clear-cut to the *divergent* thinker who prefers complexity and generates explanations that encompass each of the possible answers to the question. The divergent thinker has considered the problem from all angles and made connections between the question and *each* of the potential answers. He has now spent four times as long on the question as the person who is tuned to think convergently, and his likelihood of choosing the "right" answer is still no better than chance. Instead of eliminating some of the answers to improve his chances of making the correct choice, his divergent thought processes have brought *all* answers into the realm of possibility.

Does this sound familiar? If you're primarily a divergent thinker (if your score on the quiz from Chapter Two indicated you prefer the *connect* brainset), you may have had a *lot* of trouble with convergent tests such as the SAT. You may have been considered an underachiever in school precisely because most scholastic tests are based on *convergent* thinking principles.

The divergent thinker sees a rich tangle of possibilities in every situation. The divergent thinker is often highly creative. However, we live in a convergent-thinking world for the most part. And if you're a divergent thinker who spends a great deal of time in the *connect* brainset, you may feel that others don't understand you. In fact, many of the highly creative individuals that I work with attest to feeling like a round peg in a square hole. (One screenwriter actually related that he felt like "an octagonal peg with conical appendages in a square hole"![10]) If you feel like this—and the *connect* brainset is your mental comfort zone—we will address your problems in the next two chapters where you will learn some *convergent*-thinking skills. However, right now we need to convince the 60 to 80% of you who find divergent thinking uncomfortable[11] that you can increase your creative capacity by learning to access the *connect* brainset during creative problem solving (just don't do it when you're taking the SAT!).

Speaking of creative problem solving, before we continue let's take a look at three different types of problems that can be solved creatively. These include *reasonable* (or *logical*) problems, *unreasonable* (or *illogical*) problems, and *ill-structured* (or *open-ended*) problems.[12] When working on a creative problem, it's helpful to understand the kind of problem you're facing before you try to develop a strategy to solve it.

First there are *reasonable* problems (sometimes also called *logical* problems). These are problems that have a single endpoint as their solution, and you can use logic or reason to reach that solution. For these problems, there's some sort of protocol or road map you can follow to get to the solution. Mathematical equations are reasonable problems, as are many real-life problems, such as balancing your checkbook, finding a book in a library, or constructing a child's bicycle from a kit; for all of these problems there is a single correct endpoint or solution as well as a protocol you can follow to get there.

The problems on the SAT tests are *reasonable* problems, and they can be solved using convergent thinking. However, though reasonable problems always have a single endpoint and a logical road map for getting to the solution, there may be more than one protocol or road map you can follow to get to that endpoint. For instance, if you wish to go from Boston to the Metropolitan Museum in New York, the Museum is your one correct endpoint. Yet there are multiple paths you can take to get there: you can get in your car and drive down I-95 or you can drive down I-84. You can also go to Logan Airport and get on the shuttle to LaGuardia, you can take Amtrak, or you can (not recommended without an insurance policy) take one of the "dollar" buses that run between the two cities. Even though there are multiple ways to reach the museum from Boston, the problem is still *reasonable* because there is a single endpoint and set precedents for how to get there.

Some reasonable problems are very difficult, but they can still be answered using reason and established protocols. Here are a couple of examples: (1) given the diagnostic criteria for depression, determine the prevalence of depression worldwide, or (2) determine if there are additional planets in the solar system. There is one correct answer for the incidence of depression, and there is one correct answer for the number of planets . . . and there are specific methods for finding these answers; therefore, they are *reasonable* problems.

Second, there are *unreasonable* (or *illogical*) problems. These are problems for which there is one right solution or endpoint but for which there are no road maps or protocols to follow to reach the solution. These problems include what are often called "insight" problems. That is, you typically need a flash of insight—the "aha!" experience—to solve them as they can't be solved with logic. Here's one of the most popular insight problems. The goal is to connect all of the dots using four straight lines without picking your pencil up off the page.

•   •   •

•   •   •

•   •   •

As with other insight problems, this one cannot be solved by logic. It requires "thinking outside the box" literally and figuratively. (If you're not familiar with the nine-dot problem, you can find the solution toward the end of Chapter Seven.) Insight solutions arrive via the *spontaneous* pathway in a sudden burst of recognition (like "getting" a joke). You never feel like you're getting warmer to the solution until it bursts upon you. Many creative problems in the sciences fall into the unreasonable category; for these problems there is a correct solution, but no roadmap as to how to get there. As Einstein remarked, "There is no logical bridge from experience to the basic principles of theory."[13]

Finally, there are *ill-structured* or *open-ended* problems. These problems have more than one possible solution, and there are no clear guidelines for how to get to a solution or endpoint or even how to tell when you've arrived at a suitable solution. Many creative problems are ill-structured and open-ended. For example, say you are Tchaikovsky and Czar Alexander III has commissioned you to write the march for his coronation; where do you begin? Or you are Frank Lloyd Wright and you want to build a house that blends into the landscape; what roadmap do you follow? Or you are Aaron T. Beck and you know that the current treatments for depression are not very effective. You want to improve them; how do you proceed?

Ill-structured or open-ended problems are precisely the kinds of problems you need to identify and address in order to survive and thrive in our rapidly changing world. Here's the thing: you can't solve ill-structured problems with convergent thinking. You need to access the *connect* brainset and set those divergent thinking wheels in motion, even if you have to suffer temporary "square peg in a round hole" syndrome to do it!

In the *connect* brainset, ideas seem to flow and "connect" one to another (hence the name!). People who spend time thinking divergently—and thus in the *connect* mode—generate more ideas with seemingly less effort than people who dwell in the *reason* brainset.[14] This is called ideational fluency.

Ideational fluency is the production of a large number of potential solutions to a creative problem. This is important because, for the most part, the quality of creative ideas is a function of the quantity of ideas. Not only does common sense dictate that if you produce enough ideas some of them are *bound* to be good, but research upholds this relationship as well. Extensive research on the lives of musical composers by Dean Keith Simonton of UC Davis indicates that the periods of highest *quantity* of music production are also the periods of highest *quality* of creative products. Oh sure, there are a couple of "one-hit wonders," but for the most part, the more the better.[15] Research on divergent thinking problems in our lab also supports this finding: People who produce the greatest number of ideas generally produce the greatest number of high-quality ideas as well (of course, they also produce the greatest number of *low-quality* ideas, but we'll discuss what to do about that in Chapter Ten. (To improve your divergent thinking skills, see *Connect* Exercises #1–3).

If you find that you are mentally exhausted by divergent exercises, you are probably thinking too hard. This can happen when you try to approach divergent thinking problems using the *reason* brainset.

(You'll learn more about using *reason* to solve creative problems in the next chapter.) By relying on your prefrontal executive center to deliberately search for answers for which there is no known pathway or road map (especially under time constraints such as the three-minute time we set on the exercises at the end of this chapter), you may become stuck on a single solution. For instance, one divergent thinking exercise will ask you to come up with as many uses as you can think of for a soup can. When thinking *reasonably*, people tend to get stuck on seeing a soup can as a container. They will write down uses such as pencil holder, spare change holder, flower vase, water cup, ashtray, and candle holder. They will then go blank. The better way to approach divergent thinking tasks is to have your prefrontal executive send a directive to the rear of the brain where the research-and-development team can go to work and find answers. This entails defocusing attention in the prefrontal part of the brain so that more answers are allowed into conscious awareness.[16]

The more often you practice solving open-ended tasks such as divergent thinking exercises, the better able you will be to achieve the *connect* brain state. Soon you will find yourself mentally energized by them, and you will find yourself thinking divergently even when you're not engaged in the exercises.

If your mental comfort zone is either the *reason* or the *evaluate* brainset, you may feel that the divergent thinking exercises are "impractical" or "unrealistic." Because there are a number of individuals who don't see the value in divergent thinking at first, I often start divergent thinking training with a practical example from real life. Here, for instance, is a task based on something that actually happened to one of my colleagues:

> You are scheduled to give expert testimony before a Congressional committee in 10 minutes and your testimony will be broadcast on C-Span and recorded for posterity. You look down and notice your fly is broken and your slacks won't zip up. What do you do? You have three minutes to generate responses.

Here's a response of a student who had identified with the *reason* brainset:

> First, I would remove the pants and try to fix the zipper. It's easier to fix a stuck zipper when the pants are off. If the zipper was still stuck I would ask around and see if anyone had one of those travel sewing kits. If so, I would go to the men's room and try to sew the fly closed. If no one had a sewing kit, I would ask the committee chairperson if she could delay the proceedings for a moment as I was having a "wardrobe malfunction."[17]

Reasonable indeed. And this individual was pretty proud of having thrown the humorous reference to "wardrobe malfunction" into the response. Compare this response to the following response from an individual who identified with the *connect* brainset:

- Find a sewing kit (Congress probably has one that cost the taxpayers several thousand dollars)
- Put the slacks on backwards (no one will see your back)
- Glue the slacks shut
- Use Velcro
- Staple the slacks
- Use a piece of gum to stick the fly together
- Take the slacks off and speak in your underwear
- Ask a short Congressman to stand in front of you
- Tear a two-inch-wide strip out of a magazine and wrap it around the arm of your jacket and tape it in place. People will be so curious about your armband that they won't look at your pants
- Make a joke about how Congress has raised your taxes so much you can't afford a decent suit

Notice that the first respondent approached this problem as though it were a logical problem, having a single solution, namely, mending the broken pants somehow (hence the search for a sewing kit;

if one can't be found, there will have to be a delay in the proceedings). The second respondent—who is thinking divergently—treats the problem as an ill-structured or open-ended problem to which there may be a number of solutions. Notice also that the second respondent did not censor any of his responses, even though a couple of them

---

BRAINSTORMING

If the divergent thinking exercises sound like brainstorming, it's because brainstorming is actually a type of group divergent thinking. Brainstorming was first described by Alex Osborne in 1953, and promoted as a team creativity technique for businesses. As with divergent thinking, the goal of brainstorming is to generate as many ideas as possible without judging them. Everyone on the team shouts out ideas to a specified problem while one team member writes down the ideas. Later the team looks over the ideas that have been generated and begins the process of eliminating some and building off of or combining other ideas.[18]

However, research on brainstorming shows that more quality ideas emerge if individuals brainstorm alone and then bring their best ideas to the table for the group to assess. That's because even though the process is supposed to be nonjudgmental, individuals with lower status in the group may still be wary of shouting out ideas that their superiors could judge as foolish. In order to counteract this problem, a newer technique called *brainwriting* has been introduced into group divergent thinking sessions. In this technique, each member of the group generates three to five ideas on an index card. The cards are then passed anonymously to the group spokesman who introduces each idea for the group to explore. Brainwriting can also be adapted for use with groups on the Internet.[19]

---

were clearly not very practical. In fact, by generating some off-the-wall responses, he was increasing his ideational fluency through the use of humor. (Luckily my colleague who actually had this experience seems to be a divergent thinker. He was able to generate several ideas for dealing with the broken fly. He reports that a few well-placed staples did the trick, and further, that every Congressman's office has a stapler. Crisis averted!)

The point is that the more ideas you can come up with, the more likely it is that at least one will be a quality idea that can solve your problem. The take-home message from the broken fly incident is this: try to view every problem in life as an ill-structured or open-ended problem for which there are multiple potential solutions. Try to think divergently and generate multiple solutions—even if some of them seem "stupid" or "impractical."

Einstein said: "The formulation of a problem is often more essential than its solution . . . To raise new questions, new possibilities, to regard old problems from a new angle . . . marks real advance in science."[20] You can use divergent thinking to find or define a creative problem as well as to solve one (see *Connect* Exercise #3 to practice problem finding).

Finding Unusual Associations

Why is it that unique and original ideas for both creative problem-generation and solution-generation will surface when you're in the *connect* brainset? Part of the answer is that there is a spread of activation in both the semantic regions of the brain that store the meanings of words and the phonological regions that store the sounds of words. At the same time, the volume on the censor that limits the spread of semantic and phonological activation is turned down. This means that the connections will be opened between words and concepts that are more remotely associated in the brain than would normally occur.

Word association tasks are often used to demonstrate how a broad associational network can bring to mind a wealth of data which can be used in the creative process.[21] Here is an example from a word association task from my early creativity studies at Harvard. Ordinarily, when given the word prompt "leaf" and asked what words come to mind, subjects respond with "tree" words. Following is a diagram of a typical response.

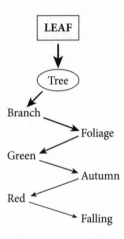

"Tree" is the most common associate to the word "leaf." And "tree" opens an associational network like the one shown above. The thickness of the arrows demonstrates the strength of the associations. Stronger associations will come to mind more quickly, while weaker associations will come to mind only when the strong associations have been exhausted. Thus, this subject responded with the word "tree" very quickly and then the responses took a bit longer until the spread of activation ended and the subject could come up with no further words associated with "leaf."

Now here is the diagram of the response of a highly creative subject[22] whose mental comfort zone would likely be in the *connect* brainset (although I tested her before I had developed the CREATES model). She demonstrated a much broader spread of activation to the word "leaf:"

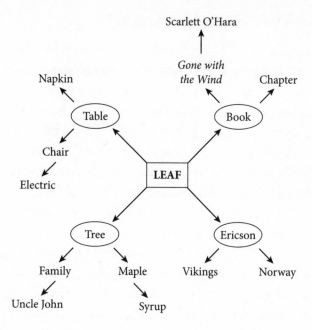

Notice that her responses included not only associations to different *meanings* of the word "leaf," but also associations to the *sound* of the word (as in Leif Ericson). This diagram is evidence of a mild state of disinhibition, where many different words clearly not directly associated with "leaf" were allowed access to conscious thought. Further, the strength of the associations was about equal, so the reaction time for all of these words was very rapid, each following the response before it without a pause.

Many of these responses may seem somewhat inappropriate (who would ever associate Scarlett O'Hara with a leaf?). Nevertheless access to this broad associational network is enormously beneficial to the creative process, which is dependent upon the ability to connect disparate pieces of information to come up with novel ideas. One of the most powerful ways to come up with creative and innovative ideas is to make a habit of forming connections between ideas and objects that are seemingly unconnected. (See *Connect* Exercises #4 and #5 for fun word games that will help you activate associational networks and facilitate connection making.)

Motivation or Goal-Directed Activity

Scholars and business executives used to see word games (like those in *Connect* Exercises #4 and #5) as time wasters rather than serious brain work. However, thanks in part to the findings of neuroscience (and thanks in large part to the success of companies such as PIXAR, where animators get to design their own huts and caves as office spaces), the serious value of "play" and "games" is beginning to receive recognition.[23] Play and games, as it turns out, increase activation in the very parts of the brain associated with creative thinking. Playfulness also increases your motivation to pursue and persevere in a creative project by turning on your internal reward system.[24]

Eating chocolate, receiving an unexpected gift, or having a good laugh can make you more creative (temporarily). I found *un*scientific evidence for this idea one semester when I gave an exam in my creativity course. On the occasion of one midterm exam, I brought in a large bag of chocolate candies and passed them out before the exam, while students received no unexpected candy before a second midterm. Into each exam I slipped a question that tested students' ideational fluency. I found that more ideas were generated during the "chocolate" exam than during the "no-chocolate" exam. Now it's hard to tell whether students were more creative in the chocolate exam because they were on a sugar high, or because chocolate acts as a stimulant (which it is), or because students were pleased that they got something they weren't expecting . . . or because I wanted the chocolate experiment to work and so I unconsciously made the chocolate exam easier or more fun. (These reasons—and the fact that I didn't get clearance from the Committee on the Use of Human Subjects in Research to run this as an "official" experiment—are why I call my subtle chocolate experiment "unscientific.")

However, there is also actual scientific evidence that indicates you're more likely to generate a large number of ideas and to make unusual associations when you receive an unexpected reward or when you're in a good mood. Alice Isen and her colleagues at Cornell have studied the effects of positive mood on different aspects of cognition. They've found that people do better on tests of divergent thinking after positive mood is experimentally induced by giving subjects in their experiments an unexpected gift.[25] Other studies have found that people score better on divergent thinking tasks after laughter or a good joke. In a large meta-analysis of the effects of positive mood on creativity, Matthijs Baas and his group at the University of Amsterdam found that positive mood significantly enhanced ideational fluency and originality in the bulk of the 102 research studies they investigated.[26]

Conversely, rapid thinking of the type that's associated with divergent thinking tasks can increase positive mood and other aspects of creativity. In a recent experiment, Emily Pronin of Princeton and Dan Wegner at Harvard ran an experiment with Princeton undergrads in which they were forced to think much more rapidly than normal by reading statements that scrolled across a computer screen at a fast pace. They found that thinking quickly increased positive feelings. It also increased some other effects, including feelings of creativity, feelings of power, higher self-esteem, and a heightened sense of energy.[27] (See *Connect* Exercise #6 to practice a rapid-thinking exercise.)

A side effect of pairing this upswing in mood with a creative project in the *connect* brainset is that your motivation to work on and complete the project is enhanced. Positive mood and the self-esteem that accompany it lead to an increase in *agency*—or the belief that you have the power to overcome obstacles and achieve your goals.[28]

Psychologist Norbert Schwarz of the University of Michigan and his associates suggest that positive mood allows for more divergent and playful thinking because it signifies that all is well. When you aren't worried about threats in your environment or how you're going to put the next meal on the table, you have the leisure time to devote to exploration of new ideas. You can play around with alternate solutions to problems and make playful connections between ideas because your mind is not occupied with survival.[29]

We've now seen that the *connect* brainset involves divergent thinking, unusual associations, and motivation in the form of internal rewards and positive mood. There are exercises following this chapter that can help you activate this set of creativity-enhancing factors. However, there are also some other methods of entering the *connect* brainset. Neurologist Alice Flaherty from Harvard Medical School and I found that subjects in a study we have been running increased their divergent thinking scores and had increased energy and positive mood after two weeks of exposure to 10,000-lux bright light. (This is the same intensity of light that is used to treat seasonal affective disorder.) Although we haven't tested this, our study would suggest that spending more time outdoors in the sunlight (with sunscreen of course, which doesn't interfere with the therapeutic effects of bright light) might have the same effect on divergent thinking.[30]

Speaking of the outdoors, other research has investigated the effect of surroundings of natural beauty on cognition. As it turns out, spending time in areas of beautiful scenery—such as the ocean, the woods, or in the presence of a beautiful sunset—releases endogenous opioids that increase positive mood and decrease cognitive inhibition,[31] making the *connect* brainset easier to utilize.

You can also use any of the rewards on the Small Pleasures list you made in Chapter Two (Cluster Two, Exercise #9) to induce a positive mood. However, the results of experiments seem to indicate that simply *being* in a good mood does not evoke divergent thinking and the *connect* brainset; rather you have to *change* your mood in a positive direction to get this effect. Listening to upbeat music, hearing a good joke, and engaging in physical activity such as dancing can also be beneficial in elevating your mood.

Strangely, you would think that taking drugs that have been deemed "uppers" would also do the trick; however, studies that have looked at the way amphetamine affects divergent thinking have found no significant positive *or* negative results. Perhaps this is because of the dose-dependent effect of amphetamine-type drugs. In very small doses, amphetamines can lower cognitive inhibition (this, according to our model should enhance divergent thinking); however, in slightly greater doses, amphetamine drugs *increase* inhibition (which should have a negative effect on creativity). In fact, there is a growing what-if-Einstein-took-Ritalin public debate about the effect of amphetamine-based treatments for attention-deficit hyperactivity disorder (ADHD) on children's creativity.[32] There is a lack of research on the effects of caffeine on creativity (although one study found that artists tend to use more caffeine than members of a control group). However, the dose-dependent effects of this drug on other aspects of cognition have been studied; small doses have a beneficial effect while higher doses hamper effective thinking.[33] The bottom line on "uppers" is that science hasn't provided evidence to support their use in enhancing associational thought. There appears to be a dose-dependent response to such substances, such that minor variations in the dose may restrict rather than enhance creative thought.

Neuroscience of the Connect Brainset

What does your brain look like when you access the *connect* brainset? The *connect* brainset appears to combine elements of both the *spontaneous* and the *deliberate* pathways described in Chapter Four. On the one hand, there is considerable evidence for an increase in alpha wave coherence in the prefrontal lobes when individuals who score high in divergent thinking skills engage in divergent thinking problems.[34] This suggests a defocusing of attention and a mild deactivation of the lateral executive areas involved in the *deliberate* pathway.[35] On the other hand, the *connect* brainset does not reflect a completely *spontaneous* state in which ideas spring unbidden into mind. It is, rather, a state in which you are actively searching for connections in a semi-spontaneous manner.

Kalina Christoff and her colleagues at the University of British Columbia have proposed that there is a type of creative thinking lying somewhere between the *deliberate* and *spontaneous* pathways.[36] I believe that the *connect* brainset may embody this creative thinking pattern. This in-between-state interpretation would account for some seemingly contradictory findings that show increased alpha coherence in prefrontal areas on the one hand (suggesting deactivation), but *increased* prefrontal activation relative to resting state in other studies.[37]

A second finding is that there is an increase in ratio of right-to-left hemisphere activation of the prefrontal cortex in the tasks that we've associated with the *connect* brainset. For instance, the right prefrontal cortex increases in activation when subjects are asked to find associations between unrelated words or when they are asked to incorporate a group of unrelated nouns into a short story. This makes intuitive sense, because activation of the right hemisphere is known to evoke a broad attentional focus, whereas left hemisphere activation evokes a narrowing and focusing of attention. Broadening of attentional focus would lead to a wider ranging search for potential connections between ideas. Right hemisphere activation has also been shown to facilitate the processing of distant semantic associations.[38] (So Daniel Pink may have been on target when he said in his 2005 best-seller *A Whole New Mind* that "right-brainers will rule the future"![39])

Finally, the *connect* brainset is characterized by activation of the associational centers, just as we would expect from a state of brain that is devoted to making associations! These areas are clearly activated during association exercises, especially on the left side of the brain where semantic information is stored.[40]

The main *connect* brain pattern then consists of defocused attention (as demonstrated by increased alpha wave coherence in the prefrontal lobes), preferential activation of the right hemisphere prefrontal area, and activation of the association centers in the temporal and parietal lobes (especially in the left hemisphere). What I am suggesting is that the relative deactivation of the prefrontal lobes in the left hemisphere disinhibits the actions of the right hemisphere to allow for a broadening of attentional focus and the greater activation of associational areas.

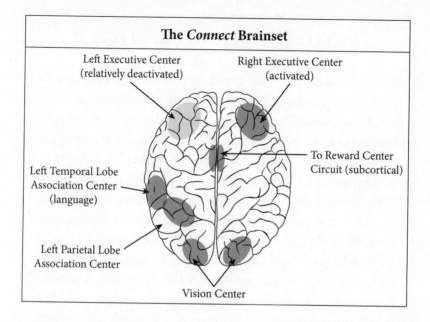

The *Connect* Brainset

Left Executive Center (relatively deactivated)

Right Executive Center (activated)

Left Temporal Lobe Association Center (language)

To Reward Center Circuit (subcortical)

Left Parietal Lobe Association Center

Vision Center

Some corroborating evidence for the disinhibitory explanation comes from an interesting case reported by neurologists William Seeley and Bruce Miller of UC San Francisco.[41] Anne Adams, a scientist and artist, suffered from a degenerative brain condition called primary progressive aphasia that affected the language centers of her brain. As the disease was wreaking devastation to the left prefrontal cortex and part of the left temporal lobe, Anne developed an intense drive to create art. Further, she began expressing unusual cross-modal themes in her art, such as rendering music and mathematics through paint. Somehow, the deficit in the left frontal lobe led to strong creative motivation and extremely creative associations of remotely related concepts through art. Notice also that Anne's cross-modal art expression is reminiscent of the cross-modal experiences of synaesthetes, who "see" music and "hear" numbers (see Synaesthesia and Creativity).

Anne Adams's sudden creative motivation is rare but not unique. Other cases of what's called "sudden artistic output" have been reported after the disease frontotemporal dementia (FTD) strikes the left hemisphere.[42] It seems that the deactivation of parts of the left

SYNAESTHESIA AND CREATIVITY

Synaesthesia is an unusual condition in which different sensory and verbal systems in the brain seem to be cross-wired. Thus, synaesthetes may "hear" colors, or different words may evoke the sound of notes on a musical scale. Some synaesthetes see letters of the alphabet as colors, so when they read they may be bombarded with a rainbow of colors or musical notes uncontrollably. Synaesthesia runs in families and is seven to eight times more prevalent among highly creative individuals than among the general population. Neuroscientist V. S. Ramachandran of UC San Diego has studied synaesthetes at great length and has found that their brains are wired differently in the left association center (left angular gyrus and supramarginal gyrus).[43] This is exactly the region that lights up when people are making unusual associations during creativity testing. (Note that this is also the only part of Einstein's brain that was found to be larger than average.) Back in Chapter One, we mentioned Sarnoff Mednick's theory that the ability to synthesize remotely associated elements of thought into new and useful combinations is the basis of creativity.[44] The fact that synaesthetes have unusual brain connections in the association centers of the brain may explain their overrepresentation among creative achievers.

prefrontal lobes by disease allow creative drives that may have been inhibited to come to the forefront. One question that has yet to be answered is whether we all have this creative drive that is currently inhibited by our high-functioning left hemisphere or whether the drive to create is unique to only certain individuals who just happen to contract FTD.

The case of Tommy McHugh may shed some light on this question. Tommy was a construction worker in Liverpool, England, with no stated interest in art or poetry until an event in 2001 changed his life. Tommy then suffered an aneurysm that affected his frontal lobes and required brain surgery to save his life. About two weeks after the surgery, Tommy began to fill notebooks with poetry and to draw hundreds of sketches. Upon returning home, he filled every square inch of wall space in his house with paintings and continues to paint obsessively. He also became interested in sculpting with clay. His desire to be engaged in creative work appeared to be on an obsessive level.[45]

My connection with Tommy began when Alice Flaherty, the Harvard neurologist with whom I conducted the light therapy study, asked me if I'd be interested in testing Tommy on standard creativity tasks. The question everyone involved with Tommy wanted to know was whether his drive to create was caused by the disinhibition of an innate creative drive or whether it was an indication of a compulsive disorder, similar to what we might see in an OCD patient who has to turn off a light switch over and over again. Unfortunately, we have not been able to scan Tommy's brain since his drive to create began due to the presence of a metal shunt installed to stop the bleeding in his brain (metal can be dangerous in a brain scanner). If we could see his brain, we could tell more about the origin of his continuing desire to paint, sculpt, and write. My sense from communicating with Tommy and observing his work is that he is thoroughly enjoying his new talents and creative drive (this is evidence *against* the compulsion explanation and *for* the disinhibition theory) and that his artistic work is continually improving. When asked about his new art-based life in an interview with reporter Jim Giles of *Nature*, Tommy reported, "My life is 100% better."[46]

The damage done to Tommy's frontal lobes appears to have disinhibited both his reward-based motivation to create and his verbal and visual ideational fluency. I would say that he seems to be living in a permanent condition of the *connect* brainset. I'm happy to report that Tommy's artwork is now receiving international recognition.

When to Access the *Connect* Brainset

The brain model of the *connect* brainset is characterized by defocused attention, increased right hemisphere activation, and increased activity in the association areas of the brain. This activation pattern can be helpful any time it would be beneficial to come up with more than one option for creative problem finding or problem solving in your professional or personal life. It will be most beneficial, though, when you're trying to find solutions to ill-structured open-ended creative problems. Remember, though, that you can use it to work on any of the three types of problems: reasonable (logical problems with a single correct solution), unreasonable (illogical problems with one right solution that is not evident unless you "think outside the box"), and ill-structured (open-ended problems for which there is more than one right solution). Finally, try using the *connect* brainset during the elaboration stage of the creative process, when you need to flesh out an idea or project. There may be more than one direction you could take the elaboration, so why not use the *connect* brainset to explore?

> Caveman #1: I don't understand it, Folg. You failed the standardized test for skinning a saber-toothed tiger. And you seem so bright. . . .
>
> Caveman #2: I don't do well on standardized tests . . . but have you read my latest work?

201 RECIPES FOR BARBECUING SABERTOOTH TIGER

In this chapter you've seen that divergent thinking, making unusual associations, and a rise in motivation are all connected to each other and are facilitated by the brain changes modeled in the *connect* brainset. The *connect* brainset is the ideal brain state in which to generate abundant creative ideas and get excited about your creative project. But generating ideas is only part of the creative process. It's possible to get stalled in an extended whirlwind of generating ideas but fail to act on them. In the next two chapters, you'll learn about brainsets that keep your creative project moving forward in a positive direction.

Exercises: The Connect Brainset [47]

Connect Exercise #1: Divergent Thinking: Alternate Uses

Aim of exercise: To improve ideational fluency and divergent thinking skills. You will need a stopwatch or timer, three pieces of paper, and a writing utensil. This exercise will take you nine minutes.

Procedure: Set the timer for three minutes and then write down all the uses for a soup can that you can think of. Don't stop writing until the timer sounds.

Immediately reset the timer for three minutes and write down all the white edible things you can think of on the second sheet of paper. Don't stop writing until the timer sounds. Finally set the timer again for three minutes and, using the third sheet of paper, write down all the consequences you can think of that would occur if humans had three arms instead of two.

When the timer sounds, check how you're feeling. Did the exercise energize you or exhaust you?

Continue to practice divergent thinking exercises every other day by considering alternative uses for other common household objects (examples include a newspaper, a paper clip, or a brick) and other unusual physical conditions (for example, the consequences if humans had six fingers instead of five on each hand).

If you are using the token economy incentive, give yourself one *connect* token for completing this exercise and one additional token for each time you practice divergent thinking exercises. Additional divergent thinking training can be found at http://ShelleyCarson.com.

Connect Exercise #2: Divergent Thinking: Loquacious Friend

Aim of exercise: To help you generate multiple solutions to an open-ended problem and to improve your divergent thinking skills. You will need a stopwatch or timer, a piece of paper, and a writing utensil.

Procedure: Consider the following dilemma. Your friend Ron always sits next to you during the weekly production briefing. Ron really likes to talk to you, and he distracts you so that sometimes you miss an important part of the briefing. Also many times you don't finish your work because he constantly drops by your desk to talk. But because he's your friend, you don't want to offend him.

○ Think of as many ways as you can to solve this problem. Don't judge your answers and try to be creative. Set the timer for three minutes and do not stop writing answers until the timer sounds.

○ When the timer sounds, look over your list. Did you write down some ideas that surprise you? Give yourself one *connect* token in the Rewards section of the journal.

○ Try to spend at least 15 minutes every other day purposely thinking divergently about a practical problem (this could be a problem from your own life or one that you make up).

○ If you are using the token economy incentive, give yourself one *connect* token for completing this exercise and one additional token for each time you practice the divergent thinking exercise. You may want to check out the divergent thinking training program available on the http://ShelleyCarson.com Web site.

Connect Exercise #3: Divergent Thinking: Creative Problem Finding

Aim of exercise: To help you recognize the large potential for creative innovation that exists all around you and to improve your divergent thinking skills. You will need a stopwatch or timer, a piece of paper, a writing utensil, and your journal.

Procedure: Wherever you are (it could be on a subway, in a shopping mall, at your desk at work, or in your own living room), sit down and prepare to write.

○ Set the timer for three minutes and do not stop writing until the timer sounds.

- Look around you and list all the objects, situations, or procedures within your current environment that could be improved, changed, or replaced to make life run more smoothly. Be as creative as possible and do not judge any of your ideas.
- When the timer sounds, look over your list. Are there some ideas that you might actually be interested in pursuing? If so, transfer them to your journal in the area for Creative Problems. Write today's date and be sure to include your current location.

If you are using the token economy incentive, award yourself one *connect* token each time you complete this exercise.

Connect Exercise #4: Activation of Associational Networks: Word Association

Aim of exercise: To practice activating broad associational networks and to increase divergent thinking skills. You will need a stopwatch or timer, a piece of paper, and a writing utensil.

Procedure: Set the timer for three minutes and do not stop writing until the timer sounds.

- Write down all the words that come to mind when you think of the word "spring."
- When the timer sounds, look at your list of words. Now make a map of your associations similar to the one shown earlier in this chapter using the word "leaf."
- Look at your map. Did words associated with different meanings of the word "spring" come to mind? Take note of your most unusual associations.

You can perform this exercise using any noun as a prompt. If you are using the token economy incentive, award yourself one *connect* token each time you complete this exercise.

Connect Exercise #5: Activation of Associational Networks
Exercise: Degrees of Separation

Aim of exercise: To practice activating broad associational networks and to increase divergent thinking skills. You will need a piece of paper and a writing utensil.

Procedure: Open any book and point to a word. If the word is not a noun, pick the noun closest to the word you chose in the text (note that the noun should not be a proper noun). Write the word down. Make room for three words to the right of that word by drawing dashes. Now open the book to a different page and select another noun. Try to connect the two nouns by using no more than three connecting words. Here's an example using the two random words "fish" and "money."

Fish   (Ocean)   (Yacht)   (Wealthy)   Money

Now try to find two words to connect your nouns. For example:

(Shark)   (Loan)
or
Fish   (Stream)   (Bank)   Money

Finally, try to connect your nouns with just a single word. For example:

Fish   (Gold)   Money

As a variation on this exercise, you can use two nouns suggested by your environment. For instance, if you're driving you can pick words off billboards or signs. This is a great car game to do with kids.

If you are using the token economy incentive, award yourself one *connect* token each time you complete this exercise.

Connect Exercise #6: Increasing Speed of Thought Exercise

Aim of exercise: To increase your thinking speed, as well as to enhance positive mood and motivation. You will need a stopwatch or timer and a novel that you have enjoyed reading in the past. This exercise should take you around 12 minutes, depending upon your reading speed. The purpose of this exercise is not to read fast; it is to speed up your thinking. So don't concern yourself if your initial reading speed seems slow.

Procedure: Set your timer for five minutes, and open the book. Begin reading at your normal pace at the top of the left-hand page and continue to the end of the right-hand page. You should be reading at a speed that allows you to savor and comprehend the material. Check the timer and see how long it took you to read these two pages. Write down that time.

- Now set the timer for 10 seconds less than it took you to read the first two pages. Try to read the next two pages before the timer sounds, retaining comprehension of the material.
- Now set the timer for 20 seconds less than it took you to read the first two pages. Try to read the next two pages before the timer sounds, retaining comprehension of the material.
- Finally, calculate how long it would have taken you to read four pages at your original speed (in other words, double your original time). Set the timer for 60 seconds less than that time. Try to read the next four pages before the timer sounds, retaining comprehension of the material.
- At the end of this exercise, you will have read 10 pages of your book, eight of them at an accelerated speed. You should feel somewhat energized and excited by this exercise. That is a sign

that you're entering the *connect* brainset. Try to do this exercise once a day for a week or until you get used to the feeling of your thoughts speeding up. If you are using the token economy incentive, award yourself one *connect* token each time you complete this exercise.

Solution to the Nine-Dot Problem

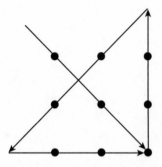

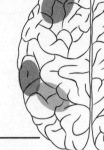

*⁂ 8

Shaping the Creative Idea: Accessing the Reason Brainset

. . . from the wheel to the skyscraper, everything we are and everything we have comes from one attribute of man—the function of his reasoning mind.

—AYN RAND, *THE FOUNTAINHEAD*[1]

IF THE CONNECT BRAINSET is the activation pattern for *divergent* thinking, the *reason* brainset is the activation pattern for *convergent* thinking. In the *reason* brainset, your executive center in the prefrontal cortex solves convergent, logical problems, with all the resources of your stored memory, knowledge, and learned skills at its disposal. Thinking in the *reason* brainset is conscious, deliberate, and sequential. And regardless of whether you're arranging flowers in a new way, writing poetry, or developing a new rocket to put humans on Mars, you will have need of the brain activation pattern of the *reason* brainset as you complete your creative project.[2]

The Thinker

For many people, the *reason* brainset comprises their mental comfort zone. Here mental life is orderly and transparent, with no unpredictable surprises seeping or leaping in from the back rooms and subterranean regions of the unconscious. The *reason* brainset allows you to control what thoughts inhabit your mental workspace. If you don't like what you're thinking, you just banish the thoughts and go in another direction.

For other people, though (including many artists and musicians I have worked with), the *reason* brainset is foreign territory. A substantial number of artistic individuals spend much of their time in what I am calling the *transform* brainset, perilously riding waves of emotion and *reacting* to their environment rather than consciously acting to guide their mental ship (see Chapter Ten). If you fall within this category, please pay special attention to this chapter. You do not have to become Mr. Spock to take advantage of the benefits of the *reason* brainset. Your emotions will survive intact; they just won't be steering the ship.

Likewise, if the *connect, absorb*, or *envision* brainset is your mental comfort zone, you need to read this chapter carefully. You'll get some tips on how to engage in the logical, step-by-step thinking that will help you get past the idea-generation stage and into the action stage of making your creative dreams come true.

While the *reason* brainset is modeled as the seat of convergent thinking, your brain is not limited to thinking convergently when it is in the *reason* mode; it can also tackle ill-structured or open-ended problems. However, it does so by generating one possible solution at a time and using trial-and-error techniques rather than by the rapid generation of multiple solutions that we see in divergent thinking. The *reason* brainset is the principal activation mode for the *deliberate* pathway to creativity (discussed in Chapter Four). While we've heard about many highly creative people who prefer the insights and "ahas!" of the *spontaneous* pathway (accessed through the *absorb* brainset), there are probably an equal number of creative luminaries who have preferred the *deliberate* process.

Many innovators (certainly Thomas Edison and other inventors) prefer to work toward solutions using a logical trial-and-error method. Likewise, many composers, such as Bach, have used a logical approach to writing music, in which new compositions—I've already mentioned the Brandenburg Concertos—are developed by following explicit conventions. Art in the styles of Realism and *Trompe l'Oeil* is also generated primarily through the *reason* brainset.[3]

However, even if you prefer the *spontaneous* pathway to creativity, you will need to spend considerable time in the *reason* brainset as you revise, elaborate, and implement your creative ideas. One of the most controversial cases of *reason* improving on *spontaneous* insight is that of Samuel Taylor Coleridge's classic poem fragment *Kubla Khan*. According to the Coleridge, as he woke from an opium-induced sleep (opium was not illegal then and was prescribed for a variety of ills— apparently the Romantic poet was suffering from an anything-but-romantic bout of dysentery at this time), the vision of *Kubla Khan* came to him spontaneously. He experienced it simultaneously as both

David Brega's Colors *(1999–2000) is an example of Trompe l'Oeil art that uses logic and information from the science of optics and perception to fool the eye into seeing a three-dimensional representation.*
PHOTO CREDIT: Photograph by Rick Kyle/5000K Inc.

a visual image and a verbal description (which he subsequently wrote down) without any sensation of consciousness of effort.[4] The essence of pure spontaneity!

However, critics who don't believe in the *spontaneous* pathway (yes, there are such individuals even among creativity researchers) have pointed out that the published poem is quite different from the version written down by Coleridge after his so-called vision. Apparently, he did considerable rewriting and editing of the vision material. Why would anyone, the critics ask, mess with a vision?[5] Isn't this evidence that there was, in fact, no *spontaneous* production? However, my response to such criticisms is this: A creative idea can arrive *spontaneously* and appear to be quite complete; that doesn't mean it can't be improved with a little *reason* brainset activity! Even my songwriter from Chapter Five, who claims she gets her songs from the angels, edits some aspects of the music. The point is that no matter how you come up with your original idea, if it is worth creating, then it's worth improving, reworking, and elaborating . . . and that all happens in the *reason* brainset.

Defining the Reason Brainset

The *reason* brainset is the brain state that you access when you engage in everyday problem solving. You use this state to plan your day (pick up the dry cleaning, attend the conference, pick up the dog from the groomers, stop for Chinese takeout, and so on). You also use it to make decisions (study for the bar exam tonight versus watch reruns of *Lost*; watch CNN versus watch Fox News), and to solve problems (what shall I serve for the dinner party on Saturday; how can I get little Britney to do her homework).

However, the *reason* brainset does more than perform these daily housekeeping functions. It is also the mental home of philosophers, mathematicians, and scientists who follow ideas to their logical conclusions. In other words, this brainset is active when you are consciously thinking things out, from the mundane to the earthshaking. It is the brain activation pattern you access when you are thinking intentional thoughts.

Before I continue, let me clarify what I mean by the words "reason," "rational," and "logical." These terms are used more or less interchangeably in modern parlance, although they do have specific meanings in the field of philosophy. I will use them interchangeably as well. What I mean by "reason" is a type of thought in which you arrive at hypotheses and conclusions based on observations and knowledge that you believe (correctly or incorrectly) justify those conclusions. This can include both deductive and inductive reasoning. *Reason* also employs cause-and-effect thinking. Things don't just happen without pattern or purpose in a reasonable world. *Reason* assumes that every effect has a cause, even if the cause is unknowable at the present time. Therefore, much thought that is *reasonable* is an attempt to determine either causes or effects.

Let me give an example from the research of my friend and former office mate at Harvard, Susan Clancy. Clancy studied the memory patterns of individuals who believed they had been abducted by aliens from outer space. Many of these people, she found, were very reasonable. They held good jobs and had friends and secure family relationships. They were not, as a rule, psychotic. In her book *Abducted: How People Come to Believe They Were Kidnapped by Aliens*, Clancy states, "Alien-abduction beliefs reflect attempts to explain odd, unusual, and perplexing experiences."[6] In other words, abduction beliefs were an attempt to use *reason* to find the cause for unusual effects. These unusual effects included waking in the night with large-eyed strangers bending over their beds, being paralyzed and unable to move but still able to perceive, awakening in the morning to find strange marks and bruises on their bodies, strange compulsions to drive to remote spots out in the country, unexplained nosebleeds, and unexplained feelings of violation, terror, and helplessness. Just as a scientist collects data and fashions a hypothesis to explain the data, Clancy's subjects collected data in the form of unusual experiences and fashioned a hypothesis to explain them. *Reason* dictates that there is a cause for these effects, and the alien-abduction hypothesis fits the data. *Reason* doesn't always lead to truth. But, hey, the Truth is out there!

The *reason* brainset, then, reflects a type of thinking in which hypotheses and conclusions are formed on the basis of evidence (in the form of past experience or knowledge). Likewise, ideas, decisions, and plans for the future formed in the *reason* brainset are also based on evidence from your bank of past experience and knowledge.

Three factors define the *reason* brainset: conscious and intentional control of thought processes, realism or practicality, and sequential processing. Let's look at each factor separately.

Conscious Control of Thought Processes

Cogito ergo sum (I think therefore I am)

—RENE DESCARTES[7]

Descartes' famous one-liner was originally written as evidence that we exist. Thought exists (it must because I am thinking, he reasoned). Thought cannot be separated from me, therefore, I exist. Pretty cool. Such thinking about thought is called metacognition. Conscious direction of thought is presumably a human characteristic (although see Irene Pepperberg's cognition work with Alex the grey parrot to change your mind about what it means to be a bird brain!).[8] However, creativity is also a human characteristic and, as we've seen, one of the keys to entering brainsets often associated with creativity—including the *absorb*, the *envision*, and the *connect* brainsets—is the willingness to relinquish conscious cognitive control to allow ideas to enter consciousness uncensored (or at least only partially uncensored). What you are striving for is the ability to switch between brainsets that allow uncensored ideas into awareness and those in which you are actively controlling thought. (See *Reason* Exercise #1 for practice in controlling the flow of uncensored thoughts.)

Realism or Practicality

When you're in the *reason* brainset, you tend to think in realistic and practical terms. This state is not characterized by flights of fancy (note that Susan Clancy's alien subjects only settled on the alien abduction hypothesis after other more practical explanations failed to explain the data);[9] rather, you look at things analytically. Your thoughts are pragmatic; you think in terms of what will or might work rather than how you would *like* things to work. This does not mean that you ignore fanciful or imaginative ideas. In fact, the *reason* brainset is the perfect place to take a fanciful idea to flesh it out and make it practical.

Remember the example of talking trash cans from Chapter Five? Well, I have no idea how the innovative folks at Solar Lifestyle came up with that idea, but once they had it, they were able to couch it in a sensible and realistic business plan that appears to have worked well for the people of Berlin. Solar-powered talking trash cans are now common in many cities throughout the world. Trash cans in Shanghai not only thank people for throwing their trash away, but they have built-in solar trash compactors for easy trash pickup (they also direct pedestrians to the nearest public restroom, although no one is sure what that has to do with trash disposal). Finnish trash cans sport voices of Finnish celebrities, and they even throw in some political commentary when passersby deposit their rubbish.[10] Talking trash cans have the very practical outcome of keeping the city streets clean. This is just one example of how a fanciful idea—perhaps conceived in a different brainset—can be "practicalized" in the *reason* brainset.

One of the greatest examples of how an imaginative idea (originating in the *envision* brainset) can be elaborated by *reason* is the work of J.R.R. Tolkien. He invented the fantasy world of Middle Earth, which has captivated several generations of readers with tales of hobbits, fairies, elves, and wizards. Yet the details of Tolkien's fantasy world are so realistic as to astound his followers. He created entire languages for the species of his world, each with its own rules of syntax and grammar. He created detailed maps of his world, and his characters have observable and consistent (one would assume genetically endowed) temperamental characteristics.[11] In short, the elaboration of Middle Earth and its inhabitants is incredibly realistic and practical, even though Middle Earth itself is a fantasy.

One of the practical functions of the *reason* brainset is problem solving. Although most people have figured out effective methods for solving problems on their own, other people—often highly creative individuals—seem to have difficulty solving problems in reasonable ways. One chef I interviewed related that he solved problems by throwing a temper tantrum. That works . . . for a little while. Although many people find anger very uncomfortable and will bend over backwards to assuage anger in others, they will eventually start avoiding the angry person, who will then be left—like my chef—wondering why their coworkers abandon them. A musician told me that she solves problems by bursting into tears; then either her husband or her manager will take care of things. Other people have told me their strategy for dealing with problems is to get drunk! These coping mechanisms are ultimately not practical. They either don't solve the problem or they throw your problems onto someone else. It's amazing how much more productive you'll be if you have a reasonable strategy for solving problems. (See *Reason* Exercise #2 to practice steps in practical problem solving.)

Sequential Processing

You think sequentially when you're in the *reason* brainset.[12] That's because you can really only consciously focus your attention on one thing at a time. Okay, I know that it feels like you're focusing on three or four things at once sometimes. One of my best friends claims she can talk on her cell phone, paint her fingernails, and drive on I-95 at breakneck speed all at the same time. Brain research indicates that you can, in fact, have several motor programs running simultaneously (stepping on the accelerator, applying nail polish, and moving your mouth to talk), but you can only focus your conscious attention— your thought—on one thing. What feels like mental multitasking is really a sequential shift of attention back and forth among several streams of thought and action.[13] (My friend with the nail polish shall remain nameless so as not to alert the state troopers.)

Not only does the conscious brain think sequentially, it plans sequentially. Being able to plan for the future is one of the great accomplishments of the executive center in your prefrontal cortex. Because time is experienced sequentially and appears to proceed in a straight line (at least until we are able to build a workable time machine), the executive center makes plans sequentially. Planning for the future is basically just setting goals, and the executive center of your brain sets hundreds of goals for you each day.[14] When you wake up in the morning (something the executive does not have control over . . . unless it has directed you to set an alarm clock), the executive sets a goal that you will get out of the bed without falling over and make it to the bathroom to prepare for the day. Each willful act you perform is a goal accomplished, from brushing your teeth, to getting to work, to eating dinner. Of course, the executive can plan much loftier goals as well. Perhaps your executive is planning law school for you or planning for you to become a millionaire or to get through the year without smoking.

Goal setting is the act of making a sequential plan for the attainment of an action or state that is important to you. Goals are essential to creative work. However, again, if you are someone who is more comfortable in the *absorb, envision, connect,* or *transform* brainsets, you may not give much conscious thought to setting goals. Yet here are some of the things that goal setting can do to help you achieve your creative objectives:

○   Motivate action
○   Help you manage time
○   Increase chances for success
○   Increase self-confidence
○   Increase sense of control over your life[15]

The trick is to have written and specific goals, and you achieve this in the *reason* brainset. (For practice in setting written and specific goals, see *Reason* Exercise #3.)

Neuroscience of the Reason Brainset

Exactly what does your brain look like when you access the *reason* brainset? The main finding is that the part of the brain we have dubbed the executive center and the circuits attached to it are highly active. This activation is especially apparent in the left hemisphere, because for all right-handed and many left-handed people, the language production center is located in the left frontal cortex. Even if you're not speaking out loud, this area is activated when you're thinking with words.[16]

While many people consider themselves visual thinkers, they are generally still using verbal thoughts in conjunction with visual thoughts. Therefore, the use of language and the use of the left hemisphere predominate when you are directing your thoughts consciously. However, your right executive center may be recruited if the information you're thinking about is quite complex.[17]

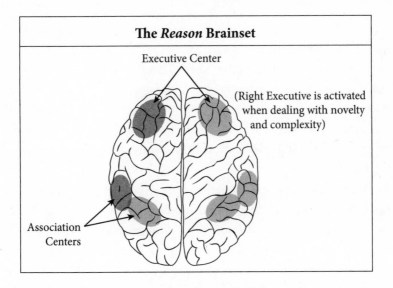

The *Reason* Brainset

Executive Center

(Right Executive is activated when dealing with novelty and complexity)

Association Centers

When people are solving problems in the brain scanner, the executive center and the left association areas light up. Conscious problem solving is also associated with increased high frequency/low amplitude *beta* wave activity in the prefrontal cortex and decreased *alpha* and *theta* wave activity. This pattern of brain waves indicates that the prefrontal cortex is more active during purposeful thinking than it is during rest. Note that while *beta* waves predominate during the *reason* brainset, it is the slower waves that characterize the *absorb* brainset. Again, this may be indicative of the prefrontal brain activation and deactivation that accompany these brainsets.[18]

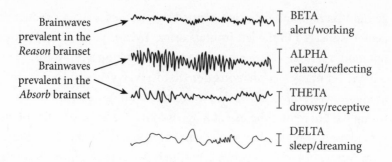

Finally, the *reason* brainset is an active brainset (as opposed to a resting brain activation pattern). Therefore, it requires a certain level of physiological and mental arousal. There is an increase in the so-called arousal neurotransmitters, including glutamate, dopamine, and norepinephrine. There are a number of methods you can use to effect this arousal. The most effective and important is moderate physical exercise. Taking a walk will reliably activate the frontal lobes of your brain.[19]

What else? We mentioned caffeine in the last chapter. That works . . . but watch out for the dose-dependent "jitters." And what about classical music—the so-called "Mozart Effect"? Well, it looks like Mozart may be good for waking up your brain and putting you in a better mood—*if* you like Mozart. Does it make you reason better? A study by Edward Roth and Kenneth Smith of Western Michigan University found that listening to Mozart significantly increased scores on a portion of the standardized GRE exam; but so did listening to traffic sounds. Basically, any noise will increase your arousal level, which in turn increases the activation of the prefrontal lobes and your executive center.[20] So if your favorite nonvocal music doesn't distract you too much, it may be helpful in getting you into the *reason* brainset. (For other methods of accessing the *reason* brainset, try *Reason* Exercises #4 and #5.)

Freud, Reason, and Neuroscience

Because Freud's theories figured prominently in early twentieth-century thinking about creativity, I want to bring him into our discussion here. I was taught in grad school that "serious" cognitive scientists didn't discuss Freud (concepts like "the unconscious" were considered untestable and therefore unscientific). He has, however, regained some respect among scientists as we are finding out more about the mental processes that occur below the level of conscious awareness (yes, there *is* an unconscious aspect to brain function, and, as suggested by Freud, that is where a lot of the action is going on!). I will no doubt be criticized by both Freudians (who will feel I'm oversimplifying extremely complex psychoanalytic material) and by brain researchers (who will say I am conflating questionable theory with actual neuroscience findings). However, I see Freud's thinking as a precursor to some of the ideas we've been discussing, so with apologies all around, here goes:

Freud's ideas of "primary process" and "secondary process" thinking were quite descriptive of what neuroscientists now refer to as the *spontaneous* and *deliberate* pathways. According to Freud, secondary-process thinking includes rational, sequential, and realistic thinking that is actively controlled by the *ego* (the reality-based conscious part of the personality). Secondary-process thinking is precisely the type of thinking that occurs in the *reason* brainset. This is in stark contrast to primary-process thinking, which is primitive, irrational, nonsequential, unrealistic, imaginative, and controlled by the *id* (the fantasy-based unconscious part of the personality that strives for self-gratification).[21]

Primary-process thinking, according to Freud, is evident in very young children, whose brains and ego defenses have not developed sufficiently to allow secondary-process rational thinking. After the full development of the ego, primary process can be accessed only through dreams, drug-induced mental states, psychotic episodes, and high fevers. For the most part, the mature ego is protected from primary-process material; however, every once in a while, primary-process content makes an end run around the ego defenses and careens into conscious awareness.

This sounds very much like a bolt of insight from the *spontaneous* pathway to creativity, doesn't it? In fact, Ernst Kris, in his 1952 book *Psychoanalytic Explorations of Art*, suggested that creative individuals are prone to primary process thinking that explodes into consciousness. He believed that creative individuals have the ability to switch between secondary-process and primary-process thinking more easily than their less creative counterparts; he called this switching into primary process "regression in the service of the ego." The "regression" process involves two parts: (a) the ego withdraws its control and allows the psyche to slip into the more childlike and imaginative state of primary-process thinking where material wells up from the unconscious (this corresponds to the "insight" stage of the creative process), and (b) the ego resumes control and works with material generated in the primary process (this corresponds to the "verification" stage of the creative process; see Chapter Four).[22]

Regression in the service of the ego approximates the process that Coleridge went through with the *Kubla Khan* fragment. And, in fact, it also approximates what neuroscientist Arne Dietrich of the American University in Beirut believes actually happens in the brain during insight and verification: the executive centers in the prefrontal cortex momentarily and purposely deactivate to allow material to feed forward from TOP association areas into conscious awareness. (Dietrich refers to this as the Transient Hypofrontality Hypothesis.) The prefrontal lobes then reactivate to work with this new material.[23]

Thus Freud, long criticized by scientists for his decidedly non-scientific, nonverifiable theories, may prove to have been prescient in his explanation of brain mechanisms. Indeed, a whole branch of Freudian psychology, called neuro-psychoanalysis, is devoted to mapping Freud's theories onto current knowledge of brain functioning.[24]

When to Access the Reason Brainset

Although the other brainsets that we've looked at so far (*absorb, envision,* and *connect*) get billing for being the "creative" brain activation patterns, the truth is that the *reason* brainset is, as Ayn Rand put it at the beginning of this chapter, where "everything we have comes from." Our ability to reason, to plan, and to make decisions directs any creative efforts in which we may engage.

By careful observation of your environment, you can determine practical new areas that are ripe for change. This will help you find problems that can benefit from creative input.

Next, the *reason* brainset is crucial in the *deliberate* pathway to creativity. You can come up with creative ideas through reason, and through trial and error. Sometimes taking your creative problem and "thinking it through" will yield an original and useful solution.

Think about the creative act of writing a paper for your business or telling others about your work. Both writing and speech involve creativity as you choose how to arrange the words in an orderly progression. Although the idea you talk or write about may be inspired, your grammar and syntax are organized by the *reason* brainset. Others couldn't understand what you're saying if it weren't for this organization.

Once you have obtained a creative idea, you will find that you need the *reason* brainset to decide what to do with it. If the idea passes the muster of evaluation, then you will need to revise and elaborate it. You will need to implement it in some way so that it can be available to others. All of this will take your best *reason* brainset thinking.

The take-home message of this chapter (and one of the main points of this book) is that, however creative inspiration occurs, whether through the *spontaneous* or the *deliberate* pathway, the *reason* brainset, and its reliance on the executive center in the prefrontal brain, is a necessary and vital participant in converting an original thought into a creative accomplishment that can benefit yourself and others.

"After I invented the "Graphic" novel, it was
only **reasonable** to invent the literary agent."

But we get ahead of ourselves—before you put the time and effort into elaborating and implementing your ideas, you need to check them for worthiness. Judging your ideas is the province of the *evaluate* brainset, and that is a different state of mind altogether. In the next chapter, you'll learn how to enter a brainset that is helpful for evaluating your work. You'll also learn how to handle evaluation and criticism of your work from others.

Exercises: The Reason Brainset

Reason Exercise #1: Conscious Control of Thought: Thought-Stopping[25]

Aim of exercise: To improve your ability to direct your thoughts consciously and help you stop unwanted thoughts that interfere with your ability to think logically. This technique, called "thought-stopping" is a behavioral tool used in clinical psychology to help patients control their angry or anxious thoughts. You will need a three-by-five index card and a writing utensil. It will take you about five minutes to prepare your thought-stopping card. You can practice using it whenever unwanted thoughts enter your mind. Try to do this for the next two weeks.

Procedure: In this approach, you will simply tell yourself to stop particular thoughts as soon as you notice them. You can do this through a set of verbal self-commands or through mental images that direct you to stop paying attention to thoughts that are upsetting or distracting. Let's look first at some verbal commands you might give yourself to stop negative or distracting thoughts.

"I need to stop thinking these thoughts."
"Don't buy into these thoughts."
"Don't go there."
"Stop this thought now!"
"Mentally walk away."
"Don't buy into this thought."
"These thoughts won't help the situation."
"I need to stop thinking these thoughts."

○   Imagine saying each of these commands to yourself when you're having thoughts you don't like. Select at least four that you think would be effective for you and write them on one side of your index card.

○   Now take a minute to write down at least two other commands you could give yourself that would help you stop thinking negative thoughts. Write these below the commands you've already chosen. You should now have at least six mental commands you can use if negative or otherwise unwanted thoughts enter your mental workspace.

Some people prefer to use visual rather than verbal commands to stop unwanted thoughts. These could include visualizing:

A stop sign
A red stop light
A hand raised in the Stop position
The words "negative thought" with an X through them or with a super-
 imposed international "no" sign (a circle with a diagonal slash)
An arrow directing you to a calming vision such as a waterfall
A person listening to soothing music through headphones

- Imagine visualizing each of these image commands when you're having thoughts you don't like. Select at least three that you think would be effective for you and write them on the opposite side of your index card.
- Take a minute to write down at least two other things you could visualize that would help you stop negative thoughts in their tracks. Perhaps an image of the bad thought scrolling across the screen of your mind and breaking up into tiny crystals and falling out of sight.
- Each time an unwanted thought pops back into your mind, use a thought-stopping command or visual, and keep doing this until the negative thought runs out of steam. This could take as long as fifteen minutes or so. But be persistent: Refuse to let the negative thoughts regain control of your attention.

If you are using the token economy incentive, give yourself one *reason* token for creating the thought-stopping card and one token each time you use the technique successfully.

Reason Exercise #2: Steps in the Problem-Solving Process[26]

This process is straightforward and produces results. The more you practice problem solving, the more easily you will be able to apply this skill to both your personal and your creative problems. The following problem-solving process is adapted from work I did with the *afterdeployment.org* project. If you have trouble meeting your problems head-on—and especially if your mental comfort zone is in the *envision, connect,* or *transform* brainset—you should find this process quite helpful.

Step 1: Recognize when you have a problem. One of the clearest signs that you have a problem is the presence of negative emotions. When you feel stressed, anxious, ashamed, or depressed, it may signal that a problem needs to be addressed.

Step 2: Define the problem. Decide what the problem actually is and be very specific about what has caused (or is causing) it.

Step 3: Set a goal. Set a very specific goal for dealing with the problem. Make sure that this goal is something that is within your power to achieve.

Step 4: Brainstorm possible solutions. Use a little *connect* brainset and brainstorm possible solutions to the problem that will satisfy the goal you have set. Open your mind and get really creative about possible solutions. When you brainstorm, *do not judge* any of the solutions you come up with, just let them flow. Even if some of your ideas seem ridiculous, write them down without judging them.

Step 5: Evaluate possible solutions. Use a little *evaluate* brainset and make a list of the pros and cons for each of the possible solutions from Step 4.

Step 6: Choose the best solution based on pros and cons. Once you have looked at the pros and cons of all reasonable solutions, choose the best one. (*Note:* Problem-solving experts suggest giving special consideration to the solution with the *least* cons rather than the solution with the most pros.)

Step 7: Make a plan to implement the solution and try it! You now need to create a specific plan to implement your solution. You may need to divide the plan into steps. Set a deadline for the completion of each step. (See more about this under *Reason* Exercise #3: Steps in Achieving Your Goals.)

Step 8: Assess success. After giving your solution a fair try, the next step is to decide if your solution worked. Did you meet the goal you set in Step 3?

Step 9: If the first solution didn't work, try another! If your solution worked, your negative feelings should be diminished. If it did not work, you can always try the second and then the third solution from Step 5 until you find one that will work for you. Make sure to create a specific plan and give it adequate time to work!

Problem solving is a skill. And, like all skills, it needs to be practiced before it becomes mastered. Practice meeting your problems face-to-face and using this process. You will soon become a master at coming up with reasonable and practical solutions.

If you're using the token economy incentive, award yourself five *reason* tokens each time you solve a problem using the Steps in the Problem-Solving Process. (Note that the reward for this exercise is large because problem solving is such an important skill not only for creativity but also for all aspects of your life.)

Reason Exercise #3: Steps to Achieving Your Goals[27]

Step One: Write down a creative goal that is important to you.

- Give your goal some thought. Imagine what you'd like your life to look like five or six years from now. What would you like to have accomplished?
- Make your goal a positive statement rather than a negative statement.
- Make sure that your goal reflects *your* desires, *not* the wishes of someone close to you and *not* what you think society would

expect you to do. In order to achieve its full effectiveness, your goal has to come from within.

○ Make your goal as specific as possible.

○ Make sure your goal is challenging but at the same time realistic. If your goal is too difficult, you'll feel anxious and frustrated. If it's too easy, you'll become bored and lose motivation. You want your goal to be a stretch but not impossible.

Example: Lorne is a talented sculptor. Years ago he had drawn a series of sketches that he thought would make great bronze garden sculptures, but he kept putting off doing anything about them. When he lost his job as a graphic designer due to downsizing, he decided to get busy on his old idea. He wrote his goal as follows:

"My goal is to produce and sell at least three of my garden sculptures within the next two years." (Notice how his goal is positive, specific, and reasonable.)

Step Two: Create a plan for the attainment of your goal.

○ First, write down all the intermediate steps, called mini-goals, that you will need to accomplish in order to make your main goal a reality. This may take some research.

○ Once you have a list of mini-goals or steps toward your main goal, put them in chronological order. What sequence do you need to follow to arrive at the big goal?

Example: Lorne's mini-goals included: making models of each sculpture from his sketches, molding a cast for each, locating a foundry that could cast his statues with sufficient detail, having the pieces cast, and selling the sculptures.

○ Next you need to get really specific. Again, this part of the step may take some research. Make a list of everything you need to do to accomplish *each* of your mini-goals.

- Then set up a timetable for the completion of each step in your first mini-goal. You may want to use a spreadsheet for this work.

Example: This is Lorne's timetable for one of his mini-goals:

Mini-Goal: Get Statues Cast at Foundry	Date Due
1. Finish bird sketches for Claude to pay for foundry	Sept 10
2. Take casts to foundry	Sept 12
3. Check proofs	Sept 30
4. Pick up from foundry and pay	Oct 10

- As you near the completion of your first mini-goal, you can work on setting up a timetable for the completion of the steps in the second mini-goal.
- Be sure to schedule in time for contingencies and setbacks. If you plan for snags ahead of time, they will not be so upsetting when they inevitably occur.

Step Three: Implement your plan.

- Begin as soon as possible, but pace yourself. Many people start off working toward their goals with a flurry of activity and at a pace that they can't maintain. Try to march slowly and steadily toward your goal.
- Schedule the time into your calendar on a regular basis to make sure the journey toward your goal remains a priority. Also, if an unforeseen obstacle crops up, you can go back and change the target dates on your goal plan. Don't let an obstacle squash the entire plan!
- Write down your goal and post it where you can review it daily. Each morning when you wake up, look at your goal and visualize it as though you had already completed it. Then each night, right before you go to bed, look at it again. Each time

you make a decision during the day, ask yourself, "Will this take me closer to or further from my goal?"

º Reward yourself when you reach each of your mini-goals. And when you complete your goal, give yourself some time to savor your accomplishment, then set another challenging goal.

If you're using the token economy incentive, reward yourself with five *reason* tokens for writing out each of your creative goals and setting a timetable for its achievement.

Reason Exercise #4: Executive Center Activation: Memorization

Aim of exercise: To improve your ability to activate the prefrontal circuits associated with the executive center. (Note that the subcortical areas associated with learning—such as the hippocampus—are also activated with this exercise.) You will need copies of 10 poems that you enjoy and that you do not know by heart. Sources may include a book of poetry or the Internet. Copy the poems so that you have printed or handwritten paper copies to refer to. This exercise is variable in time commitment.

Procedure: As access to electronic information becomes more and more available (through computers and now Smartphones), the need to memorize material has decreased. However, memorization is an effective tool for activating brain circuits associated with learning and executive functions.

º First, make a stack of your poems in order of their length, with the shortest poem on top. This is your "poem of the week."

º Memorize the poem over the course of one or two days. If you have chosen a poem of considerable length (for example, the "Rubaiyat of Omar Khayyam," which has some 100 verses), you may need to delegate more days to its memorization.

o Once memorized, recite your poem to yourself each day for
   seven days.
o Continue to learn and recite one of your poems each week for
   10 weeks.

The acts of learning and memory retrieval will strengthen your
cognitive skills and also get you into the *reason* brainset. In addition,
you will have committed to heart work that inspires or moves you,
which can in turn influence your own creative work.

If you are using the token economy incentive, give yourself two
reason tokens for each poem you learn and recite for one week.

Reason Exercise #5: Executive Center Activation: Become an Expert

Aim of exercise: To improve your ability to activate the prefrontal circuits associated with the executive center. (Note that the subcortical
areas associated with learning—such as the hippocampus—are also
activated with this exercise.) You will need Internet access and a
variable block of free time.

Procedure: Pick a topic that you know nothing about or would
like to know more about. This should be a relatively restricted topic
that you can get a grasp of without researching for a dissertation. Here
are some topics chosen by others: tree-climbing lions, the life of
Beethoven, the "lost wax" process, North American wildflowers, cell
phone radiation.

o Use both Internet sources and scholarly sources to learn about
   this topic. However, be careful to stay on topic. If you start to get
   distracted by another topic while you're doing your research,
   make a note of it and return to your chosen topic.
o Take notes and make a computer file on your topic. Be thorough.
   You don't want all your information from one source. Your investigation should include a number of sources.

○   Choose a new topic every two months.
○   Keep an eye out for new developments in your chosen topic areas and periodically update and review your topics of expertise.

This exercise is fun to do with another person with whom you can share your acquired knowledge. Not only does this exercise activate the *reason* brainset, but it will increase your intellectual curiosity. Your newfound expertise will also make you a more interesting person and may also suggest areas for potential creative development. If you are using the token economy incentive, give yourself three *reason* tokens for each topic you research.

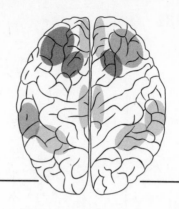

* 9

Recognizing Useful Ideas: Accessing the *Evaluate* Brainset

Good judgment comes from experience, and a lot of that comes from bad judgment.

—ATTRIBUTED TO WILL ROGERS

Not All Ideas Are Good Ideas

YOU HAVE NOW SPENT some time in the *absorb, envision, connect*, and *reason* brainsets and you've generated a collection of original and novel ideas that you're really excited about. Now what? Generating novel ideas is essential to the creative process, but knowing how to hone down your collection of bright ideas to those that have a chance of being workable is also essential. Generating a number of novel ideas is not much use without the ability to tell a good idea from a bad one. So how do you accomplish this without doing injustice to those unique brainchildren you've just produced?

181

"After further consideration, Caveman #2
decides there's something wrong
with his wheel idea ..."

As it turns out we are equipped with incredible brain machinery to make judgments. In fact, a substantial part of our prefrontal cortex is devoted to this because making rapid but accurate decisions is so important to survival. It was essential, for example, for our Caveman #2 to be able to judge whether that moving shape behind the ginkgo tree was a potential meal (good) or a carnivorous predator (not so good). Likewise, it was important to judge whether those luscious berries growing on the vine were prehistoric blueberries (good) or poisonous pokeweed berries (ugh—not so good) or whether the approaching stranger was friend or foe.

To determine how good we are at making quick judgments based on first impressions, Nalini Ambady and Robert Rosenthal conducted a series of experiments at Harvard on our ability to make rapid assessments. They had undergraduates watch very short video clips of high school teachers lecturing in a classroom. The audio was removed so that the undergrads couldn't hear the teacher's voices, and the clips were randomly selected from long lectures so as not to focus on particular positive or negative behaviors of the teachers. Yet the undergrads were able to reliably judge which teachers received high ratings (based on performance evaluations by the school principal) and which received low ratings after watching a 10-second video clip. Ambady and Rosenthal then repeated the experiment using five-second and then two-second video clips. Untrained undergrads were still able to judge the good teachers from the bad teachers in just five seconds (although their judgment was less reliable at two seconds).[1]

Clearly humans would not be able to make such accurate and speedy judgments if being able to "size things up" were not an important aspect of all our endeavors. That is certainly the case with endeavors pertaining to creativity and innovation. Yet many people—and especially many of the highly creative people I work with—have a great deal of difficulty with this component of the creative process. One of the reasons for this difficulty is that their mental comfort zone is one of the idea-generating brainsets (especially *absorb, envision,* and *connect*), and they don't know how to get into the *evaluate* brainset.

Defining the Evaluate Brainset

The *evaluate* brainset is basically a brain state in which you are focused on judging an aspect of your environment.[2] As part of the creative process, the aspect of the environment you'll be judging, of course, is your own work. This is always very tricky and has implications for self-esteem. Because self-esteem affects motivation, you run the risk of stalling your whole creative career if you are overly critical (the quintessential Type II error). On the other hand, if you're not critical enough, you may waste valuable time pursuing ideas or projects that have a low probability of panning out (the less emotionally devastating but still unpleasant Type I error).[3]

Three factors that are necessary for creativity and innovation define the *evaluate* brainset: active judgment, focused attention, and impersonality. On its surface (and indeed in its underlying brain activation pattern) the *evaluate* brainset is the mirror opposite of the *absorb* brainset, which is nonjudgmental and defocused. Let's look at each factor of the *evaluate* brainset separately.

Active Judgment

The goal of making judgments is to improve our ability to predict the future. It is a human tendency to categorize and judge things and experiences—to put them in neat pigeonholes so that we know what to expect from them if we encounter them again.[4] Categorization is a form of judgment that improves our future speed of decision making based on past experience. If, for example, you stayed in a hotel in Costa Rica that featured lines of roaches streaming up the wall, you would categorize that place as "bad." If, on the other hand, you stayed at a hotel that met your expectations, you would categorize it as "good." Either way, your categorization effort will make your decision about where to stay on your next trip to that location easier and more efficient.

While improving the efficiency of decision making, however, judging decreases flexibility and closes doors. Judging decreases the possibility that a thing could be other than that which is dictated by the pigeonhole into which you have put it. Thus, by judging a novel as "bad," you are dismissing the possibility that it might contain a great character or scene that you would like to revisit in the future. When you are in the *absorb* brainset, you loosen your need to judge things, and category boundaries become porous. In fact, you tend not to categorize at all. You are able to tolerate ambiguity about whether things are good or bad, right or wrong. You accept *everything*. This promotes intellectual curiosity; you won't automatically reject points of view because of some past categorical judgment. If your mental comfort zone is the *absorb* brainset, you are probably cringing right now at the thought of passing judgment on *anything* (let alone your own ideas)— you can just hear those doors of possibility creaking to a close!

There comes a time, however, when decisions have to be made and the next step has to be taken in order to progress. The *evaluate* brainset not only allows this, it enables it. In the *evaluate* brainset you are internally rewarded for making judgments. There is thus a pressure or drive to make judgments. You *absorbers* out there, get ready to put on your black judge's robes; you may find it very difficult to make categorical decisions, but no pain—no gain! Because making judgments and evaluations is difficult for many people who engage in creative work (simply because culling ideas seems totally opposite to generating ideas), I've divided the Active Judgments section into two parts: first, we'll look at how to force yourself to make judgments in general; then we'll progress to how to judge and evaluate your own creative ideas.

Making Judgments in General

In order to practice getting into the *evaluate* brainset, you can try some exercises that are based on work with hoarders. Hoarding is in many ways the opposite of the *absorb* brainset in that *absorbers* are so flexible in their thinking that they don't want to judge things for fear of limiting possibilities. Hoarders, on the other hand, are very rigid in their thinking; yet they also have trouble judging things— but their trouble is based on anxiety. Hoarders suffer from a type of anxiety disorder that makes it extremely painful for them to throw anything away, even meaningless candy wrappers, scraps of paper, or (yes, I'll say it) empty soup cans (remember all the uses for them you discovered in Chapter Seven?). They cannot judge these items as expendable because, for them, everything is imbued with emotional meaning. The attempt to throw away some of their trash can elicit extreme anxiety and even a panic attack. As a result, hoarders often live in homes that are piled to the ceiling with junk, creating a fire hazard and impossible living conditions.[5]

One way of dealing with this problem is to present a forced-choice scenario. In one component of cognitive-behavioral therapy, for instance, hoarders are presented with items that need to be removed from the living space and asked to categorize them into three groups: one group they will keep, one group they will sell or throw out, one group they will store to go through again later. In this way, hoarders make difficult judgments—under the watchful eye of a therapist—that ultimately allow them to remove over half of their stuff, improving their living conditions.[6]

Although you will not have a trained therapist to help you sort through your creative ideas, you can still take advantage of the forced-choice technique. (This is helpful not only to *absorbers* but also if your mental comfort zone is the *connect* brainset and you have a huge accumulation of ideas that are going nowhere.) You can sort your creative ideas into "keep," "throw away," and "store" categories to help you narrow down the ideas that are most worthy of your current development and attention. (For practice in categorizing and prioritizing, see *Evaluation* Exercises #1 and #2.)

Evaluating Your Own Ideas and Your Ongoing Work

In his 1996 book on creativity, psychologist Mihaly Csikszentmihalyi reports that at Nobel Prize–winning chemist Linus Pauling's 60th birthday party, a student asked him, "Dr. Pauling, how does one go about having good ideas?" Pauling replied, "You have a lot of ideas and throw away the bad ones."[7] In fact, the difference between being creatively productive and nonproductive may hinge on your ability to evaluate your ideas—to "throw away the bad ones." To do that, of course, you have to have some idea of what constitutes a good and a bad idea.

One of the ways you do this is to learn as much as you can about the domain or area of creativity in which you're working. It's important to know the "rules" of the domain and how experts in that area evaluate creative work. (This of course takes time and experience in that domain: see the "10-Year Rule" and Exceptional Performance in Chapter Eleven).

You may be questioning this premise. After all, don't revolutionary and innovative ideas occur "outside the box"? Don't creative people break the established rules when they create? Yes—but they use "poetic license." That is, they *know* the rules and *choose* to break them to solve a creative problem; that is more creative than not knowing the rules to begin with. Consider the poet who knows the rules that comprise a sonnet but chooses to break the rules for effect; that will generally produce a higher level of creative work than the novice who has no idea of what a sonnet is but writes a poem and calls it a sonnet anyway.

If you're totally unfamiliar with what constitutes good work in your field (whether that field is music, sales, or parenting, or any other area to which creative ideas can be applied), then you are not taking advantage of all the work that has been done by those who have gone before you. You also run the risk—excuse me, Caveman #2— of reinventing the wheel. You may put a great deal of effort into the production of something that's already been done.

Unfortunately, I see this all the time with novice psychology students in my classes. They come up with what they think is a revolutionary new idea and spend weeks developing their idea. When they finally show it to me, I have to inform them that if they'd just done a little more research they would have found their idea had already been fully explored. Sadly, the only way to know what constitutes a good idea in your field, what's been tried already and what hasn't, is to do your homework and know the background of the area in which you're doing creative work.

So, the first method of evaluating your creative idea is to determine how it would stack up next to other work in the same area of endeavor. But what if your creative idea isn't related to any established domain of work? That may certainly be the case if you're working in a relatively new genre or a new area of technology. (How, after all, could Steve Jobs and Steve Wozniak have evaluated their idea for personal computers against an established domain of work?) Here are some general tips for evaluating your ideas.

GENERAL TIPS FOR EVALUATING CREATIVE IDEAS

Deliberate judgment of your creative ideas requires comparing your idea to some criterion of acceptance. You can't judge whether an idea is good or bad unless you have some concept of what constitutes a good idea. If you had a specific goal in mind before you generated your creative solution, you can measure it against that goal. If you did not have a specific goal in mind (as is often the case when ideas "pop into your head" via the *spontaneous* pathway), you can measure them against the standards for all creative products:

Is this idea original?	Yes	No
Is it adaptive or expressive in a way that will be useful to someone?	Yes	No
Will this idea change the way people think about things?	Yes	No
Does this idea meet the goal that I set ahead of time?	Yes	No
If not, does it meet a goal that might be useful to pursue at another time?	Yes	No
Is it beautiful (does it have aesthetic value)?	Yes	No

If your answer is no to all of these questions, then you should reject your idea. If the answer is no to the first four questions but yes to one of the last two, decide whether this idea is worth dropping your current plan to pursue or whether you should record it and store it to pursue at a later date.

The criteria you will use to evaluate whether your creative ideas are worth pursuing are different from the criteria you will use to evaluate aspects of your ongoing work once you've decided to accept and build on a creative idea. In general, you should be more lenient in your acceptance of ideas and then become a somewhat harsher critic of aspects of your work in progress.

Here are some guidelines for evaluating your ongoing work that I've developed to help both novices and professionals constructively critique their creative projects:

1. *Get some distance.* Put the work aside for a few days before you evaluate it. You cannot be objective when you are recently emerging from the throes of creative engagement. You will be too close to your work to give it a fair appraisal.

2. *Evaluate your work with respect.* Give your work the same respect that you would give if someone you admire asked you to evaluate their work.

3. *Don't decide to throw out a work midway through the project.* Discouragement may cause you to believe that the work will never amount to anything. However, remember that before you began the elaboration work, you evaluated this idea and gave it a thumbs-up; therefore, it must have some value. Tell yourself that you can always throw it out when it's finished if it doesn't meet muster.

4. *Look at individual parts of your work.* Evaluate each part for its quality. Then look at how the part relates to the whole. Does each part contribute to the whole in a meaningful way? There will be many parts of which you're very proud and which are in fact very good, but if they don't relate to the whole work in a meaningful or satisfying way, then judge them accordingly. Remember that these parts can be preserved through photography or keyboard or recording to be part of a future project if they're that good (see Dealing with "Pets").

5. *Look at the work from the point of view of the audience.* Who will benefit from this work? If you can identify who will be the benefactors (your audience) then try to look at your work from their perspective. Does that change the way you evaluate the individual parts?

6. *Be flexible.* Sometimes a work gets pulled by its own weight in a direction you weren't expecting. You may have a mental vision of what the final product is supposed to be, but that vision may be as much of a "pet" as the individual parts that don't fit in are. Be willing to alter your vision if the work is going in an interesting direction. You can always come back to your vision if the new path doesn't pan out. Novelists often claim that their story gets a life of its own and goes in a new (better) direction than the one they had originally envisioned. You can tentatively follow the new direction and retreat to the original idea if the new direction doesn't pan out.

7. *Decide whether to consult others.* This is tricky. What are you going to do if the person you consult says the work is garbage but deep down inside you think it's good? Likewise, there's no benefit in consulting a "yes" person who will tell you your work is great no matter what they really think. And if someone tells you what they honestly think, it might destroy your momentum. If you're going to consult someone, it's best to ask them to give you concrete suggestions for improvement of your work rather than asking them to render judgment on a partially completed work-in-progress. Professional editors working with their authors know how make corrections and suggestions without destroying fragile egos; if your consultant will not be as delicate, you might consider waiting until the work is completed to show it to critics.

8. *Be hard on your work,* not *on yourself.* Remember that it is the work you're judging. Put your best effort into the work and you'll be successful as a person regardless of how you ultimately judge this one piece of work.

One additional problem that often pops up during the evaluation of your work is how to handle an idea or an elaboration to which you are inappropriately attached. This could be the result of having a *spontaneous* idea (remember that *spontaneous* insights often arrive with a strong conviction of "rightness") or it could be a paragraph, musical phrase, or other element of creative work that you worked really hard on and feel is perfectly executed. Here is some information on dealing with these "pet" creations.

DEALING WITH "PETS"

You have written a perfect mini-speech. It is witty and concise and written for the main character of your novel. You love this speech. The problem is it doesn't really fit into your plot. You spend days manipulating the plot just so that you can include this little speech. When you finally figure out how to fit it in, you've veered so far off course that you have to spend more days getting back to the original plotline of your novel.

Think about what you've done: you ruined the forest to save one tree. Everyone has their pet creations, something that they can't let go of despite all evidence that the "pet" is mucking up the works. It's a real problem.

However, modern technology has given us a way to deal with inappropriate "pets": the answer is to put them on an *outtakes* reel. I recommend that my students have an *outtakes* file for every chapter, for every scene, for every painting, for every piece of music, and for every invention they create. When you realize that your pet has to go, simply copy and paste (or photograph and scan) your work into an outtakes file before deleting it from your work. Make sure that you have a method for preserving your unused pets. That way you can always reinstate them or go back to them for a later project, and parting with them is not such sweet sorrow.

(By the way, the concept of storing "pets" on an outtake reel has an analogy in our larger culture. It is an interesting

(continued)

phenomenon that at the cultural level, creativity has increased as a function of knowledge transmission. When all information had to be held in the head and passed on in the oral tradition, there wasn't much room for innovation and unproven "pets." Only so much knowledge could be retained in the head to be passed down. However, when the written word developed, people could record both traditional knowledge *and* new ideas; in case the new ideas didn't pan out, the traditional ways were still preserved. This led to greater cultural creativity.[8] Finally, with the advent of the Internet, even minor variations on new ideas (such as "pets") can be retained, so we are able to branch further and further from tradition without fear of losing information valuable to our culture. Thus, culturally, we have access to even more information to combine and recombine in novel and creative ways.

Now that you have some ideas about how to force yourself to make decisions, how to evaluate your work, and how to deal with pet creations that are slowing down your progress, let's look at other aspects of the *evaluate* brainset that will help you make appropriate decisions about your work.

Focused Attention

When you're in the *evaluate* brainset, your attention is very focused, allowing you to hone in on small details rather than defocusing attention to let peripheral information into your cognitive workspace. Focused attention keeps you on task and concentrating on the pros and cons of your solution or project, which is what evaluation is all about. Focusing on a single item, aspect, or detail is quite difficult for people who are used to thinking in terms of imagination (*envision* brainset) or of connections between concepts (*connect* brainset). However, if your goal is to judge the worthiness of your idea or part of your idea, you need to stay focused on it and compare it to the standards you have set for appropriateness (more on that in a few minutes; for practice on maintaining focus, see *Evaluate* Exercises #3 and #4.)

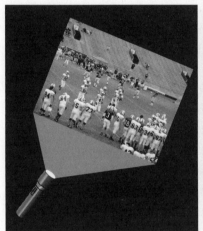 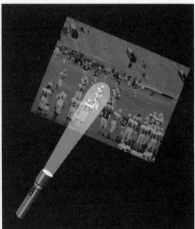

Defocused attention is like a light with a broad but dim beam that allows many objects to be illuminated at once.

Focused attention is like a light with a narrow intense beam that can only illuminate a single object at a time.

Impersonality

Creative and innovative work takes courage. You are venturing into unknown territory when you create, and you are leaving yourself open to criticism, ridicule, failure, and all the other perils that can accompany breaking with established patterns of doing things. One of the perils that you are most open to is self-rebuke and self-criticism. It's extremely important to remain impersonal in the *evaluate* brainset; remaining impersonal entails keeping the volume turned down on the self-evaluative "Me" center in the brain. You are evaluating an idea or a piece of work—you are *not* evaluating yourself or your abilities.

You have to give yourself the freedom to fail. Failure is part of the idea-development process of creativity. Thomas Edison made literally thousands of mistakes as he sought to perfect the electric lightbulb. When asked about his failures, he is cited as responding, "I have not failed. I've just found 10,000 ways that won't work."[9] The Wright brothers, likewise, sustained many failures in their attempt to create controlled and sustained flight. You're going to be coming up with lots of new ideas. Remember what we said back in Chapter Seven; the number of good ideas and products you create is a function of the quantity of ideas and products. So the more you produce, the more "hits" you'll produce. Also the more you'll fail. Failure is expected and allowed! It only takes a small number of good ideas to make you successful, and then you'll forget about all those that didn't work. So do not self-flagellate when one of your ideas doesn't pan out.

Self-rebuke will stall your creative efforts. You need to monitor yourself, especially when you're in the judgmental *evaluate* mode to make sure (1) that you're not coming down on yourself for ideas that don't work, and (2) that you're not taking personally any criticism from others about your creative work.

If you start feeling low or discouraged about your idea or product, listen to the running commentary of thoughts in your mind—psychologists call this "self-talk." Are you thinking negative things like "I'm no good at this," "I might as well give up," or "How can I be so stupid!"? If so, take a moment to consider what you're saying. Is there really any evidence for your negative thoughts? Because that's what the *evaluate* brainset is all about: making judgments based on evidence. So gather evidence for and against your negative self-talk, and then try to replace that self-talk with more positive and realistic statements, such as "Well, that's one idea that didn't work . . . on to the next one" or "That was a mistake—but if I don't make mistakes, I won't learn anything."[10] (For practice monitoring your negative self-talk and evaluating it, see *Evaluate* Exercise #5).

Finally, you need to know how to handle criticism from others about your creative ideas and work without taking it personally. This is quite difficult because even the best creative ideas are often met with skepticism, and it is painful to think that others don't have the same enthusiasm for your ideas that you have. Regardless of what others may say about embracing change, people are naturally cautious about accepting new ideas that threaten their old and comfortable ways of thinking or doing things. Learning to handle negative evaluation of your work in an impersonal but gracious manner is an important skill. Because criticism is inevitable when you're breaking new ground with creative ideas, it's a skill that will serve you well throughout your creative endeavors. Here are the rules I've developed for handling negative evaluation from others:

Rule #1

If someone is criticizing something you've done, that's a sign that you've *done* something to criticize! You've taken a risk and chosen something that's a challenge. Receiving criticism is therefore a badge of courage. **Congratulate yourself!** Doing something new and challenging, even if you're not yet good at it, is infinitely more rewarding than being praised for doing the same old thing well.

Rule #2

Consider criticism to be valuable feedback. If you don't take criticism as a personal attack, but rather look at it as an indicator of an area in which you need to improve or change course, you can use the feedback to self-correct. Think about a guided missile system. It has built-in monitors to detect when it's heading off course so that other parts of the guidance system can make the correction and get back on track. If you can put aside feeling personally attacked, you can use the feedback in criticism as part of your own self-correcting guidance system.

Rule #3

Do not defend yourself if criticized. When you receive criticism, it's very easy to feel as if you're being put on the defensive; this can make you feel that you need to take a stand and defend your work or your actions. Once you begin to defend your work, it is very unlikely that you will learn anything from the information others are trying to give you. Instead, you will entrench yourself in the position *against* the criticism. You learn nothing and your critic has wasted his or her breath in trying to give you some feedback. The worst-case scenario is that you'll actually launch a counterattack, and the person who was offering you feedback will become your adversary. Even if someone has delivered hostile or unjust criticism (perhaps out of jealousy or spitefulness), do not defend your position. Rather, thank the person for their feedback (see Rule #5) and ignore the criticism. Do not be pulled into battle by a hostile critic.

Rule #4

Rephrase the main points of the criticism. In most cases, spitefulness or hostility is not the motive for the criticism. Therefore, listen actively to what the person delivering the criticism has to say (that means you don't spend the time while they're talking to you planning what you're going to say back to them). When they're finished, paraphrase in a neutral (not angry or sarcastic) tone the points you think they were making. Example: "Okay, it sounds like you think my novel moves too slowly and that I need to develop the character of Edward more. You also think the description of the dinner party is too long. Is that right?" Now the person delivering the criticism can straighten out any misunderstandings, and he or she will feel that they've been heard. Note that this rule also applies if the person has delivered their criticism via e-mail, letter, or newspaper opinion column. This rule has two advantages for you: first, it takes the personal sting out of the criticism; it's much easier to hear the criticism when it's voiced in your own words. Second, it defuses the confrontational aspects of the criticism and makes the criticism part of a collaboration; it puts you and the critic on the same team working together to make your work better. When engaging in creative work, it's always better to have helpers rather than adversaries.

Rule #5

Thank the person criticizing your work for their feedback. Note that by thanking the person, you are not agreeing to incorporate their criticism. In private, you can analyze the criticism and decide whether to use it or disregard it. This step is also a good way to deal with blowhards and naysayers who are criticizing you for criticism's sake or to make themselves look important.

Rule #6

Determine the value of the criticism objectively. Once you've received criticism, look for the evidence for and against its validity. Try to do this objectively, and analyze each point of criticism separately. Even blowhards can offer valid points of criticism. After you've done an evidential analysis, you can decide whether to make changes based on the criticism. This rule also removes the subjective sting of the criticism and helps you deal with it objectively.

Neuroscience of the Evaluate Brainset

Exactly what does your brain look like when you access the *evaluate* brainset? Remember that the *evaluate* mode is characterized by active judgment, focused attention, and impersonality. The brain activation patterns of people when they're in the *evaluate* brainset reflect these characteristics. The *evaluate* brainset is similar to the *reason* brainset in activation pattern; this is because evaluating and making judgments are actually functions of the executive center that is so active during reasoned thought. Therefore, the areas of the prefrontal lobes that control decision making and inhibition are highly active. There is also preferential activation of the left hemisphere with relative deactivation in the right hemisphere when individuals are making categorization judgments. The orbitofrontal and anterior cingulate cortex, areas that we named as part of the judgment center in Chapter Three, are active as well.[11]

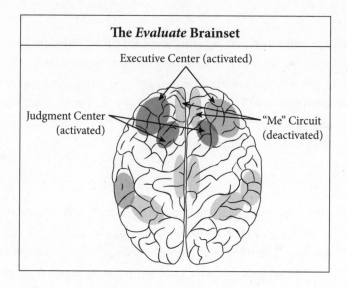

The *Evaluate* Brainset

Executive Center (activated)

Judgment Center
(activated)

"Me" Circuit
(deactivated)

Activation of the executive center and especially the left prefrontal cortex is an indication that this brainset is one of highly focused attention. We would expect high levels of norepinephrine and dopamine in the prefrontal cortex,[12] although studies have not been conducted to confirm this. The new field of neuroeconomics combines research from both economics and neuroscience. It is beginning to explore how making judgments affects both the fear and reward systems in the brain.[13] This new field will soon be able to tell us more about how specific neurotransmitters may facilitate or inhibit *evaluation*.

When to Access the Evaluate Brainset

Timing is important when you are accessing the *evaluate* brainset. Because it's the virtual opposite of the brainsets that you want to be using when you're coming up with creative ideas, this brainset will cut off further generation of ideas. However, it can be a useful tool for getting out of the *connect* brainset in which you just continue to spew ideas without ever acting on them.

I've worked with several artists and students who have this difficulty (including Richard, the film producer whom I mentioned in the preface). If the *connect* brainset is your mental comfort zone, you may have had this problem as well. I'm currently working with a writer who hasn't been able to get started on his next project because he's stuck in the idea-generating *connect* brainset. He keeps coming up with new ideas for the plot, and with every new idea he's off doing more research. While he's researching, he runs into something that gives him another new idea and he's off researching that. Just as when you're surfing the Net, one page leads you to another and another until you're totally off track from your initial search, stimuli in the world lead the person in the *connect* brainset on a chase far afield from his or her original intention. It feels almost blasphemous to put the brakes on when you're generating potentially good ideas (I mean, what if you never get back into that *connect* brainset?). However, you have to trust that you *will* be able to generate more ideas in the future. Note that too many ideas—as well as no ideas—can lead to creative block. And the best thing you can do now is to implement your best idea of today. If you have several ideas, begin evaluating *now*.

Besides getting you out of the idea-generating phase of the creative process, the *evaluate* brainset is, of course, where you want to be when you're deciding which idea or solution to implement. This happens during the evaluation stage of the creative process (macroevaluation) and then off and on during the editing, elaboration, and implementation stages (microevaluation).

Criticism and evaluation are important parts of the creative process. However, the *evaluate* brainset is not conducive to generating new ideas or sustaining work on a complex project, so use it in small doses. If the *evaluate* brainset is your mental comfort zone, reward yourself with items from your Small Pleasures list (from Exercise #9 in Chapter Two) each time you successfully achieve the *absorb, envision,* or *connect* brainset. Being able to view the world from different perspectives will improve your evaluative skills even if your goal is to be a professional evaluator, such as an art, movie, or music critic.

Remember that the definition of creativity is something that's both original and useful or adaptive. You cannot determine whether your idea or solution meets those criteria unless you evaluate it.

"After careful consideration, I nixed that porcupine blanket idea; but I'm moving forward with the iron tools concept."

One final reminder: judge your *work* and not your*self*. Use criticism to your advantage and *not* as an indicator of your personal worthiness. If you are finding that you take criticism (both your own and other people's) too personally, you may actually be operating in the *transform* brainset rather than the *evaluate* brainset. When you're in the *transform* brainset, everything seems personal and (usually) deflating. To learn about how you can take this self-referential brain state and *transform* it into a creative advantage, read on!

Exercises: The Evaluate Brainset

Evaluate Exercise #1: Making Judgments: Forced Choice

Aim of exercise: To decrease the need to suspend judgment and improve evaluation skills. This exercise will take you between 10 and 15 minutes. You will need a writing utensil, two pieces of paper, and a timer or stopwatch. Try to do a version of this exercise once a week until making judgments about your own things is easy or you.

Procedure: On one sheet of paper, make a list of your 10 favorite books. Take some time with this. These should be books that are really meaningful to you. When you have your list, number the books (they don't have to be in any order, just assign each a number).

When you're ready, on the second piece of paper, write a row of numbers from one to ten, and beside each number write two words: "keep" and "throw."

Now imagine that you're at sea on a small boat and you have to throw half of your books overboard to keep the boat from sinking. You will never see these books again.

Set your timer for two minutes. For each book on your list, decide whether you will keep it or throw it. Remember that you can only keep five. You must complete the list before the timer sounds.

If you are using the token economy incentive and you finish before the buzzer, give yourself two *evaluate* tokens. If you finished the list but did not complete it before the timer, give yourself one token.

This exercise is very effective in getting you to make rapid judgments about the value of your belongings; however, some people who have tried it find it somewhat traumatizing. One artist (whose mental comfort zone was the *envision* brainset) told me it reminded her of the movie *Sophie's Choice* and that she actually wept for a while over losing her beloved books. If you feel upset by the exercise (please don't laugh—*envisioners* with their strong imaginations can get caught up in the exercises), then mentally row the boat back out into the water with a grappling hook. Envision yourself retrieving the books, bringing them home and drying them by a warm, cozy fire, and restoring them to your bookshelf.

Repeat this exercise once a week with lists of other belongings that are important to you, such as: pairs of shoes, golf clubs, pieces of jewelry, or your CD collection. My clients have also used: their collection of T-shirts from bars across the globe, teddy bears, rare coins, and Mardi Gras beads. *Envisioners*, remember that you can go mentally retrieve your items from the water later, but try to sit with the discomfort of making serious judgments for a while first.

Evaluate Exercise #2: Making Judgments: Best and Worst

Aim of exercise: To decrease the need to suspend judgment and improve evaluation skills. This exercise will take you 10 minutes. You will need a writing utensil, a piece of paper, and a timer or stopwatch. Try to do this exercise once a week until making judgments about your own things is easy for you.

Procedure: On a sheet of paper, make a list of your six happiest moments from the past year. Take some time with this. These should be moments that are really meaningful to you. When you have your list, set the timer for two minutes.

Now rank the moments from the best to the worst with the best being number one.

If you are using the token economy incentive and you finish within the allotted time, give yourself one *evaluate* token.

Try to complete a version of this exercise every week until you feel comfortable rank-ordering things of personal value. You can use lists of other types of moments (most embarrassing, angriest, and so on) for the past year. This exercise will help you slip into the *evaluate* brainset more easily.

Evaluate Exercise #3: Focusing Attention: Watching the Clock

This exercise was adapted from Carol Vorderman's book Super Brain *(see Vorderman, 2007). It has worked well for my creative artists, musicians, and writers who have trouble staying focused.*

Aim of exercise: To improve your powers of concentration and focused attention. You will need an analog clock with a second hand. This exercise will take you between one and three minutes. Try to do this exercise once a day for progressively longer periods until you can remain focused for three minutes.

Procedure: Place the clock so it is in front of you. If it's on a wall, stand so that it's directly in front of you. Wait until the second hand reaches 12. Now focus all your concentration on the movement of the second hand. If a thought interferes with your concentration, stop the exercise and wait till the second hand reaches 12 again. Aim to focus on the second hand for 10 seconds without letting other thoughts intrude. Each time you do the exercise, gradually increase the time until you can focus for three minutes. If other thoughts intrude, try counting the seconds as you follow the hand. With practice, you should be able to totally focus on the second hand and nothing else.

If you are using the token economy incentive and you are able to focus for the time you stipulated for yourself today, give yourself one *evaluate* token.

Evaluate Exercise #4: Focusing Attention: Turn the Volume Down

This exercise was also adapted from Carol Vorderman's book Super Brain *(2007). Thank you, Carol!*

Aim of exercise: To improve your powers of concentration and focused attention. (This exercise may also improve your hearing.) You will need either a television or a radio plus a timer or stopwatch. This exercise will take you two minutes. Try to do this exercise once a day for two weeks.

Procedure: Turn the volume on the TV or radio down so that you can barely hear what's being said (tune to a talk station if you're using a radio). Now turn up the volume so that you can understand what's being said only if you really strain your ears and concentrate. Make a note of the volume level (many TVs and radios have a readout for volume level). Listen for two minutes, trying to decipher all that is said. Focus only on the voices you hear. If you can't understand anything, the volume is too low.

If you are using the token economy incentive, reward yourself with one *evaluate* token.

Try to do this exercise once a day for a couple of weeks, striving to turn the volume to a lower level while still being able to comprehend when you concentrate.

Evaluate Exercise #5: Self-Monitoring for Personal Criticism

Aim of exercise: To monitor your own thoughts for negative self-criticism that could hamper your creative efforts. You will need either a blank sheet of paper and a writing utensil, or you can make a copy of the following page. This exercise will take you around 10 minutes. Try to do this exercise whenever you feel discouraged about your creative problem.

Procedure: When you feel discouraged, answer the questions on the Self-Monitoring Form that follows.

Self-monitoring is a skill, and like all skills it needs to be practiced to be developed. However, once you get the hang of it, you'll find your outlook concerning yourself and your creative efforts will improve and you'll be more motivated to continue.

If you're using the token economy incentive, award yourself one *evaluate* token each time you fill out the Self-Monitoring Form to evaluate your self-criticism.

You can learn more about the technique of self-monitoring and download a copy of the Self-Monitoring Form used in this exercise on the Web site http://ShelleyCarson.com.

Self-Monitoring Form

Date

1. What was happening at the time you felt discouraged?		
2. Who was with you?		
3. What were you saying to yourself (your self-talk)? Be specific.		
4. Were you being critical of yourself rather than your creative idea or product? __Yes __No		
5. If yes, what is the evidence for and against your critical self-talk?	Evidence for critical comments	Evidence against critical comments
6. Does the evidence support your critical comments about yourself __Yes __No		
7. Replace your negative self-talk with more positive and realistic self-statements.		

10

Using Emotion Creatively: Accessing the Transform Brainset

Feeling and longing are the motive forces behind all human endeavor and human creations.

—ALBERT EINSTEIN[1]

THE *TRANSFORM* BRAINSET is a state of consciousness in which your attention is occupied by thoughts relating to yourself and your feelings (generally negative feelings).[2] In past chapters we've looked at ways you can enter brainsets that will allow you to generate creative ideas (the *absorb, envision, connect,* and *reason* brainsets), evaluate your ideas (the *evaluate* brainset), and develop and implement your ideas (the *reason* brainset). The one thing we haven't talked much about is your feelings. Your emotions color the way you see your environment, the way you recall memories, and, indeed, all aspects of your cognition. Your emotions can either get in the way of your creative efforts . . . or you can use them to enhance your creativity. In this chapter, we'll discuss both the good and the bad aspects of self-consciousness and emotions, as well as how you can *transform* emotional experience into creative products.

Let's look at some different levels of emotion and why they have an impact on your efforts to be creative.

Levels of Emotional Experience

Much of the time we're not consciously aware of our feelings; they run in the background occupying only a minimal amount of our attention. This low-level background feeling state is referred to as *stream of affect* by psychologists David Watson and Lee Anna Clark ("affect" being the psychological term for emotions).[3] We may notice this stream of affect as a mild positive or negative state (as in "I'm having a good day" or "I got up on the wrong side of the bed"), if we notice it at all. Yet, regardless of how little of our attention it is claiming, our stream of affect influences how we see the world. Positive stream of affect makes us somewhat more open to novelty, while negative stream of affect closes us up somewhat to new ideas (every teenager knows it's best to approach Dad about a loan when he's whistling than when he's scowling).

The next step up in emotional intensity is a *mood*. When you're experiencing a *mood* state, you may feel anxious, irritable, contented, self-conscious, or "blue." Mood states can be of relatively long duration, some lasting for months, and they occupy more of your conscious attention. Certain moods, such as anxiety or melancholia (a.k.a. depression), can make it difficult to concentrate. If negative moods persist for extremely long periods, they can interfere with both your work and your interpersonal relationships. In such cases, you may need to seek the help of a mental health professional (please note that modern evidence-based treatments are very effect in alleviating these debilitating and dysfunctional negative mood states).[4]

The most intense emotional state you can experience is the onset of an actual *emotion*. Note that while we refer to all feeling states as *emotional* states in everyday speech, actual *emotions* have specific characteristics (see the diagram below). *Emotions* are events of relatively short duration, usually lasting less than an hour. They are a response to a particular trigger (either in the environment or an internal event such as a traumatic memory or the experience of pain), and they are extremely intense. They are accompanied by characteristic facial expressions, thoughts, physiological changes, and subjective feelings. They also prime the body to behave in specific ways called "action tendencies" (for example, the action tendency associated with fear is the "fight or flight" response, while the action tendency for anger is aggression).[5] *Emotions* demand your attention; you will be focused on the emotional material to the exclusion of other thoughts. If the emotion is intense enough, you may feel completely controlled by it.

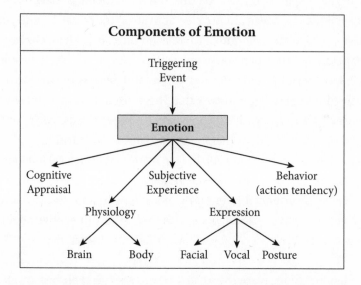

This is called "emotional hijacking." Emotional hijacking may take the form of a fit of violent rage (extreme anger), a suicide attempt (extreme despair), or a panic attack (extreme fear). When you're emotionally hijacked, your action *tendency* becomes an action *imperative*, and you have little conscious control over your actions.[6] This is, in part, the basis of the "temporary insanity" plea.

One of the functions of emotions is to alert you to the need for action (hence the *action tendency* response). Emotions, moods, and stream of affect absorb more of your attention if they have a negative valence than a positive one. That's because positive feelings suggest that all is right with your world and that you're interacting with your environment in a manner that is conducive to your survival. Full speed ahead and no action needs to be taken. However, negative moods and emotions grab your attention because they're an indicator that something may be wrong and that you may need to act. Negative moods can affect your creative efforts to the extent that they pull your attention away from the creative process. The more negative emotion you're feeling the harder it will be to focus on generating novel and original ideas.

In the chapters that precede this, one clear theme is that creativity is associated with desiring novelty, activating the reward center, and upswings in positive emotion. There is no mention of fear, anxiety, or depression. In fact, when you're in a fearful or depressed state (as noted in Chapter Nine) you avoid novelty. Fear and depression are a turnoff for the idea-generating brainsets that we've discussed. So if you're self-absorbed in some negative feeling state (in other words, you're in the *transform* brainset), does that mean you can't be creative?

NO! (that's an emphatic *no*). In fact, many highly creative individuals —both past and present—are clearly (as we used to say) neurotic.[7] They have experienced long bouts of anxiety, irritability, or depression; yet they have found ways to use their state of negative affect to enhance their creativity. They've done this in two ways:

o First, by using creative work as a way to assuage their negative feelings; in this way, the negative feelings act as a motivator to be creative and creative work acts as a type of self-administered therapy.

o Second, by using the negative feelings as subject matter for their creative work. As we shall see, many a painting, poem, novel, and musical composition has focused on its creator's state of negative emotions.

I don't recommend purposely getting yourself into a negative feeling state (unless you're using method acting to prepare for a theatrical part). But if you're already in the *transform* state, why not make the most of it and use it to your advantage? Later in this chapter, we'll examine ways you can use that negative emotion to propel yourself to a better state through creative endeavors, and we'll also look at how others have used negative moods to inform their creative work.

Defining the *Transform* Brainset

The *transform* brainset is basically a brain state in which your feelings are mildly negative and your thoughts are self-referential.[8] As a rule, you are not consciously directing these thoughts; they are rather of a mind-wandering, stream-of-consciousness nature. As with the *envision* brainset, you engage in "what if?" thinking; but rather than the purposeful imagining that characterizes the *envision* brainset, what-if-ing in the *transform* brainset is not purposefully directed and often includes themes of worry, anxiety, resentment, self-pity, or regret. At other times, themes of thinking in the *transform* brainset may tend toward fantasies of self-aggrandizement, idealized romance, power, or revenge. While this doesn't sound very healthy, neuroscience research indicates that all of us slip into these types of self-referential fantasies at times. Our idle thoughts (times when we're not consciously directing our thoughts) may reflect current mood states, frustrations, and longings. The *transform* brainset is identified by three factors: self-centered thought, negative feeling states, and dissatisfaction. Let's look at each of these factors separately and determine how you can make creative use of them.

Self-Conscious Thought

Self-conscious thought is thought that's directed toward yourself and your relationship to your environment. This can and (and generally does) include comparing yourself or your circumstances to those of other people. This can lead to resentment for those who seem to have it better than you do and to self-pity and feelings that the world is unfair. This can also lead to feelings of personal worthlessness and concern about your future. Finally, it can include excessive guilt and regret about things you have done or have failed to do in the past. When thoughts such as these begin to stream into awareness, many people have trouble turning them off. In fact, they may become caught in a downward spiral of negative self-assessment.[9]

While these particular thoughts are psychologically unhealthy and usually don't reflect your true value and worth, there is a silver lining to this state; it produces a state of internal reflection. Your internal world is where all creative ideas are generated and also where all psychic healing takes place. While you're there, how about doing a little exploring and investigating? Your investigations can yield enormous knowledge about yourself and the human condition in general. (For practice in self-investigation, see *Transform* Exercises #1 and #2. However, please note that self-investigation should take place in a state of *mild* dysphoria or negative mood. If you're feeling hopeless or out of control, you should *not* perform the *transform* exercises and you should seek the help of a mental health professional.) Note that when you've had enough self-reflection and you want to move on to thinking about other things, you can use the Self-Monitoring Exercise from Chapter Nine or the Thought-Stopping Exercise from Chapter Eight to help you get out of the self-conscious state. (By the way, you don't need to be in a state of dysphoria to engage in self-reflection; however, self-reflection often results from such a state.)

While trying to understand your complexities as a person, it is also important to recognize that you have enormous strengths as well as flaws. To focus on the negative aspects of your character is to disregard half your essence. It isn't realistic. You are a person with great potential to be creative. Use your self-knowledge of both your problems and your strengths to guide your creative expression. (To investigate your personal strengths, see *Transform* Exercise #3.)

Negative Feeling States

Negative feeling states are part of the normal ebb and flow of human emotions, of course. They provide a natural counterpoint to the joyful and happy occasions of life, and they add to the rich tapestry of human experience. Since the middle of the twentieth century, however, we seem to have developed a fear of negative mood states; when we encounter them, we immediately do everything we can to extricate ourselves from these states—with drugs, liquor, sex, or thrills—without taking time to understand what these moods are trying to tell us.[10] If you are in the *transform* brainset, you may want to give some real thought to why you are there rather than taking the first available train out of that town.

Explorations of negative feelings have been the subject matter for creative works since at least the time of the early Greeks, when Aristotle first associated poets and playwrights with melancholia. Here is a very small sample of work from creators who have used their negative mood states as subject matter to connect with others and to share their mutual experience of important aspects of the human condition:

o   Emily Dickinson's famous poem "There's a Certain Slant of Light" describes depression on a winter's afternoon (perhaps an early description of seasonal affective disorder [SAD]).

o   Edvard Munch's famous Expressionist painting *The Scream* portrays a state of high anxiety.

o   The entire genre of blues music is based on a negative feeling state. It gets its name from the term *blue devils,* which the African American community has used for centuries to denote a state of melancholy and sadness.

o   Playwright Eugene O'Neill's masterpiece *Long Day's Journey into Night* portrays an entire family's dysfunction and melancholy. O'Neill won a Pulitzer Prize posthumously for this work.

o   In 2005, a celebrated art exhibit called *Melancholy: Genius and Madness in the West,* opened in Paris at the Galeries Nationales du

Grand Palais. The exhibit was devoted to art inspired by depression and melancholy and featured work spanning 2,000 years. (Negative feelings have been around a long time!)

○ Tchaikovsky's Symphony No. 6 in B minor, "Pathétique," is often referred to as the composer's suicide note (he died nine days after conducting its premier performance). Author and musicologist Joseph Horowitz says "this is a work which cannot be listened to casually . . . here's a guy who's in an extreme personal crisis baring his soul."[11] (Again, if your negative mood is this severe, do not write music; get the help of a mental health professional.) For more information on the connection between creativity and mental illness, see Mental Disorders, *Transform*ation, and Creativity.

○ J. D. Salinger's classic 1951 novel *The Catcher in the Rye* is the consummate description of teenage angst.

You, too, can use your negative moods as inspiration to encode emotions in artistic form that others may be feeling but do not know how to express. You can do this through music, writing (both poetry and prose), art (both drawing and sculpture), and drama. Florists know how to express mood through flower arrangements, and chefs can use spices and herbs to connote different moods. You can use virtually any domain to creatively express your negative mood in a way that may resonate with the emotions of others. You don't have to have training or innate talent to do this. Personal expression of emotion is powerful, even from the untrained creator. (For practice in describing your feelings creatively, see *Transform* Exercises #4 and #5.)

Dissatisfaction

The negative feeling state of the *transform* brainset goes hand-in-hand with a basic state of personal dissatisfaction. These two factors of the brainset feed off of each other as dissatisfaction with oneself can breed negative mood, while negative mood breeds dissatisfaction. However, the up side of this for your creative endeavors is that dissatisfaction can also breed creativity. In fact, contentment is often the enemy of creative effort.[12] (Note that although creativity is associated with a positive upswing in mood, the positive mood that evokes divergent thinking is *not* in the form of *contentment* but rather of pleasant surprise, mild euphoria, pride, positive expectation, or joy.)

Creativity is predicated on some sort of dissatisfaction with the current state of things; otherwise, the impetus for creativity would be absent. The creative person is always on the lookout for life circumstances that could be improved. However, in order to improve circumstances, you need to be very clear about what it is that's causing dissatisfaction. Once you can identify the problem then you can use divergent thinking or the problem-solving steps we discussed in Chapter Eight to find and implement solutions. (For practice writing about negative experiences in a way that can improve both your physical and mental health, see *Transform* Exercise #7.)

Whether through music, art, writing, drama, a new video game, or some other medium, one of the best uses you can make of your dissatisfaction is as an inspiration to endure suffering and to prevail over it. Suffering is part of the human condition. Yet perhaps one reason we are encountering an increase in the rate of depression worldwide[13] is that our ability to endure suffering has diminished with the availability of quick fixes that promise the rapid end to all negative feeling states. If we don't learn that we *can* endure negative feelings—and come out on the other side of them stronger—then we will be subject to episodes of depression whenever the normal vicissitudes of life deal us a blow. One use of your negative feelings is as a starting point for the artistic expression of the process of humans using their strengths to overcome hardship in the modern world. (See *Transform* Exercise #8.)

Creativity as a Coping Mechanism

One of the most potent methods of dealing with negative moods and dissatisfaction is to express them in the form of creative work. As we saw from the list under "Negative Feeling States" previously in this chapter, many creative people before you have used their negative mood state as subject matter for artistic achievements. Likewise, many creative people have used their creative endeavors to soften the bitter sting of the negative mood state. For instance, the English novelist Graham Greene wrote: "Art is a form of therapy. Sometimes I wonder how all those who do not write, compose or paint can escape the madness, the melancholia, the panic inherent in the human situation."[14]

In psychoanalytic terms, the energy of negative emotions that is too dangerous or unacceptable to be expressed directly can be redirected into creative work that is more socially acceptable. This is a type of beneficial defense mechanism called *sublimation*. As an individual releases negative energy into the creative work, the power of the negative emotions is weakened.

Indeed, the experience of delving into a creative endeavor is such an effective way of coping with negative moods that dozens of creative therapies have sprung up to help individuals who suffer from depression, anxiety disorders, eating disorders, and even psychosis to cope with their demons. Therapies include art, drama, writing, music, and dance therapies. The growing body of scientific literature that reports on the effectiveness of these therapies as adjunct treatments for mental illness attests to the healing power of creative activity.[15]

The benefits of creative therapies include a group setting (misery loves company) as well as a trained therapist to encourage you and help you interpret your work. However, you don't need a therapy group or a trained professional to receive the therapeutic benefit of creative work. A pen, a guitar, a computer keyboard, or a set of colored pencils will be adequate. Nor do you need to limit your endeavors to the "arts." Eminent scientists such as Isaac Newton were able to lose themselves in their creative work for days on end.[16] The experience of losing yourself in your work will be discussed more fully in the next chapter on the *stream* brainset. For now, the take-home message is that your negative mood, your self-referential funk, and your dissatisfaction can be a potent motivation to get creative!

Mental Disorders, Transformation, and Creativity

Because we've been discussing negative moods and creative therapies in this chapter, now might be a good time to address the association between mental illness and creativity that has received so much attention in recent years . . . and, in fact, throughout recorded history. Since the days of the ancient Greeks, people have associated creative genius with eccentricity and even madness. Plato described the creativity associated with poetry as "divine madness," and Aristotle added that "no great genius was without a mixture of insanity."[17] In 1889, Cesare Lombroso, the Italian physician and pioneer criminologist, published a book called *The Man of Genius*, in which he described the odd and sometimes bizarre behavior of numerous creative luminaries of the past. He pointed out, for example, Samuel Johnson's need to touch every lamppost that he passed, and composer Robert Schumann's belief that his musical compositions were dictated to him by Beethoven and Mendelssohn "from their tombs." Lombroso believed that geniuses and violent criminals shared a common genetic inheritance. He concluded that "Unfortunately, goodness and honor are rather the exception than the rule among exceptional men, not to speak of geniuses."[18]

In more recent times, creativity has been associated with manic depression, alcoholism, and psychosis proneness. Psychologist Kay Redfield Jamison believes, for example, that many creative luminaries from the past, including Samuel Taylor Coleridge, Emily Dickinson, T. S. Eliot, Victor Hugo, Edgar Allan Poe, Tchaikovsky, Handel, Rachmaninoff, Cole Porter, Irving Berlin, Vincent van Gogh, Gauguin, and Georgia O'Keefe, suffered from manic depression or other mood disorders. Author Tom Dardis points out that of the eight American novelists who have won the Nobel Prize for literature, five have been alcoholics. And many creative luminaries have displayed psychotic-like behavior.[19] William Blake claimed that both his poetry and his paintings were presented to him in visions by visiting spirits who sometimes jostled him while competing for his attention. Tesla, the scientist credited with developing alternating electrical current, is reported to have suffered from columbiphilia (pigeon-love) and triphilia (obsession with the number three), as well as from auditory and visual hallucinations. Charles Dickens is reported to have fended off the imaginary urchins of his novels with an umbrella as he walked the streets of London. And Beethoven had such disregard for his personal cleanliness that friends had to undress him and wash his clothes while he slept.[20]

Clearly, we can find many examples of highly creative people from the past who do indeed appear to have had mental disorders. Likewise, we can cite current research that indicates that the risk of having a psychiatric disorder such as manic depression is elevated among highly creative individuals. One such study, in which Kay Jamison examined award-winning British artists and poets, indicated that the artist/poet group was six times more likely to have been treated for manic depression than members of the general public.[21] But even if we use the results of this study (which are on the extreme end of such research findings), we see that only 9% of the artists and poets had manic depression, and that over 90% had *no* such affliction. Although the eccentricities of high-profile creative individuals, such as a Howard Hughes, a Pablo Picasso, or a Michael Jackson, may receive attention from the press and publishing worlds, they do not characterize the majority of persons who make substantial creative contributions.

Why then would the rates of certain types of mental disorders be higher in at least a subset of individuals recognized for their creativity? The answer to that question is complex. However, there is some evidence to suggest that certain mental disorders may facilitate entry into some altered states of consciousness that resemble the brainsets associated with *spontaneous* thinking in the CREATES model.[22]

For example, mild alcohol or drug intoxication turns down the volume on the part of the brain that evaluates the appropriateness of ideas and behavior. This state of "disinhibition" allows more ideas to flow into your conscious awareness than would otherwise be filtered out by your brain before the ideas even reach the threshold of consciousness.[23]

Likewise, the bipolar individual who is cycling into a manic state (or more accurately, the premanic state called *hypomania*) is highly motivated to perform goal-directed activity. This activity may be in the form of prototypical creative acts, such as painting, writing, composing, inventing, or entrepreneuring. (Of course, it may also have deleterious results, such as shopping sprees that include the purchase of Lear jets and Caribbean islands, ill-considered sexual liaisons, and messianic crusades.)[24]

Psychosis-prone individuals may be privy to unusual mental associations that allow them to make connections between distal bits of information (remember that the ability to combine disparate concepts is the hallmark of creative thought). This may be due in part to a feature of the psychotic brain called *hyperconnectivity*, in which parts of the brain that are not normally connected for functional reasons light up at the same time. Though this tendency to make unusual associations can sometimes lead to novel and original ideas, it can also lead to bizarre notions, such as the belief that Martians are trying to steal your thoughts, or that Katie Couric is sending you secret love messages through the television screen.[25]

By studying creative individuals with mental disorders, we've been able to understand more about the brain states that are involved in creative thought and productivity. In fact, we owe a huge debt of gratitude to those creative pioneers who have struggled against their inner demons to bring beauty and comfort to all of our lives. These individuals have courageously taken their mental discomfort and transformed it into creative work that benefits us all. We owe them gratitude not only for their acts of creativity but for what they've taught us about the creative process in spite of their suffering. Thanks to them, we are learning more about how to access the mental brainsets that can bring forth a fountain of creative ideas. Now, with new knowledge of the brain, we can learn to control these brainsets and use them to increase innovation and productivity.

The take-home message that I want to emphasize about creativity and mental disorders is that in small doses, mood disorders or psychosis-proneness may be beneficial to creativity primarily because they facilitate entry into brain states (such as *absorb, envision, connect,* or *transform*) that allow more information that is ordinarily censored by brain filters to be available to consciousness for creative combination.[26] However, most highly creative individuals do *not* suffer from mental illness; they are able to access the appropriate brain states through mental discipline, just as you can use the exercises in this book to facilitate those same brain states.

Neuroscience of the *Transform* Brainset

In 2001, neuroscientist Marcus Raichle of Washington University in St. Louis identified a brain network that is active when the human brain isn't involved in purposeful problem solving. Raichle dubbed this brain circuit the "default mode" because the default activation pattern of the idle brain seems to include this network.[27] As we noted

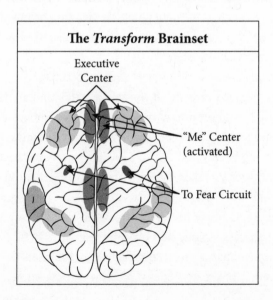

The *Transform* Brainset

Executive Center

"Me" Center (activated)

To Fear Circuit

in Chapter Four, the default mode activates when you are daydreaming, thinking about the past, or are absorbed in self-related thought. It deactivates when you actively try to solve problems.

The default mode is important in the *transform* brainset. It includes the "me" circuit described in Chapter Three, as well as parts of the temporal lobes that are involved in memory retrieval. When you're involved in the *transform* brainset, your "me" center is activated, along with emotional circuits in the limbic center deep in the brain. In particular, the amygdala and its connections to the prefrontal lobes (the fear circuit) are active as you process negative moods.[28]

The *transform* brainset also connotes withdrawal from the environment. This is directed by activation of the Behavioral Inhibition System (BIS), first described by the late British psychologist Jeffrey Gray, as a response to fear and other negative emotions. The counterpart to the BIS is the Behavioral Activation System (BAS), of which the reward center is part.[29] This system activates when you are purposefully engaged with your environment. (These two systems are the human versions of the approach and avoidance systems that are found in even very primitive organisms.) An effective way to overcome the self-referential, stream-of-consciousness anxiety state that is associated with the *transform* brainset is to purposely turn up the volume on your BAS. In other words, if you want to overcome fearful or negative emotional states, become more—rather than less—engaged with your world.[30] This takes courage, but the creative person *is* ultimately courageous (you have to be if you are planning to introduce new ideas into the world!).

When to Access the *Transform* Brainset

The *transform* brainset can imbue your creative projects with great emotional power. You can enter this brainset temporarily if you need to harness emotion for character development, musical or artistic effect, or performance realism. However, you may find yourself feeling negative and questioning your abilities if you access this brainset.

Be certain that you have developed the flexibility to change brainsets before you enter this one purposefully (see Chapter Twelve).

The exercises and reflections in this chapter have ideally provided you with some ideas about how to use negative and self-referential brain states to *transform* your negative thoughts and feelings into creative material. You can use your negative moods to create expressive materials in the form of art, writing, music, or drama that allow you to share your experience of negative states with others who may not have the talent to give expression to their deepest emotions. You can also use your experience of negative moods to depict the inherent strength of humanity by creating work that shows the journey from despair into hope. Finally, you can use creative work as a method of dispelling negative feeling states through immersion in the creative process.

"What does it look like I'm doing—
I'm preserving my misery for posterity."

Whereas the *transform* brainset is a state of negative mood and hyper-self-awareness, the brainset we'll look at in the next chapter takes you to the opposite extreme. There, you will learn to lose your sense of self in challenging and creative performance. You are about to enter the *stream* brainset, perhaps the most rewarding and delightful brain activation state that your creative brain can achieve.

Exercises: The Transform Brainset

Transform Exercise #1: Thinking About Yourself: The Wallet

Aim of exercise: To focus your thoughts on yourself and to better understand yourself. You will need a blank sheet of paper, a writing utensil, and your wallet, purse, backpack, or briefcase. This exercise will take you around 15 minutes.

Procedure: Empty the contents of your wallet, bag, or briefcase onto a table. Examine the contents.

○ Pick three items that you think are representative of your qualities, personality, or character. (Note that if something strikes you as missing from your wallet, purse, or bag that you think most other people would carry, you can also choose that missing item as one of your three choices.)

○ Now write a short paragraph about each of these three items and how each relates to your personality. Don't worry about spelling, punctuation, or grammar. Just write what you feel.

○ When you're finished, look over what you wrote. Did you learn anything about yourself? Did your paragraphs reflect a positive or a negative view of yourself? Will this exercise change what you carry around with you?

○ You can do this exercise with other places where you keep your belongings as well, such as a bureau drawer, closet, medicine cabinet, or the glove compartment of your car.

If you are using the token economy incentive, give yourself one *transform* token each time you complete this exercise.

Transform Exercise #2: Thinking About Yourself: Fictional Character

Aim of exercise: To focus your thoughts on yourself and to better understand yourself. You will need a blank sheet of paper and a writing utensil. This exercise will take you around 15 minutes.

Procedure: Think of a fictional character that reminds you of yourself as you currently are. This could be a character from a novel, a comic book, a movie, or a television show.

○   Now write a paragraph about all the things you have in common with this character. Take into consideration your physical appearance, your personality characteristics, your family and professional circumstances, your love life, your aspirations for the future, and any other points of comparison that you can think of.

○   Next write a paragraph about the ways you differ from your chosen character, using the same points of comparison listed above, plus any other differences you can think of.

○   Finally, write down whether you would like to know this person in real life. Why or why not? When you're finished writing, look over your work. Did you learn anything about yourself?

○   As a follow-up to this exercise, pick a fictional character who reminds you of the person you would like to be. Use all the same points of comparison in this second exercise that you just used in the first. When you are finished with both the similarities and differences paragraphs, look over your work. Are you more similar to your ideal fictional character than you originally believed? Can you use the comparisons in the differences paragraph as a basis for personal change in the future?

If you are using the token economy incentive, give yourself one *transform* token for completing this exercise.

Transform Exercise #3: Thinking About Yourself: Core Strengths[31]

Aim of exercise: To focus your thoughts on yourself and understand your strengths. You will need a blank sheet of paper, a three-by-five index card, and a writing utensil. This exercise will take you between 10 and 15 minutes.

Procedure: Look at the following list of personal strengths.

authentic	imaginative	street-smart
persistent	ambitious	friendly
honest	artistic	good-natured
curious	mature	sensible
open-minded	patient	able to see the big picture
creative	mentally tough	analytical
enthusiastic	bold	spunky
brave	proud	motivated
kind	responsible	supportive
generous	loyal	clever
energetic	fair	witty
compassionate	modest	adventurous
loving	humble	easygoing
considerate	grateful	resourceful
polite	spiritual	tolerant
a fast learner	sense of humor	strong
a good friend	a natural leader	logical
able to forgive	accepting of others' faults	charming
cheerful	self-disciplined	calm
optimistic	wise	rational
able to inspire others	intelligent	trustworthy

On the piece of paper, copy down all the strengths that describe you. Make sure that you include the trait "creative," even if you are new at exercising your creative powers. If you're unsure of whether other strengths apply to you, think of whether anyone has ever told you that you had this strength. If you're still unsure, ask someone who knows you well whether they would attribute this strength to you.

○   If you think of a strength trait that you possess that's not on the list, add it to your paper.

- ○ Your list should include at least 10 strength traits. If you have fewer than this, go back through the list of strengths and think about those that you rejected. You will be able to find additional strengths if you think about it.

- ○ Now look over your list and rank these strength traits according to how important they are to you in dealing with the problems you may encounter in life, with the number one trait being the most important. Make sure to choose the trait "creative" among the top five.

- ○ These top five traits are your core strengths. Write them on the three-by-five card as five sentences, each beginning with the words "I am [strength trait]." At the bottom of the card write the words "I vow to use these strengths to prevail over adversity and achieve my goals." Sign the card and date it.

- ○ Put this card in a place where you can read it first thing in the morning and last thing at night. You might keep it in your purse or pocket, on the bathroom mirror, or inside the door of a kitchen cabinet. Use it as a reminder that you have many core strengths at your disposal that you can count on when things get tough. Your creative brain is one of those strengths.

If you're using the token economy system, award yourself three *transform* tokens for completing this exercise, including the core strengths index card.

Transform Exercise #4: Feelings: Describing Your Feelings

Aim of exercise: To better understand and describe your feelings. You will need a blank sheet of paper and a writing utensil. This exercise will take you around 12 minutes.

Procedure: Sit in a quiet place and try to step outside your current feeling state and observe it objectively.

- ○ Write down a description of your feeling state. What emotions, moods, or affect are you experiencing right now? Try to write at least three sentences that describe how you feel.

o   Now write what physical feelings you're experiencing right now. Scan your body for any area that might feel tense, painful, or constricted. Write down these physical feelings. Do you think they are related to your feelings? If so, write down how you think your current physical and emotional states are connected.

o   Now think about your mental state. Are you having trouble concentrating due to your feelings?

o   Finally think about your action tendencies. Are you feeling the urge to act in a certain way? Run away or escape, lash out at someone or something, disappear into the floor, put your arms around someone?

o   The goal of this exercise is to write as detailed and precise a description of your feeling state as possible. When you've finished, read over what you wrote. Does it adequately describe what you're feeling?

o   Try to do this exercise at least once a week. It will provide insight into your feelings and also develop your skills of self-expression. This exercise will also help you develop emotional intelligence, a quality that will enhance your creative work.

If you are using the token economy incentive, give yourself one *transform* token each time you complete this exercise.

Transform Exercise #5: Feelings: Depicting Your Feelings

Aim of exercise: To help you better understand and describe your feelings. You will need a blank sheet of paper or a sketchpad and a set of crayons, colored markers, or watercolor crayons. You will also need a timer or stopwatch. This exercise will take you around 10 minutes.

Procedure: Sit in a quiet place and try to step outside your current feeling state and observe it objectively.

o   Now set the timer for five minutes and depict your feelings on the paper. (Note: If you are using colored markers, put a piece of cardboard behind your paper so the color doesn't bleed through.) Use whatever colors seem appropriate. Don't censor yourself; just get out the colors and go to town. Draw whatever comes into your mind. Your work can be abstract, representational, or anything in between, as long as it comes from your inner well. Try to draw for the entire five minutes.

○ When the timer sounds, look over your work. If you have more to add, set the timer for another five minutes.

○ When your picture is complete, look over your work. Does it adequately depict what you're feeling? Did you learn anything about yourself from examining the picture?

○ Try to do this exercise at least once a week. It will provide insight into your feelings and also develop your skills of self-expression.

If you are using the token economy incentive, give yourself one *transform* token each time you complete this exercise.

Transform Exercise #6: Feelings: Music and Moods

Aim of exercise: To help you better understand your feelings and to practice "mood flexibility." You will need access to your music library (CDs, MP3s, or tapes). This exercise will take you around 30 minutes plus the time it takes you to select music for the exercise.

Procedure: Think about the music you listen to and pick out three pieces of music from your library that are consistent with the mood or feelings you're experiencing now. The pieces could be any type of music from classical to jazz to rap. They could be instrumental or vocal. You can mix styles—the three pieces do not have to be from the same genre.

○ Now pick out three pieces of music that are consistent with the way you'd like to be feeling. It may take you a while to locate these three pieces as it is more difficult to think of positive things when you're in a negative mood (this is called mood-congruent memory).

○ Finally, select one piece of music that you don't mind listening to but that doesn't really evoke any mood or emotion in you.

○ Set up a playlist with the three pieces that match your current mood followed by the neutral piece and concluding with the three pieces that match your desired mood.

○ Now listen to all seven pieces with your eyes closed. During the mood-congruent (first three) pieces, really get into the mood they represent. During the mood-incongruent pieces (last three), try to match your mood to the music and really get into that mood.

○ When the play list is complete, check your current mood. Were you able to alter it to be more consistent with your desired mood?

○ Music is a powerful mood regulator. You can experiment with your playlist to find the music that works best for you. The point is to start with music that matches your current mood and move toward music that matches your desired state. If you just play happy music when you're in a low mood, it can backfire and lead to a deeper negative mood. The trick, again, is to match your current mood and gradually effect a change. After practice, you may be able to alter your mood with a single piece in each of the mood-congruent, mood-neutral, and desired mood categories.

If you are using the token economy incentive, give yourself a *reason* token each time you complete this exercise.

Transform Exercise #7: Dissatisfaction: Writing About Your Discontent

Aim of exercise: To practice self-expression concerning an area of dissatisfaction in your life and to promote cognitive processing of this dissatisfaction state. Note that this exercise should be done on three consecutive days at roughly the same time each day. Do not start the exercise unless you can commit 15 minutes to it every day for three days. You will need a lined notebook and a writing utensil, or you can use the word processor on your computer. This exercise is called "emotive writing." It was developed by psychologist James Pennebaker of the University of Texas. The exercise has been tested on thousands of individuals and has been shown to have beneficial effects on both physical and mental health.[32]

Procedure: Find a quiet spot where you can write uninterrupted. Set the timer for 15 minutes and begin to write using the following guidelines:

For the next three days, write about your very deepest thoughts and feelings about an extremely important issue that has affected you and your life. In your writing, really let go and explore your very deepest emotions and thoughts. You might tie your topic to your relationships with others, including parents, lovers, friends, or relatives; to your past, your present, or your future; or who you have been, who you would like to be, or who you are now. You may write about the same general issues or experiences on all days of writing or on different topics each day. No one will see your writing but you. Don't worry about spelling, sentence structure, or grammar. The only rule is that once you begin writing, continue to do so until your time is up (adapted from Pennebaker, 1997, p. 162).

When your writing is finished for the day, put it away and don't look at it again. Start your writing tomorrow without reviewing what you wrote today. The value of this exercise is in the actual writing. You never need to look at what you wrote to get the benefit of it.

If you are using the token economy incentive, give yourself six *reason* tokens for completing all three days of writing.

Transform Exercise #8: Dissatisfaction: Redemptive Story

Aim of exercise: To practice self-expression concerning an area of dissatisfaction in your life and to promote the alleviation of your dissatisfied state. You will need a lined notebook and a writing utensil, or you can use the word processor on your computer. You will also need a timer or stopwatch. Note that this exercise may take you more than one session to complete. However, once you start it, you must complete it. Plan to work on this exercise for 20 minutes at each session.

Procedure: Find a quiet spot where you can write uninterrupted. Set the timer for 20 minutes. Your goal is to write a short story, complete with character change and a plot, using the following guidelines:

Your story should have a main character who has the same dissatisfactions in life that you have. You must describe this character and his or her dissatisfactions in detail. The plot of the story is a description of how your main character changes his or her own life so that the sources of dissatisfaction are alleviated. The events of this story should be realistic (no being saved by Captain Kirk and the starship Enterprise or a knight in shining armor!). The character must *earn* his or her way out of the unbearable present to a better future. Along the way there should be some character development—that is, your main character should experience personal change in some meaningful way. You may write the story in either first- or third-person voice.

Force yourself to finish this story. Do not leave your character dangling out there in a dissatisfied state!

When you have finished the story, read it over. Did you learn anything from your character's growth that could be useful in your own life?

If you are using the token economy incentive, give yourself four *reason* tokens for completing the story.

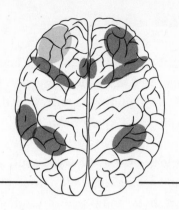

※ 11

Performing Creatively: Accessing the *Stream* Brainset

The quality of the imagination is to flow, and not to freeze.

—RALPH WALDO EMERSON[1]

AT 3:25 PM ON JANUARY 15, 2009, U.S. Air Flight 1549 took off from New York's La Guardia airport bound for Charlotte, North Carolina, with Captain Chesley Sullenberger at the helm. Within six minutes the flight would be over and the crew of Flight 1549 would make aviation history. Shortly after takeoff the aircraft hit a flock of Canada geese, resulting in loss of thrust to both of the Airbus A320s' engines. The aircraft began descending, with no chance of making it back to LaGuardia or even to a nearby private airport. With just enough altitude to make it over the George Washington Bridge, Sullenberger deftly set the large aircraft down in the Hudson, saving the lives of all 155 people on board.[2] On that day, the experience and skill of the pilot were a perfect match for a difficult challenge. On that

233

day, Captain Sullenberger and his crew were able to *stream* their moment-to-moment responses to the unfolding events of the flight in a feat of improvisational skill; the landing of Flight 1549 was a heroic and creative performance.

Creative performances can occur in virtually every area of human endeavor. Any time you apply your accrued knowledge and skills to an ongoing challenge in a novel and original way, you are performing creatively and you are operating within the *stream* brainset.

The *stream* brainset is the brain activation state for what psychologist Mihaly Csikszentmihalyi calls "flow."[3] When you're in this state, you perform a novel dance of sorts in which your responses to each nuance in a challenging situation fully occupy your attention. In this brainset, you lose both your sense of self and your sense of time as you build a set of *spontaneously* and skillfully executed responses to the challenge. When you hear the cockpit voice recordings from Flight 1549, for example, you do not hear the panicked voice of a man who is focused on the possibility that he is one minute from death; what you hear is the voice of a well-trained professional who is fully engaged in his work.

The *stream* brainset[4] allows you to piece together (or *stream*) a set of responses to a challenge, none of which may be creative in and of itself. However, the sum total of the responses results in an improvisational performance that researchers call "ecologically relevant creative behavior"; that is, the creative behavior has been shaped in part by your relationship to your current environment.[5] This is the type of creativity demonstrated by jazz musicians, improvisational actors, neurosurgeons, novelists who are writing automatically, and tennis champions who are fully immersed in their work.

Whether you refer to it as "flow," "peak performance," being "in the zone," or entering the *stream* brainset, the end result is a unique melding of self and action that feels almost religious in its intensity (or "surreal" in Sullenberger's words).[6]

Fortunately, you do not have to be involved in a near-death challenge like Flight 1549 to experience the state of flow generated by the *stream* brainset. According to Csikszentmihalyi (pronounced "Cheek-sent-me-high"), who has spent almost 30 years examining the psychological features of this state, any physical or mental activity can produce flow as long as it is a challenging task that demands full concentration and commitment, provides immediate feedback, and is perfectly matched to your level of skill. Let's look at the conditions of this state of flow as described by Csikszentmihalyi, in his book *Creativity: Flow and the Psychology of Discovery and Invention:*[7]

○ **There are clear goals**. The endpoint and intermediate goals for the activity have to be established for flow to occur. Note that this is true whether your challenging activity consists of getting a plane safely on the ground or performing a piece of music. The pilot has a checklist of procedures to accomplish and the musician has a series of notes to play. In other words, there are "mile markers" along the route to the end-point of your activity.

○ **There is immediate feedback to your actions**. You know whether or not you've reached each mile marker successfully. The musician can hear whether an appropriate note was played and the pilot gets feedback from the response of the aircraft.

○ **The level of challenge matches your skill level**. If the level of challenge is too great, you'll feel anxiety and frustration. If the level of the challenge is too weak, you'll feel boredom. Only when your skill meets the right level of challenge can you enter the flow state.

When these conditions of flow are met, the ensuing mental state includes the following characteristics:

○ **There is a merging of action and awareness**. This merge occurs when the challenge of the activity is such that it requires all of your attention and there are no attentional resources remaining with which to process other stimuli. According to Csikszentmihalyi, we can process about 110 bits of information per second. When your task requires that amount of attention, you won't have any left to devote to self-consciousness.

○ **Distractions go unnoticed**. All attention is directed to the task at hand.

o **There is no worry of failure**. Attention is focused on the here and now, and there is no room for concern. For instance, Sullenberger was asked in a CBS interview if he had worried during the minutes after the bird strike that he couldn't land the plane successfully. He stated emphatically that no such thought had entered his mind. He was certain of his ability to do the task.

o **Self-consciousness disappears**. The boundaries of the ego seem to dissolve and you become part of something bigger than yourself, in harmony with the universe. As an example, Sullenberger noted in the interview with CBS that he initially felt a wave of intense reaction to the plight of the aircraft. He had to put that aside before he could focus on landing the aircraft. Once that reaction was sidelined, his focus was entirely consumed by the work at hand and his self-conscious reactions receded.

o **Time becomes distorted**. Time may speed up so that hours seem like minutes. Or time may slow down. For example, you seem to have all the time in the world to get into position to return the serve from your tennis opponent.

o **The activity becomes an end in itself**. That is, the activity becomes intrinsically rewarding rather than being a means to an end. Sullenberger was working toward a goal of getting the aircraft on the ground—not toward getting his fifteen minutes of fame on the evening news.

Clearly, the experience of flow is possible across a large swath of human behavior that can be considered creative due to its novelty and adaptability. In this chapter, we'll examine flow and the *stream* brainset to discover how you can use this state to increase your moments of creative production and performance.[8]

Defining the Stream Brainset

I've defined the *stream* brainset as a brain state in which time disappears, you lose your sense of self, and your focus is totally on the task at hand. You become one with your work. This level of absorption is reminiscent of the *absorb* brainset. However, with the *stream* brainset you are engrossed in self-initiated activity directed *outward* toward the environment, whereas with the *absorb* brainset you are engrossed in information *coming in* to consciousness either through your five senses or through the activation of memories or visual images. The vectors of information and activity are going in opposite directions in these two brainsets.

What factors can account for this state in which you flawlessly fit your performance to the challenge facing you? First, you need the appropriate level of expertise to succeed at your task; second you need to be intrinsically motivated to persevere in the activity; and, finally, you need to act with what I call "trained impulsivity" (that is, without consciously evaluating your moves) in a series of semistructured steps as you respond skillfully to the challenging activity. In other words, you need to *improvise*. Let's look at each factor individually.

Appropriate Expertise

You need the right kind of expertise to enter the *stream* brainset. Clearly the expertise has to be appropriate for the type of challenging work in which you're engaged (expertise in playing the violin won't help you meet the challenge of landing an airplane). However, the expertise has to be more than appropriate to the task; the components of that expertise have to be represented in the *implicit* memory networks of the brain.

Implicit memory contains information that you've learned to the point that it has become automatic. This is sometimes referred to as "overlearning" or "muscle memory." You generally cannot describe the contents of implicit memory in words, but you can access it without consciously thinking about it (examples include how to ride a bike or play a musical instrument). In contrast, *explicit* memory includes information that you can access consciously. Most of what you learned at school (such as the names of the oceans or the elements in the periodic table), is represented in explicit memory, as are your personal autobiographical memories.[9] To illustrate the difference, think, for instance, of a six-year-old child who is speaking in his native tongue. He has no *explicit* knowledge of the rules of his language, yet he is able to use appropriate grammar and syntax without effort. When he speaks, he is accessing *implicit* memory to form sentences. Now compare that to the adult who is learning a second language. She will learn the rules of conjugation, grammar, and sentence structure for the new language, and she will access these *explicitly* as she forms sentences with the new language. Her speech will be more effortful and lack the smooth delivery of *implicitly* accessed speech.

Retrieval of memory from the *implicit* and *explicit* systems uses different parts of the brain. This is important. When you're engaged in a challenging activity, you don't have time to send messages from the executive center through the hippocampus to call up the information you need piece by piece (and in the right order) from *explicit* memory storage. Rather, you need the expert knowledge to *stream* automatically from *implicit* storage to the brain's premotor cortex (which will prepare the knowledge to be converted into action).[10]

As an example, when a jazz musician first learns to play an instrument, information about how to produce each note is held in *explicit* memory. However, as she grows more proficient, she no longer has to think about which keys to press to produce the B-flat scale. Similarly, a pilot like Sullenberger learns to fly an airplane *explicitly;* however, after years of practice and drills, knowledge of flying skills is gradually transferred into the *implicit* memory system. The experienced pilot automatically reacts to forces on the aircraft to maintain a desired flight path without having to consciously compute the probable effect of such forces on the trajectory of the flight.

Developing *implicit* expertise requires time, practice, and dedication. Scientific research is remarkably consistent in finding that expertise in most fields takes about 10 years to develop. The first evidence for this "10-year rule" was presented by William Chase and Nobel Prize–winner Herbert Simon in their famous study of chess players. They discovered that it takes 10 years of hard practice before a novice chess player can become an expert. This even applied to Bobby

Fischer who became a grand master at the age of 16. His youthful acquisition of expertise was the result of an early and intense interest in chess since the age of six (exactly 10 years before he ascended to grand master status).[11]

Since Chase and Simon's study, investigators have looked into other areas of exceptional performance; they have found the 10-year rule applies virtually across the board—from science to musical composition to creative writing to dance. Geoff Colvin, in his best-seller *Talent Is Overrated*, suggested that even the Beatles didn't begin producing music that transformed the domain of rock 'n' roll until Lennon and McCartney had been practicing together for 10 years. In fact, researcher K. Anders Ericsson of the University of Colorado at Boulder and his colleagues found so much evidence for the 10-year rule that Ericsson claims the difference between the elite performer and the novice is not so much innate ability as it is the hours of serious practice put into the domain.[12] Finally, Howard Gardner notes how surprised he was to find evidence for the 10-year rule in individuals as diverse as Albert Einstein, T. S. Eliot, Pablo Picasso, and the other creative luminaries whom he studied for his book *Creating Minds*.[13]

Although there have, of course, been some exceptions to the 10-year rule (it seems to take somewhat less time to develop expertise in writing poetry than in performing heart surgery), the point is that it takes many years of practice to internalize skills in a particular domain of work to the point that they are represented in the *implicit* knowledge base. Once you have assimilated the complex level of knowledge that constitutes expertise, you are in a position to begin to develop your own style and produce innovations that will rock your field.

While it may be discouraging to consider the length of time necessary to become an elite expert in any given domain, remember that everyday creative acts (the kind that can enrich your life and contribute to your family's and community's well-being) can be accomplished with implicit skills that don't achieve world-class status. A novice can surely enter the *stream* brainset while participating in a creative activity. Even if you have not mastered the more complex aspects of a domain, you still likely have mastery over elementary aspects of an activity.

For instance, when I took watercolor lessons for the first time several years ago, I was able to spend one highly enjoyable afternoon painting a planter of geraniums that sits on my front porch. I became so involved that I totally lost myself in the activity. Time and distractions did indeed dissolve, and before I knew it, the sky was getting dark—six hours later! I ended up framing that painting—not because it was a masterpiece of art, but because I had had such a phenomenal time painting it. So how could I—a novice watercolor artist—get into the *stream* brainset? After all, it's not like I didn't have *any* relevant implicit skills: I had had years of experience holding drawing utensils in the form of pens, pencils, and crayons. I could draw lines and circles, and I also had years of experience applying colors to surfaces (I have painted every room in my house at least twice and I put on makeup almost every day). Bottom line: if you have some skills partially represented in *implicit* memory and you have a challenging task that employs those skills, you too can access the *stream* brainset.

Besides having information stored in *implicit* memory for instantaneous retrieval, there is a second reason that you need to develop some expertise in the domain in which you face challenging activity. If you have internalized the expertise, you have also internalized the understanding of what makes a good performance in that area. In other words, you automatically *know* if you're doing it right. Why is this important? It allows for continuous feedback as you perform the activity. In some instances, the continuous feedback will come from the environment. For instance, if you're playing tennis, the feedback will come from the effectiveness of your volleys and the accumulation of points. If you're playing in a jazz ensemble, the feedback will come from the way your work blends with that of other musicians.

However, if you're writing Chapter Sixteen of your novel, continuous feedback will only come from your own appreciation for the "rightness" of your sentences and paragraphs as they stream from your pen or keyboard. And that comes from knowing what makes good writing (see Chapter Ten). Indeed, for many areas of science, invention, and the arts, the *only* feedback the creator receives during the challenging activity is his or her own internalized knowledge that the work is going well.

Csikszentmihalyi is adamant that this continuous feedback is necessary for the experience of flow; it provides the motivation to continue despite the challenging nature of the activity. When you see that work is progressing well, you are intrinsically motivated to continue it.[14]

Intrinsic Motivation

Besides requiring that you possess *implicit* skill, the *stream* brainset demands that you be engaged in an activity that is intrinsically motivating to you. Intrinsic motivation means that you are involved in the activity because of some internal reward you get from the work rather than from some extrinsic reward (such as fame, fortune, or staying out of jail). When you are in the *stream* brainset or flow, the activity in which you're engaged becomes, according to Csikszentmihalyi, "autotelic." That is, performing the activity becomes an end in itself.[15]

Psychologist Teresa Amabile, a professor at the Harvard Business School and consultant to high-tech companies such as E Ink (the group that developed the innovation behind electronic reading devices like Kindle), has done extensive work on the role of intrinsic motivation in creative work. Her research has repeatedly demonstrated that when individuals are intrinsically motivated they perform more creatively than persons with the same skill level who are working merely for extrinsic rewards such as prizes or money. For example, in a series of studies during the 1980s, Amabile demonstrated that grade school–age children who were allowed to work on a creative project such as a collage produced more creative results (as judged by artistically trained raters) than children who were offered prizes for their work. Amabile has also studied motivation in artists, writers, and creative workers in consumer product and high-tech companies.

This research also indicates a correlation between intrinsic motivation and creative involvement. In an interview with Bill Breen of *Fast Company*, she reported that creative thinkers "don't think about pay on a day-to-day basis. And the handful of people who were spending a lot of time wondering about their bonuses were doing very little creative thinking."[16]

How can you increase your intrinsic motivation in the activities that fill your daily life? There are two basic ways: first, you can spend more time doing activities that you truly enjoy, and second, you can increase the motivational salience of the activities you are already doing. (To work with both of these options, see *Stream* Exercises #2 and #3.)

One aspect of intrinsic motivation is finding activities in which you achieve an optimal level of arousal. If the level of challenge in an activity is too great, you will feel anxiety and frustration (too much arousal). If the level of the challenge is too weak, you will feel boredom (too little arousal).[17] To the extent that you have control over the challenge, try to arrange a match between the challenging aspects of the task and your own personal level of expertise. If the task seems too simple, find a way to kick the challenge up a notch so that it will occupy your complete attention. There are several ways to do this:

○ **Set time limits on the task or establish deadlines**. *Example*: you've been tasked with putting together 50 copies of your report on the environmental impact of bird control on airport property (ask the pilots of Flight 1549 about this one!) to present at a conference. Time yourself to see if you can get one copy collated and into its bright yellow folder every minute. Can you beat a 50-minute self-imposed deadline? The time will go much more quickly if you set a timed goal for yourself and treat it as a challenge rather than as a dull chore.

○ **Increase your appreciation for the task**. *Example*: if your task is to dust the house, take time to appreciate each piece of furniture as you dust it. Think back to how you acquired each piece and allow yourself to indulge in memories of that time in your life. Also, as you move each item to dust under it, think about how fortunate you are to have that item. The gratitude you feel for all that you own will increase your intrinsic motivation in the task and you will begin to lose yourself in the work.

- ○ **Increase your standards for task performance.** *Example*: if your task is to write 120 thank-you cards for your wedding gifts, rather than just reeling off the same formulaic sentiments on each card, try to make each card different with a special twist or well-worded original message. As you take more pride in your work, your intrinsic motivation will rise and you'll begin to lose yourself in the task.

On the other hand, if you're concerned that the task seems too challenging for your skill level, find a way to bring the challenge down a notch so you won't feel anxious or overwhelmed by it.

- ○ **Break the task down into smaller manageable parts.** *Example*: if your task is to have your 70,000-word nonfiction manuscript completed in six months, break it down into chapters, and break each chapter down into segments. Although it's still important to keep in mind how the individual parts relate to the whole, working on one part at a time is a much less daunting and more intrinsically motivating task than facing an entire overly challenging project.
- ○ **Reinforce your skills.** It may be wise to postpone a significant challenge if you feel that you really don't have the implicit resources to handle it. However, it's more likely that you just need to remind yourself of your own existing resources. One way to do this is to read your Successful Challenges list (see *Stream* Exercise #4).

Improvisation

So far we have talked about ways to enter the *stream* brainset through matching your skill to a challenging and intrinsically motivated task. When you are *streaming*, you lose yourself in the activity and your moment-to-moment responses seem automatic and appropriate. What we haven't discussed is the mental vehicle you use to make this happen. That vehicle is *improvisation*.

Improvisation is a series of sequential responses to either internally or externally generated stimuli that is performed extemporaneously. What's interesting to note is that the individual responses that make up the improvised performance are not necessarily creative; it is the *accumulation* of a series of responses, each being limited to one of several choices, that comprises the creative product. Consider, for example, the improvisation of the jazz musician. Each step of the improvisation is limited not only by the 12 possible notes on the scale and the finite number of beats to a measure, but also by the note that was previously played (jazz progressions follow certain rules even though there is choice in which progression to select). Each note or each progression of notes is not creative . . . but the way the progressions are assembled *is* creative!

Although it is more commonly associated with the performing arts, improvisation can occur in virtually any domain of endeavor. Improvisation is the prototypical creative behavior. It involves freely generated choices, which are adapted to ongoing conditions and directed toward the accomplishment of a specific goal. Once initiated, improvised responses seem to *stream* from the *implicit* memory system as a series of "actions performed without delay, reflection, voluntary direction or obvious control in response to a stimulus." This is actually the definition of "impulsivity,"[18] and, in fact, improvisation includes responding with "trained impulsivity."

Unlike the impulsive behavior evident in disorders such as attention-deficit hyperactivity disorder (ADHD), the impulsive behavior associated with improvisation and the *stream* brain-set is nonrandom. It is based on a limited set of possible responses represented in expert training "programs" residing in your *implicit* memory. To put it more succinctly, when a challenging activity is encountered for which you have developed expertise, you will respond impulsively and automatically with one of your implicitly stored expert training programs. These programs are activated in rapid succession in response to the fluid challenge of the situation.

Now of course, "impulsive" is a dirty word to some of you even when paired with the word "trained" (especially if the *evaluate* or *reason* brainset is your mental comfort zone). If that's the case, you're in good company. Fear of impulsively uttering the wrong sequence of words, for example, is one of the main reasons that public speaking is the number one social phobia among adults.[19] If you find that you have trouble letting go of planned and consciously controlled behavior, then one of your missions has to be to loosen up and learn to trust the expertise within you.

In order to move more easily into the *stream* brainset and the state of flow, you need to feel comfortable with improvisation. You can start by thinking about how you respond when playing a video game. Take the popular game Tetris, for instance.[20] Each move has only a small number of possible responses; yet it's your ability to string the responses together in rapid order that indicates mastery of the game. It's impossible to play at a high level without disengaging your need to consciously plan and make decisions. The game moves too fast. Yet once you develop the skill to make moves without thinking about them, your skill level matches the challenge of the game and a state of flow results. (This is no accident, by the way; video game designers purposely build the conditions of flow into their game programs.) So is the secret to the *stream* brainset to play more video games?

Well, no! But you may be able to get a feel for *stream*ing responses through small doses of video game exposure. You can get practice at improvisation by joining a local improv theater group, taking improv lessons, or studying jazz or other forms of improvisational performance. (To practice improvisation, see *Stream* Exercise #5.)

We have now seen that the combination of implicitly stored expertise, a challenging activity that provides intrinsic motivation and the optimal level of arousal, and the willingness to let go of tight cognitive control (thus allowing yourself to improvise) can lead to the experience of flow. Because *you* control intrinsic motivation and optimal arousal level, you can increase your experience of flow by purposely entering the *stream* brainset.

Neuroscience of the Stream Brainset

While we can't (yet!) scan the brains of tennis champions that are "in the zone" as they volley with their opponents, or of pilots as they are guiding a crippled aircraft to safety, researchers *have* been able to look at the brains of another group of creative performers as they engage in the improvisational behavior associated with the *stream* brainset. The interesting findings from studies of highly trained pianists during musical improvisation show a brainset that is defined by the following:

- Deactivation in the left executive center (the big honcho of consciously directed behavior)
- Activation of the premotor areas (involved in selecting motor action programs)
- Activation of the temporal lobe association center (which helps process music but may also be helpful in other forms of improvisation)
- Mild but continuous activation of the reward center[21]

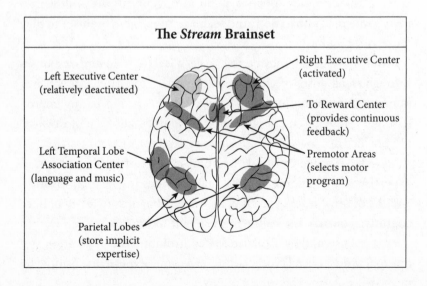

The *Stream* Brainset

Right Executive Center (activated)

Left Executive Center (relatively deactivated)

To Reward Center (provides continuous feedback)

Left Temporal Lobe Association Center (language and music)

Premotor Areas (selects motor program)

Parietal Lobes (store implicit expertise)

In a 2007 study of classically trained musicians, Swedish investigators Sara Bengtsson and Frederic Ullen of the Karolinska Institutet in Stockholm teamed up with Csikszentmihalyi to study classically trained concert pianists as they played a specially made piano keyboard in an fMRI scanner. In another study, conducted in 2008 by Charles Limb and Allen Braun of the National Institutes of Health, researchers looked specifically at highly trained jazz pianists. In both studies, the brain activation patterns of musicians during improvisation were compared to the patterns generated by music played from memory. This allowed researchers to subtract the parts of the brain that are lit up during music production and to isolate brain areas activated solely in response to improvisation.[22]

The results of both studies indicate that the left executive center is not involved in improvisation. In fact, the one study that looked at *deactivation* patterns showed a decrease in activity in the left DLPFC, a condition that neuroscientist Arne Dietrich[23] refers to as "transient hypofrontality" (we discussed the transient hypofrontality hypothesis way back in Chapter Five in conjunction with the *absorb* brainset). *Hypo* (low) + *frontality* = (prefrontal cortex) = low activation of the prefrontal cortex. This state results in cognitive disinhibition (also discussed in Chapter Five and elsewhere), which allows information assembled in other parts of the brain to *stream* forward without being censored by the executive and the judgment centers.

Why would you want to deactivate the executive center—that most modern and sophisticated of all brain regions—during a time when sophisticated and complex behavior is most desired? The answer is that the executive center is limited in the number of elements it can process at one time. (This is due to the limited capacity of working memory, which has been shown to hold only around four chunks of information at once.)[24] *Implicit* memory systems, however, are not limited in capacity and can process many elements in parallel. If we assume that each of these elements represents an action program that is well represented in implicit memory, we can see why it's important to allow them to feed forward in rapid succession in response to a challenging situation that requires multiple ongoing responses—without the meddling of the capacity-limited executive center.

Another area of the brain that is active during flow is the reward center of the brain. Ongoing positive feedback (from either the environment or your own expert knowledge of how the work is going) causes mild but continual activation of the reward center. The firing of the reward center may be so mild that it doesn't even register in conscious awareness. But it's sufficient to affect behavior and motivate you to continue in your ongoing efforts.[25] As Csikszentmihalyi points out, people who are in the midst of a flow experience are not aware of intense pleasure. However, once the flow activity is completed, they look back on it as an exceptionally positive experience that they will do almost anything to repeat.[26] In this way, the *stream* brainset provides motivation for you to gain more expert knowledge and seek ever more challenging activities. Thus progress—on the personal and the societal level—advances.

When to Access the *Stream* Brainset

Whenever you must perform a challenging task, either on the job or in your personal life, remember what you've learned about accessing the *stream* brainset. Use the strategies outlined in this chapter to bring the challenge in line with your skills, and try to increase your intrinsic motivation in the task. The more you can become absorbed in the task, the more enjoyable it will become and the higher your performance level will be.

You can also use this brainset in the elaboration phase of the creative process to flesh out your ideas. Once you have your creative idea (from the *absorb, envision, connect*, or *reason* brainset), and you've evaluated it, try to lose yourself in the process of bringing it to life. By using all your implicit resources and by becoming one with the work, you can, say, develop the characters of a novel, create a moving musical arrangement for your new melody, add a cool fort and a picnic table to that backyard swing set project, or make your "better mousetrap" more attractive and user-friendly. Whatever your idea, make your effort in the elaboration phase of development a flow experience.

Finally, access the *stream* brainset in the implementation phase of your creative project. If you can be completely engaged with your creative idea when you present it to others, the enthusiasm will be contagious. You will be able to get your work out there in a way that inspires excitement and appreciation.

In this chapter, you've seen how implicitly learned expertise, intrinsic motivation, and the ability to improvise can lead to creative performance in the *stream* brainset. Entering this brainset takes practice. However, as you acquire expertise and practice improvisation, you will find your level of intrinsic motivation for challenging activities is rising. You will find that engaging in creative actions will become its own reward as you slip ever more easily into the flow of the *stream* brainset.

"I don't know that one, but if you hum
a few bars I'll improvise."

You have now seen how each of the CREATES brainsets affects and enhances your ability to be creative, innovative, and productive. But the brainsets don't operate in isolation. In Part III—"Putting the CREATES Brainsets to Work"—you'll learn strategies for switching brainsets at appropriate times and applying them to your real-world work and leisure. You're about to put it all together to make Your Creative Brain work for you!

Exercises: The *Stream* Brainset

The following sequence of exercises, developed as part of a creativity workshop, work best to promote the *stream* brainset when completed in order. Very much like *streaming* itself (in which each response you make to a challenge is a function of the previous choice), each exercise in this chapter builds on the previous one and prepares you for the next exercise.

Stream Exercise #1: Implicit Expertise

Aim of exercise: To discover areas in which you have expertise that can be utilized in flow experiences representative of the *stream* brainset. You will need a piece of paper and a writing utensil. This exercise will take you 10 minutes.

Procedure: Make two columns on your paper. Label one column "Areas of Acquired Expertise" and label the second column "Areas of Developing Expertise." In the first column, list all the areas in which you have acquired *implicit* expertise. Note that these areas must have a "performance" or execution element to them rather than being areas of general *explicit* knowledge. Examples of *implicit* expertise would include activities that most of us can already perform using implicit memory, such as walking, reading, speaking in our native language, driving a car, riding a bicycle, eating with utensils, and drawing basic symbols. Add any specialized expertise you may possess by virtue of your profession, such as skill at flying, dry cleaning garments, performing heart surgery, or welding metal.

Next, list expertise you may possess by virtue of your hobbies or interests, such as playing an instrument, skateboarding, skiing, speaking fluently in a second language, telling jokes, or belly dancing.

In the second column, list all the areas of expertise that you are currently acquiring. These would be areas in which you are a novice but are working toward greater *implicit* expertise. These could include any area in which you are currently taking lessons or in which you're interested but have not yet committed the skill to *implicit* memory.

When you've completed your lists, look over the Acquired Expertise list. Note just how multifaceted your current skills actually are. Next, look over your list of Developing Expertise. Add one activity to this list in which you would like to develop skill.

If you are using the token economy incentive, give yourself one *stream* token for completing the exercise and one *stream* token for actually taking the first step toward developing your newly chosen skill.

Stream Exercise #2: Intrinsic Motivation: Identifying Intrinsically Motivating Activities

Aim of exercise: To explicitly determine what activities are intrinsically motivating for you. You will need a piece of paper and a writing utensil. This exercise will take you between 10 and 15 minutes.

Procedure: At the top of your paper, write the heading "Intrinsically Motivating Activities." Now it's time to figure out what you *love* to do. Think about the following questions: what do you look forward to doing each day? Your list should consist of activities in which you are an active rather than a passive participant. (Passive participant activities include sitting in front of the television and zoning out, getting drunk, binge eating, and sleeping. Active participant activities include just about anything that involves moving your muscles or exercising your mind.) Make sure to include activities that you look forward to at work, as well as during leisure hours and on the weekends. Check the list of activities you wrote down in the Implicit Expertise exercise for additional ideas of what motivates you.

On the other side of the paper, start a second list headed "Potentially Motivating Activities." On this list include any activities that you think you would be interested in trying. Be sure to list several activities that involve creative work. These could include writing, drawing, playing music, cooking, sculpting, pottery, quilting, woodworking, dancing, and so on—any type of creative work that you think you would find interesting. It doesn't matter if you think you wouldn't be good at them. Don't let fear of failure limit your list!

When you're finished writing all the activities you can think of that are intrinsically appealing to you, put your list aside for a few days. If you run across activities that look interesting, add them to your list. Try to think about your list as you go through each day this week and add activities as appropriate.

If you are using the token economy incentive, give yourself one *stream* token for completing this exercise.

Stream Exercise #3: Intrinsic Motivation: Doing What You Love[27]

Aim of exercise: To increase intrinsic motivation in your daily activities. One of the most validated findings in research on highly creative people is that they are intrinsically motivated in what they do. They also arrange their lives so that they can do more of the work that they find intrinsically rewarding. You will need a highlight marker and two copies of the Daily Activities Calendar from Appendix Three. (You can also print out the calendar from the Web site http:// ShelleyCarson.com.) This is a two-part exercise. Part One will take you 10 minutes a day for seven days. Part Two will take 20 minutes during the day following completion of Part One.

Procedure: Part One: Fill out the Daily Activities Calendar each day for one week. Each two-hour block of time should reflect the major (most time-consuming) activity you engaged in during that time. Try to fill in the calendar at approximately the same time each day—either just before you go to bed or upon rising in the morning.

When you've completed the seven-day Calendar, take a few minutes to go through your weekly activities and highlight those you enjoyed. In other words, mark activities that were intrinsically motivating. You now have an idea of how much of your time you spend doing activities that you love. If less than half of your time was highlighted during the last week, continue with Part Two of this exercise.

Part Two: Your goal in this part of this exercise is to increase the number of hours you spend involved in activities that you love during the upcoming week. You must replace one of the two-hour segments that were not highlighted last week with an intrinsically rewarding activity for the upcoming week. Take the blank copy of the Daily Activities Calendar and schedule in an intrinsically motivating activity right now. You can choose any activity that you identified in *Stream* Exercise #2.

You can repeat the exercise by continuing to fill in the Daily Activities Calendar each day for the next week, making sure to increase the amount of time you spend doing things you love. (The goal is to work toward spending more and more time in activities that are meaningful and rewarding.)

If you are using the token economy incentive, give yourself two *stream* tokens for completing the Calendar for one week. Give yourself one token for scheduling in an additional intrinsically motivating activity. Finally, give yourself two tokens for actually engaging in that intrinsically motivating activity during the upcoming week.

Stream Exercise #4: Intrinsic Motivation: Successful Challenges

Aim of exercise: To increase your intrinsic motivation in challenging activities by reinforcing your confidence in your implicit resources. You will need a paper and writing utensil, or you can complete this exercise on your computer's word processor. It will take you approximately 30 minutes.

Procedure: You're going to make a list that you'll want to refer to in the future. Make a heading at the top of your paper titled: "Successful Challenges."

○ Make a list of five different situations in which you were able to use your internal resources to deal with a serious challenge. Make each challenge a subheading on your paper. For each situation:

- ○ Describe the challenging situation.
- ○ Describe your response and the implicit skills you used (these could be physical, mental, or interpersonal skills).
- ○ Describe the positive outcome of this challenge in detail.

Whenever you worry that a current situation is too challenging for you, get out your list and remind yourself of your great store of personal resources.

If you are using the token economy incentive, give yourself one *stream* token for completing this exercise.

Stream Exercise #5: Practicing Improvisation: TV Narrator

Aim of exercise: To improve your ability to improvise by responding to a series of changing stimuli. You will need a stopwatch or timer and a television. This exercise will take you between five and 10 minutes.

Procedure: Turn your television on to a drama or comedy show. This can be a movie, a sitcom, or a soap opera. However, it has to be a movie or episode that you've never seen before. Wait until a commercial break is over so that you'll have a period of 10 minutes of commercial-free time. When the show resumes after the commercial, set the timer for five minutes and turn down the TV volume so that you can no longer hear the sound.

Now narrate the show out loud. Describe all the action, the emotions of the characters, and how the plot is progressing as it happens. Don't stop talking until the timer sounds.

Try to do this exercise once a week and work up to 10-minute narrations to improve your ability to respond spontaneously to the action on the television. This will help you develop improvisation skills.

If you are using the token economy incentive, give yourself one *stream* token each time you complete the exercise.

PART 3

Putting the CREATES Strategies to Work

* 12

Flexing Your Creative Brain

IT'S THE YEAR 1925. An 18-year-old woman who is planning to study medicine is riding in a bus in Mexico City with her boyfriend. In an instant, her life is changed forever as the bus collides with a trolley, injuring the woman's spinal column, legs, ribs, collarbone, and abdomen. She is bedridden for months and confined to a painful full-body cast. To take the woman's mind off the pain, her mother has a special easel built over her daughter's hospital bed. She brings paint and canvasses so the girl can pass the time. After she leaves that hospital, Frida Kahlo has transformed into a painter, her former plan of studying medicine forgotten. She will spend the rest of her life depicting her pain and her joy on canvas, often in the form of self-portraits. She will work tirelessly on her art, despite constant physical and emotional pain. She will imbue her work with the symbolism of her native country and her religion. But in her lifetime, she will be recognized as Mrs. Diego Rivera, wife of the famous Mexican muralist. She will not be recognized by the art world as Frida Kahlo until several decades after her death.[1]

Fast forward a couple of decades. It is 1941. George de Mestral, a Swiss engineer, returns from a hunting trip with his dog. As he tries to remove burrs from his jacket and his dog's fur, he becomes fascinated by the persistence with which the burrs cling to both fur and fabric. He examines them under a microscope and discovers their secret: from each burr, hundreds of tiny hooks protrude that latch onto any rough surface they encounter. De Mestral immediately sees the possibilities of this concept for a clothing fastener. Put together two pieces of fabric—one with hundreds of little hooks and one with closed loops as found in many woven materials—and you have a zipperless zipper! Of course, no one takes his idea seriously, but de Mestral does not give up on it. First he tries to render his fastener idea in cotton. That doesn't work. Through trial and error, he eventually lands on the newly developed synthetic fiber nylon as a possible material for his fastener. It takes him another eight years to figure out how to mechanize the manufacture of the hooked material. In 1955, after fourteen years of work, de Mestral finally receives a patent for his newfangled fastener, and Velcro (*vel* from the French word *velour* or velvet + *cro* from *crochet* or hook) is born.[2]

Flash forward three more decades. It is now the fall of 1984. A Southern street lawyer overhears a young black witness in a Mississippi courtroom describe a horrific tale of attack and gang rape. The lawyer can't stop thinking about the incident. He imagines what he would have done if he'd been the victim's father. And he begins to write about his imaginings. He wakes every morning at 5AM to get in a few hours of writing before his long day as a small-town lawyer begins. He steals time whenever he can get it to write just a few more words. It takes him over three years to write his story. When his work is finished, he types it up and sends it off to publishers. Rejection after rejection ensues. Finally a small publishing house agrees to print 5,000 copies of his book, but only if the manuscript is cut down to one-third its original size. And the publisher won't promote the book. John Grisham has to buy up many of the copies of *A Time to Kill* himself and sell them practically door-to-door at ladies' tea parties and library readings. No matter. He is a writer, and he is already hard at work on his second novel, *The Firm*, long before the contract for his first novel is signed.[3]

The stories of Kahlo, de Mestral, and Grisham, along with countless other examples we could discuss, indicate how important brain states such as the *absorb, envision,* and *connect* brainsets are in generating creative ideas. They also point out how important the *transform, reason, evaluate,* and *stream* brainsets are for planning, maintaining motivation, producing, and implementing a creative idea.

De Mestral, for example, appears to be very much in the *absorb* brainset as he returns from his hunting trip and cleans burrs off his dog and his jacket. Rather than treating this as a humdrum chore, he *notices something new.* He is not irritated by the burrs, he is fascinated by them, even putting them under the microscope to see what structure makes them so sticky. (Note that this is reminiscent of how Alexander Fleming, discoverer of penicillin, noticed mold growing in a petri dish of bacteria in his lab.[4] Both de Mestral and Fleming were interested in—not dismissive of—these pesky intrusions into their lives, and they paid off big time in creative currency.) Interest in the burrs sparks the *connect* brainset as he sees right away the connection between the stickiness of the burrs and a possible fabric fastener. Now he has an innovative idea, but it will take years of trial-and-error work in the *reason* and *evaluate* brainsets to bring Velcro to the world.

Grisham, in contrast, begins with the *envision* brainset. When he overhears testimony in a Mississippi courtroom, he imagines a scenario based on that testimony (pure "what-if-ing"!). Grisham now has *his* creative idea. He gets up early each morning to write before spending a full day at his regular job. He writes whenever and wherever he can: "If I had 30 minutes to an hour, I would sneak up to the old law library, hide behind the law books and write *A Time to Kill,*" he reports (challenge, skill, and obsessive motivation meeting in the *stream* brainset.)[5] Grisham then used the *evaluate* brainset to trim away two-thirds of his novel for the only publisher who would take a chance on it. Finally, Grisham planned and executed the promotion of his book in the *reason* brainset.

When we look at Kahlo, we see a woman whose art was motivated by the *transform* brainset, but who used the *envision* brainset to visualize her work. She constantly improved her skill and used her art to enter the *stream* brainset as a way to find release from personal pain.

Kahlo, de Mestral, and Grisham have all made substantial creative contributions to the world. What makes a person who is considered to be "creative" different from the person who does not consider him- or herself to be creative?

Consider this possibility: the difference between the creators and the noncreators is the ease with which creative people can enter the altered states of consciousness we've been describing in this book. Your brain is constantly computing possible combinations of stimuli from the environment, along with information already stored in your cortex, in an effort to predict the most likely scenarios facing you. Most of those possible combinations are deemed irrelevant and are filtered out before they reach your conscious awareness. (Remember that our filters are based on internalized codes of rightness and wrongness as well as on sensory irrelevance.)[6] What if you had conscious access to more of those "possible combinations" that are filtered out before you got a chance to see them? What if you then had the mental flexibility to return to a focused state of mind to think through those possibilities?

This is exactly what some neuroscientists believe distinguishes people who have a propensity to think creatively from those who tend to think in the more traditional, convergent way. It seems likely that highly creative people can purposely turn down the volume in their executive center long enough to let valuable (OK, sometimes not so valuable) information into their mental workspace that would ordinarily not make it through the middle-management cognitive filters.[7]

This explanation is, of course, not the whole story of creative achievement. A confluence of factors has to come together for major creative achievements to occur. These factors include individual differences in early exposure to creative domains, education, enough leisure time to devote to training, the right temperament, timing, and a little bit of luck.[8] All of these things, of course, make it *easier* to be creative, but they do not in and of themselves make a person "creative." What *does* make a person creative is the ability to generate novel and original thoughts and then figure out what to do with them and how to get them out there so that they benefit society. Easy entry into brain states that facilitate creative ideas *and* flexibility between brain states that allow for practical deployment of those ideas are the keys to productive creativity. Creative thinking is at the heart of creative achievement.

For the most part, individual differences in creative thinking are not the result of variations in neuroanatomy (the brains of highly creative people have more or less the same structural makeup as the brains of their less creative counterparts); they are rather variations in the activation patterns of different neuron networks within the brain. And brain activation is the result of: (1) learning (which creates connections between neurons), and (2) fluctuations in neurotransmitters, the chemicals that surge through the brain.[9]

We'll talk about the learning aspect in just a minute. As for fluctuations in neurotransmitters, brain studies have shown that you have more control over the variation in these neurochemicals than previously thought. For example, we now know that a certain type of psychological therapy, called cognitive-behavioral therapy or CBT, can in some situations change the level of neurotransmitters and receptors for those neurotransmitters *as effectively as drugs*.[10] (Note that the whole token economy system you have worked with throughout this book is one of the cognitive-behavioral techniques that has been shown to be effective—using those tokens to reward yourself can actually change your brain!)[11] The bottom line is that you have the ability to control your brain state and thus your level of creativity!

This will, of course, be more difficult for some of you than it will be for others. Some people may have a natural ability to manipulate their brainset through neurochemical control. Dr. Kenneth Heilman of the University of Florida suggests in his book *Creativity and the Brain*, that fluctuation of norepinephrine may be a factor in creative brain states.[12]

Norepinephrine is the neurochemical associated with focused concentration and attention (remember that the *reason* and *evaluate* brainsets are defined by focused attention, whereas the *absorb* brainset is defined by a state of *de*focused attention). By modulating the release of norepinephrine from its origins in the brain stem, Heilman believes that highly creative individuals may naturally be able to control how focused or defocused their attention level becomes. If you could, for example, temporarily dampen the flow of norepinephrine, it would facilitate entry into the *absorb, envision, connect,* or *stream* brainsets. However, Heilman also suggests that just as some individuals have innate control over this fluctuation in norepinephrine, we can also *learn* to manipulate the fluctuation. Norepinephrine becomes more available in the brain during states of high stress.[13] This creates an evolutionary advantage by helping you to focus your attention on the stressful situation to the exclusion of distracting stimuli. (For instance, Caveman #2 doesn't want to be distracted by a pretty cavewoman when he is fighting off a saber-toothed tiger.) By manipulating our stress level we may be able to regulate the flow of norepinephrine to our prefrontal lobes. (Chapter Five contains several exercises that reduce stress in addition to facilitating the *absorb* brainset.)

Besides the innate ability to regulate norepinephrine, genes that control other neurochemicals also contribute to the ease with which you can enter certain brainsets. Investigations into the molecular biology of creativity are still in their early stages, but we have already seen some interesting results. We've learned, for example, that variations in genes that control the availability of neurotransmitters such as dopamine and serotonin are associated with a variety of factors affecting creativity, including greater attraction to novelty and the tendency to be open to new ideas (the *absorb* brainset), working memory and reasoning (the *reason* brainset), the tendency to experience negative mood states (the *transform* brainset), and the ability to shift from one idea to another.[14] However, we've also learned from these new studies that these genetic variations can be moderated by your environment and your behavior; that means that your creativity is not *dependent* upon your genes but is only *influenced* by your genes.[15] You still have the capacity to be creative regardless of whether you were born into the Mozart family or into the Archie Bunker family. You may just have to work a little harder at it.

Is creativity worth the extra work? Look back at the hard work displayed by our examples from earlier in this chapter: George de Mestral, Frida Kahlo, and John Grisham. Each labored for years to see their creative ideas come to fruition, and there is no evidence that their prime motivation was a quest for fame or fortune (although they may have ultimately received it). All evidence indicates that they worked because their creative ideas had intrinsic value for them. Each of them would undoubtedly say that yes! the expression of creativity is worth the hard work. Notice also that each of our examples found creative satisfaction in work that lay outside of their original career intentions, indicating that you don't have to quit your day job to pursue creative aspirations.

Your new knowledge of brainsets can help even out the genetic differences that may make some of you natural-born idea generators and others of you natural-born critics. Remember that both of these tendencies are necessary to be creatively productive—your goal is to be flexible. Let's quickly review some of the main points concerning the CREATES brainsets.

Dimensions of the CREATES Brainsets

The CREATES brainsets model consists of seven theoretical brain activation states, each of which, I hypothesize, makes a substantial contribution to the creative process. They represent altered states of consciousness which, like other altered states such as dreaming, intoxication, and meditative trance, can change the way you see your world and the problems that you face. The brainsets differ from each other across several different dimensions:

o   *Cognitive or mental disinhibition*—stimuli from the environment (coming in through our sensory organs) and from our own internal thought processes (memories, associations, mental images) are continually filtered through the process of cognitive inhibition so that we don't become overwhelmed by stimuli in our conscious workspace. Cognitive disinhibition refers to the relative loosening of these filter mechanisms so that more stimuli (often irrelevant to our current goals) are allowed into consciousness.

o *Hemispheric activation*—each hemisphere of the brain is specialized for certain functions. For most people, regardless of whether they are right- or left-handed, the left hemisphere is the dominant hemisphere. It is specialized for language, analysis, details, and sequential thinking. The right hemisphere is specialized for spatial skills, analogies, big picture, and nonsequential thinking. In normal convergent thinking, the left hemisphere is more highly activated than the right hemisphere, often to the extent that right hemisphere ideas and skills don't get represented in conscious awareness.

o *Positive or negative mood*—the positive or negative valence of moods affects other aspects of cognition. When mood is elevated, attention becomes somewhat defocused so that we can take in more information in search of novel opportunities. When mood is more negative, attention becomes more focused so that we can concentrate on addressing stressors that are impacting our well-being. Negative moods are also often accompanied by more self-referential ("it's all about me") cognition.

o *Degree of perceived mental effort*—when we are consciously directing our thoughts, we perceive our thinking as effortful and active. When our thoughts seem to be flowing without conscious direction, we perceive them as less effortful and we feel like passive observers of our thoughts.

No two brainsets have the same pattern of brain activation or the same role to play in your creative brain. In the following chart, the CREATES brainsets are described in terms of the four dimensions described above. Notice that the *envision* and the *connect* brainset are described as both active and passive. That's because you can consciously direct thought within these brainsets or you can allow your thoughts to wander within them, leading to perceived passivity. You may question why the *reason* brainset is not associated with positive mood. While it's certainly possible to be in a good mood when you're in the *reason* brainset, the cognitive tendency is to shift into the *envision* or *connect* brainset and to thinking about connections and "what ifs" when you are joyous; focusing on *reason*-based decision making and planning becomes more effortful when you have to fight the natu ral expansive tendencies associated with joy.[16]

Brainset Dimensions

Brainset	Disinhibition			Right Activation			Positive Mood			Mental Effort	
	None	Moderate	High	None	Moderate	High	None	Moderate	High	Active	Passive
Connect	○	●	○	○	○	●	○	○	●	●	●
Reason	●	○	○	●	○	○	●	○	○	●	○
Envision	○	●	○	○	○	●	○	●	●	●	●
Absorb	○	○	●	○	●	○	○	●	○	○	●
Transform	○	●	●	○	●	○	●	○	○	○	●
Evaluate	●	○	○	●	○	○	●	○	○	●	○
Stream	○	●	○	○	●	○	○	○	●	○	●

You have already studied ways to enter the CREATES brainsets. And you know that each can support your creative brain in a significant way. Now let's look at why learning to flexibly switch between brainsets is so important. If, for instance, some brainsets allow more information into conscious awareness that inspires original thoughts, why shouldn't we stay in these brainsets all the time? There are four reasons:

First, memory may be encoded differently in the cognitive disinhibition states associated with creative idea generation (*absorb, connect, envision*). Tests that we're conducting at Harvard indicate that people whose mental comfort zone is one of these states tend to remember gestalt (big-picture) aspects of experiences and to encode them as broad patterns. They also have memory for the tone or feel of an event but less memory for the details.[17] Reduced memory for details may be due to the partial deactivation in these brainsets of the left executive center, which is specialized for processing details. It may also be due to fluctuations in norepinephrine as suggested by Heilman. High levels of the neurochemicals norepinephrine and dopamine allow you to focus in on details, whereas lower levels may be associated with encoding the broad overview of an event.[18] Depending upon how you want to encode information, you need to switch from a disinhibited brainset back into a focused brainset. If, for example, you're studying for a test in which you need to recall names and dates, the focused state is appropriate. However, if you're looking for patterns of events throughout history, the disinhibited defocused state may serve you better.

Second, without the ability to switch out of one of the disinhibited, defocused brainsets, you'll never move forward with your creative ideas. They will remain just that—ideas—because you need to focus to plan and make decisions in order to bring ideas to fruitfulness.

Third, if you remain in a cognitive disinhibition state, you run the risk of being overrun with irrelevant stimuli and ideas, which will make daily living decisions difficult if not impossible. In fact, several mental disorders are defined by just this problem of too much irrelevant stimuli coming into the cognitive workspace. These include attention-deficit disorders and disorders associated with psychosis-proneness[19] (see "Mental Disorders, Transformation, and Creativity".)

Finally, the flexibility to shift brainsets is associated with higher overall cognitive functioning. In an ongoing study, we are currently looking at the ability to shift between the *connect* brainset and the *reason* brainset (divergent and convergent thinking). In our study, subjects switch repeatedly between divergent and convergent tasks. Our preliminary data on about 80 subjects indicates that the group that is able to shift back and forth between brainsets gets better over time at thinking divergently, and the group that is not as able to shift back and forth gets worse at divergent thinking over time. Both groups maintain their original convergent thinking level.[20] Because we have established that both convergent and divergent thinking processes are important for creativity, the ability to shift flexibly between these thinking states is a primary factor in creative work.

The best way to practice flexibly moving between brainsets is to practice exercises related to brainsets that you find uncomfortable.[21] If you only practice the exercises within your mental comfort zone, you will not learn the basic lesson of this book: namely, that **to enhance your creativity it is important to be able to move into each of the brainsets *and* to move flexibly between them**. (This is the reason that if you're using the token economy incentive, you need fewer tokens from *un*comfortable brainsets than from comfortable ones to achieve a reward.) Here's a chart to help you practice brainset flexibility based on your personal comfort zone:

If your mental comfort zone is:	Practice exercises in the following brainsets to promote brain state flexibility:
Connect	Reason, Evaluate
Reason	Absorb, Connect, Envision, Stream
Envision	Reason, Evaluate
Absorb	Reason, Evaluate
Transform	Absorb, Reason, Stream
Evaluate	Absorb, Connect, Envision, Stream
Stream	Reason, Evaluate

For additional practice in cognitive flexibility, see *Flexibility* Exercises #1 through #5. They will help you learn to shift between brainsets regardless of your mental comfort zone. The more you practice them, the more easily you'll be able to slip in and out of brainsets as appropriate for idea generation and creative productivity.

The exercises at the end of this chapter are designed specifically to help you switch rapidly between brainsets. Doing activities that guide you into different brainsets automatically affects the flow of neurochemicals. However, earlier I mentioned another way of affecting your brainset: through learning. By increasing your knowledge base and learning new sports, artistic, and musical skills, you will also improve brain state flexibility and ward off cognitive decline in your later years.

The Importance of Continual Learning

One of the most important things you can do is **continue to learn!** Intellectual curiosity is a trait of virtually every highly creative person. It has the added benefit of reversing cognitive decline and slowing the progression of dementias such as Alzheimer's. There are two types of learning that are going to help you become more creative:

First, learn about many different types of things. Increase your general knowledge! In Chapter Eight I presented an exercise called Become an Expert, in which you are directed to learn as much as you can about a new subject (anything you choose!) every two months. (Now clearly you will not become an Einstein-type expert in two months—remember the 10-year rule from the last chapter) but what you will be doing is adding to the breadth of your knowledge—an important characteristic of your creative brain!) This is not just an exercise, it should become a way of life. Every few months you can add a new topic to your list. Keep notes on your topics of expertise—start a computer file for each one, and don't stop learning about an old topic just because you add a new one. This is the essence of being "self-taught."

The second type of learning that spurs creativity is the learning of a new skill. Learn to play the guitar, or cook Tuscan cuisine, or quilt, or repair motorcycles. The acquisition of a new skill stimulates different parts of the brain than does the acquisition of semantic knowledge. If you alternate focusing on a new skill and practicing skills you already possess, you will also be getting practice in brain state flexibility.

Both of these types of learning will increase the potential for making unusual associations that can result in creative ideas.

The world's most creative people have serious interests in multiple domains. They are polymaths (*poly* = many + *mathes* = to learn). Einstein the physicist also played the violin. Benjamin Franklin was both a writer and an inventor. Leonardo da Vinci was an inventor and an artist. Michael Crichton was both a medical doctor and a fiction writer.[22] (Many physicians and medical researchers write for a hobby. Each year Dr. Julie Silver, at Harvard Medical School, hosts a three-day workshop for doctors who want to become writers that is attended by hundreds of members of the medical community.)[23]

Diversity of interests within an individual mind has the same effect as diversity within a community or a nation. Ideas cross-pollinate. In fact, Dean Keith Simonton, in his studies of the Golden Ages of human culture, notes that two of the requirements for a cultural Golden Age include an openness to new ideas in the culture (a sort of culturewide *absorb* brainset) and intercourse with other cultures (many Golden Age civilizations were located on land or sea trade routes). So the combination of *exposure* to new ideas and *openness* to those ideas has—throughout the ages—led to explosions in creativity![24]

Due to the availability of information in the twenty-first century, it is within your reach to become a one-person Golden Age. The world of both new and old ideas is literally at your fingertips. Now you can access not just information but real knowledge through the Internet: Google has a goal of making every book ever written available through their browser. Jimmy Wales's Wikipedia and other open source innovations are making the body of human knowledge available to you.[25] You can even take piano lessons or classes in Western art over the Internet. Your life has so many possibilities for enrichment. And each area of enrichment that you pursue adds to the library of information and skills that you can combine to come up with creative and innovative concepts. What are *you* going to do with this opportunity?

"I just LOVE a man who can paint AND
hunt mammoths!"

In the next chapter we'll look at ways you can put all your new information about Your Creative Brain to work. You'll see how the CREATES brainsets play out in each stage of the creative process, and you'll get tips for enhancing creativity in your daily life.

Exercises: Flexing Your Creative Brain

Flexibility Exercise #1: Crossword Puzzle

Aim of exercise: To promote cognitive flexibility by shifting quickly between two different brainsets. You will need a stopwatch or a timer, a challenging crossword puzzle that you haven't worked on previously (you can use puzzles from your daily newspaper, the *New York Times*, or a crossword puzzle book), a pencil or pen, and blank paper. This exercise will take you 30 minutes.

Procedure: Set a timer for five minutes.

- Concentrate on filling out your crossword puzzle until the timer sounds.
- Note the answer to number one *across* (if you didn't get that answer yet, go to number two) and the answer to number one *down* (if you didn't get that answer yet, go to number two). Reset the timer for five minutes.
- On a blank sheet of paper begin writing a short story that incorporates the answers to number one *across* and number one *down and* includes someone being wiretapped by the FBI or CIA. Continue writing your story for five minutes.
- When the timer goes off, reset it and work on the crossword puzzle. Make sure to concentrate on the puzzle without thinking about your story.
- When the timer sounds again, reset it for five minutes and return to your story, incorporating the answer to number two *across* and number two *down*. (If you have not yet answered #2 down and across, or if you already used these answers in the first five minutes of story writing, go on to #3 down and across.)
- Alternate between the crossword puzzle and writing your story for 30 minutes.

This exercise forces you to shift between the *reason* brainset (solving the crossword puzzle) and the *connect* brainset (making unusual associations between the crossword puzzle answers and the FBI/CIA). You will also cycle through the *absorb* or *envision* brainset as you envision a story line. Try to do the exercise once a week. Use a different crossword puzzle each time, and center your story around the answers to the crossword plus one of the following themes: being abducted by aliens from outer space, being elected to the National Football League Hall of Fame, being chosen as Jennifer Aniston's hairdresser for her upcoming movie in Romania, finding an authentic painting by van Gogh hidden in a closet, and hearing footsteps outside your bedroom when you're home alone.

If you're using the token economy incentive, give yourself one *flex* token each time you complete the exercise.

Flexibility Exercise #2: Brainstorm and Judge

Aim of exercise: To promote cognitive flexibility by shifting quickly between two different brainsets. You will need a stopwatch or a timer, a pencil or pen, and blank paper. This exercise will take you nine minutes.

Procedure: Set the timer for three minutes.

o   Brainstorm answers to this question: Where can I go for vacation this year?

o   Spend three minutes listing answers to the question **without judging them**. Try to generate as many answers as possible. No answer is too wacky or out of line. When the timer sounds, set it again for three minutes.

o   Now judge your answers. Are some of them impractical? dangerous? illegal? immoral? Cross out at least half your answers and prioritize the answers that are left with number one being your first choice. When the timer sounds, set it one more time for three minutes.

o   This time, imagine that your first choice solution is actually occurring. Visualize a scene from this vacation with as much detail as possible. Immerse yourself in the visualization—nothing is out of bounds to think about. Continue to visualize until the timer sounds.

This exercise forces you to shift between the *connect* brainset (generating answers to the creative problem), the *evaluate* brainset (evaluating and ranking your solutions), and the *envision* brainset (visualizing your solution). Try to do this exercise at least once a week, using different creative problems that pop up during the week.

If you're using the token economy incentive, give yourself one *flex* token each time you complete the exercise.

Flexibility Exercise #3: Noun Fluency

Aim of exercise: To promote cognitive flexibility by shifting quickly between two different brainsets. You will need a stopwatch or a timer, a pencil or pen, and blank paper. This exercise will take you 30 minutes.

Procedure: Set the timer for three minutes.

- ○ Write down all the nouns you can think of that begin with the letter "F." Keep writing until the timer sounds.
- ○ Set the timer for three minutes again. Now put all the nouns into two categories. Use whatever distinction you wish to make the categories (good-bad, living-not living, brown-not brown, and so forth).
- ○ When you're finished, set the timer again for three minutes. Now recategorize the words into two *different* categories using some different basis for categorization. Think about how all things can be members of multiple categories.

This exercise provides experience moving between the *connect* brainset (writing out all the nouns) and the *evaluate* brainset (categorizing the nouns). Finally, the recategorization is indicative of the *absorb* brainset, as your categorization must be flexible in order to see how the same items can be members of multiple categories. Try to do this exercise once a week, using different consonants to generate the nouns and using different categorization strategies.

If you're using the token economy incentive, give yourself one *flex* token each time you complete the exercise.

Flexibility Exercise #4: Tetris and Trivia

Aim of exercise: To promote cognitive flexibility by shifting quickly between two different brainsets. You will need a stopwatch or a timer, access to the Internet, and the computer game Tetris (you can download a free version if you do not have one on your computer). This exercise will take you 25 minutes.

Procedure: Set the timer for 15 minutes.

○ Play the video game Tetris for 15 minutes, attempting to improve your score with each game. Play until the timer sounds.
○ When the timer sounds, set it for 10 minutes. Now find the answer to the following three questions before the timer sounds again. You can use any resources you wish to find the answers:
  ○ What are the names of four of Brad Pitt and Angelina Jolie's children?
  ○ How tall are each of the heads sculpted into Mount Rushmore, South Dakota?
  ○ Write out one recipe for New England clam chowder and one recipe for Manhattan clam chowder.

This exercise provides experience moving between the *stream* brainset (Tetris pretty reliably establishes a *stream* brainset) and the *reason* brainset (finding answers to convergent questions). Try to do this exercise once a week, with different trivia questions to look up in the second part of the exercise. You can generate your own trivia questions (make sure you don't know the answers already!) or you can ask others to provide trivia questions for you.

If you're using the token economy incentive, give yourself one *flex* token each time you complete the exercise.

Flexibility Exercise #5: Central Park Pad

Aim of exercise: To promote cognitive flexibility by shifting quickly between two different brainsets. You will need a stopwatch or a timer, a pencil or pen, and blank unlined paper. This exercise will take you 30 minutes.

Procedure: Set a timer for 15 minutes.

o   You have just inherited a fabulous 2,000 square-foot condominium in Manhattan overlooking Central Park. Your building is being renovated, and you have the opportunity to design your own floor plan. For the next 15 minutes design the floor plan of your unit. It is 40 feet by 50 feet. Draw the dimensions on a blank piece of paper and design your floor plan. Remember to include closets!

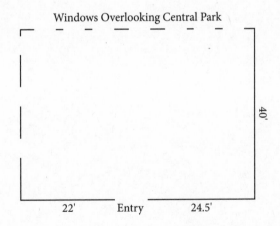

o   When the timer sounds, look over your floor plan. Set the timer for five minutes.

o   Now close your eyes and picture one of the rooms in your Manhattan apartment. How high are the ceilings? What kind of moldings are used? What is the floor made of? Wood? Tile? Carpet? What color are the walls? How will you furnish the room? What will you hang on the walls? Remember that you can decorate the room any way that you like. Take five minutes and picture each aspect of your new room. Try to see it as vividly as possible in your mind.

This exercise combines the *reason* brainset (making all rooms fit within the stipulated space of the floor plan) with the *envision* brainset (decorating your room). Try to do this exercise once a week using a different setting each time for your imaginary home (it could be a villa in Spain, a log cabin in Montana, or a houseboat on the Seine River).

If you're using the token economy incentive, give yourself one *flex* token each time you complete the exercise.

✳ 13

Applying the Brainsets to Real-World Creativity

Happiness lies not in the mere possession of money; it lies in the joy of achievement, in the thrill of creative effort.

—FRANKLIN DELANO ROOSEVELT[1]

AS WE ENTER INTO THE final chapter of our creative journey together, take a minute to think of how far you've come: You started with a mental comfort zone that consisted of a single brainset. Now—even though some of the brainsets may still be more comfortable for you than others—you have an entire toolkit of brain states from which to choose as you engage in the process of creativity and innovation.

Now you won't be as reluctant to step outside of your mental comfort zone because you have the skills to mentally go wherever you choose, and feel confident that your flexibility will give your creative brain more power and options. As you go forward you'll be able to use each of these brainsets as a tool to unlock the power of your unique set of skills and knowledge to make your contribution to the twenty-first-century Golden Age. Congratulations on this wonderful accomplishment!

Before you head out to conquer the world creatively, let's quickly review the each of the brainsets:

Absorb: When you access the *absorb* brainset, you open your mind to new experiences and ideas. You become receptive to more of the information coming in through your senses from the environment and to information from within your own (usually unconscious) thought processes. You view your world in a nonjudgmental manner, and everything fascinates you and attracts your attention. You are open to insights and the "aha!" experience that has led to so many exciting creative ideas in the past.

Envision: This is the brainset of imagination. When you access the *envision* brainset, you think visually and with your senses rather than verbally. You are able to see and manipulate objects in the theater of your mind. You use the mental format of "what if?" to envision not just how things are but how things could be.

Connect: This is the brainset of divergent thinking, where you generate multiple uncensored solutions to open-ended problems. This brainset allows you to see the connections between objects or concepts that are quite disparate in nature. Because the ability to combine and recombine remote bits of information into new and useful ideas is the essence of creativity, this brainset may be one of the most useful tools in your creative brain's toolbox. The ability to generate multiple solutions is combined with an upswing in positive emotion that also provides incentive and motivation to keep you interested in your creative project.

Reason: In the *reason* brainset, you consciously manipulate information in your working memory to solve problems in a logical and sequential way. You can use this brainset to generate ideas or to plan and make decisions about how to execute an idea. Even though the trial-and-error method of this brainset may be slower and more effortful than generating ideas from the *absorb, envision,* or *connect* brainsets, *reason*-generated ideas have the potential to be just as creative. This is the brainset in which Thomas Edison worked as he invented the electric lightbulb. Charles Darwin, who is certainly considered one of history's most creative thinkers, also wrote about his painstaking trial-and-error development of the concept of his origin of species. Even Bob Newhart, the accountant turned award-winning actor and comedian, originally worked from this brainset.

Evaluate: This is the state in which you consciously judge the value of ideas, concepts, products, behaviors, or individuals. It is the "critical eye" of mental activity, and it is necessary for deciding which of your creative ideas is worth pursuing and for constantly monitoring your creative projects to make sure they meet your criteria for usefulness and appropriateness.

Transform: In this brain state, you find yourself in a self-conscious and dissatisfied—or even distressed—state of mind. Many highly creative writers, artists, musicians, performers, and scientists have transformed the negative energy generated in this state into great works and great performances. Even though you are painfully vulnerable in this brainset, you are also motivated to express in creative form the pain, the anxieties, and the hopes that we all share as part of the human experience.

Stream: This is the brain state of flow, where your thoughts and actions begin to stream in a steady harmonious sequence, almost as if they were orchestrated by outside forces. In this brainset you improvise to produce creative material, such as jazz improvisation, narrative writing (as in novels or short stories), sculpting or painting, and the revelation of scientific discovery.

Here are some additional advantages to understanding these brainsets that have been reported by others:

° You now know that there is more than one brain state you can use to address problems. You can now recognize your current brainset as well as determine whether it is advantageous for your present task—and you'll have an idea of how to get into a better brain state for your task if necessary.

° You may also be able to recognize different brain states in others.

○ By understanding conceptually what's going on in your brain in any brainset, you may feel as if you have more control over both the content and the process of your creative thinking.

○ You can use the diagrams of activation that accompany each brainset to mentally visualize turning up the volume in the relevant parts of your brain to help you change brain states. (This is an especially good tactic for *envisioners!*)

Setting the Mood: Tips for Establishing a Creative Environment

Now that we've reviewed the brainsets, let's talk a little about how to set up both a physical and emotional environment that's conducive to creativity.

The first step in enhancing your creativity is to ensure that you're living and working in an environment that facilitates creativity and innovation, or at least one that does not actively discourage it. Here are some of the things you can do to enhance your creative environment:

○ ***Increase your exposure to creative work.*** Your own creative work will improve in fairly direct proportion to your exposure to creative excellence. Go to concerts (classical and jazz as well as popular), visit art galleries and museums, read books (the classics and poetry as well as popular fiction and self-help), go to the theater (mix live productions, opera, and of course movies), and go to science museums and lectures.

○ ***Create an environment that values and expects creative behavior.*** If you have children, make sure to include them in outings to experience creative work. Let them see you reading, painting, tinkering, or studying. Reward members of your family for thinking outside the box rather than chastising them for not doing things "the right way." Insist that everyone in your environment respects and encourages creative behavior, even when the results do not pan out. Give yourself and everyone in your environment the freedom to experiment and fail without ridicule.

○ *Avoid premature evaluation of ideas.* Statements such as "that's a stupid idea" or "it'll never work" are toxic to creativity. Negative and premature judgments should be challenged. If someone in your environment makes such statements (or if you catch yourself making them), challenge them by requesting evidence. "What is your evidence that this is a stupid idea?" Or "Can you provide evidence that this won't work?" After a few challenges, naysayers usually keep their unfounded and corrosive opinions to themselves. Don't let premature judgments poison your creative environment.

○ *Provide time and opportunity for solitude.* Creative ideas often occur during moments of solitude and contemplation. But that is not the only reason that creativity demands solitude. You should build in some time each day for thinking over the events of today or yesterday. Contemplate underlying associations and meanings. Connect the pieces of your daily life into a meaningful mosaic.

○ *Spend time in places of natural beauty.* The effect of natural beauty on the mind inspires creativity. Time spent in the mountains, at the seashore, gazing at the stars, walking in the forest, or watching a colorful sunset releases endorphins in the brain that contribute to the upswing in mood that generates creativity. Even if you are a city dweller, parks and gardens provide quiet islands of natural beauty. Places of natural beauty are portals to the *absorb* brainset.

○ *Spend time with other creative individuals.* Although a certain amount of solitude promotes creative thinking, we are at heart social beings. There is no doubt that the opportunity to play your ideas off of another creative brain promotes the *connect* brainset. When you surround yourself with other creative thinkers, ideas are cross-fertilized and you pick up grains of thought that can grow into pearls. Nancy Andreasen, of the University of Iowa (and one of the most widely respected figures in brain research), believes that a critical mass of creative people is what spurs a Golden Age. You can experience a taste of this critical mass for yourself by joining a writers' group or an art society, volunteering at a museum, or joining an amateur orchestra, theater group, or jazz band. If you can't find appropriate groups in your area, start one yourself.

Armed with a creative environment and confidence in your own creative mastery, it's time to revisit the creative process one final time to put together all you've learned. The major stages of the creative process include: Preparation, Incubation, Insight (Illumination), Evaluation, Elaboration, and Implementation.[2] As you remember from Chapter Four, you can take two pathways through the process: the *deliberate* pathway (in which you work consciously and sequentially through the process) and the *spontaneous* pathway (in which you allow ideas to feed forward from associational areas of the brain into conscious awareness as the result of cognitive disinhibition.[3]

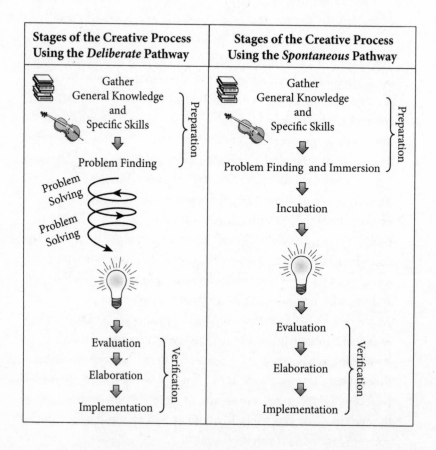

The Preparation Stage

The Preparation stage of creativity includes four processes: gathering general knowledge, acquiring specific skills and information, problem finding, and problem immersion.

Because creativity involves taking information (about things, concepts, or patterns) and combining or recombining it in original and useful ways, it stands to reason that you can't be creative unless you have something to be creative with—and that's why gathering knowledge and learning new skills is so important. Use the *absorb* brainset when you're gathering big-picture information and want to relate it easily to other concepts; use the *reason* brainset when you want to remember specific facts and figures. Remember that *nobody* has your unique combination of knowledge, memories, and skills stored in their brain. This unique combination is what you will share with the world—if you don't do it, your unique combination will be lost forever.

How do you find a "creative problem"? Because this is a challenge when you're first starting to think creatively, here are some tips for getting started.

○ **Keep a list of things that bother you.** Do you consistently get annoyed with something? Do you have pet peeves? Write them down. Periodically look over your list when you're in the *absorb* brainset. Is there a pattern in these irritations that you could do something about? Are there procedures or changes in objects that would remove the source of annoyance? Think about the de Mestral and Alexander Fleming examples from the last chapter. Rather than letting small things like burrs or mold bother them, they became fascinated by them . . . and the rest is history.

○ **When something goes wrong, brainstorm possible causes.** Even minor things, such as breaking a glass, could have causes (for example, slippery floor, shape of glass, and so on) that might suggest a creative problem. When something goes wrong, rather than getting angry, slip into the *connect* brainset and generate a list of potential causes. Once you have a list of potential causes, you also have a list of creative dilemmas that could be worked on.

○ ***Think about what slows you down.*** Do unexpected things happen during your day that keep you from being as productive or efficient as you might be? Those unexpected things could involve a creative problem that you could solve. Enter into the *envision* brainset and imagine what could be done differently to speed up whatever procedure was time-consuming.[4]

○ ***Pay attention to your negative emotions.*** Are you experiencing anxiety, sadness, or frustration that others have faced? Can you express this in a creative manner—with paint, music, or pen? Don't just be a victim of your negative moods; get into the *transform* brainset and use them to be creatively productive. Remember that you don't have to have expertise to express your emotions in a way that will resonate with others.

○ ***Scan your environment regularly for things that could be changed and improved.*** Most of the time we are so busy in our daily tasks that we forget to problem find. Sometimes just remembering to take a few minutes and look for "problems" will yield a number of interesting possibilities. And remember that when you're thinking creatively, "problems" are opportunities.

The last step in the preparation stage is to immerse yourself in your creative problem. Work on it from every angle you can imagine. If one thing doesn't work, try something else. You can use the Steps in the Problem-Solving Process from the *reason* chapter (Chapter Eight) as a guide. In addition to the *reason* brainset, you can actively try to generate solutions using the *connect* brainset or the *envision* brainset.

The Incubation and Insight Stages

If you run out of ideas of how to solve your creative problem, just put it aside. The incubation stage is most productive if you can enter the *absorb* brainset. Besides the exercises in Chapter Five, here are just a few other hints on how to enter the *absorb* brainset and prepare for insight while you are allowing ideas to incubate.

○ *Make a "creativity" playlist of music that inspires you and allows your mind to wander.* Many people find that the best music genres for this may include piano or acoustic guitar instrumentals. Orchestral soundtracks (background music from movies) may also be helpful. Avoid music that elicits negative emotions; also avoid vocal renditions as lyrics may interfere with the unconscious thought processes.

○ *Find a place of natural beauty.* As we discussed earlier in the chapter, this stimulates neurochemicals that evoke the *absorb* brainset.

○ *Take a walk.* Mild repetitive physical exercise stimulates blood flow to the brain, but does not lead to overstimulation or stress. Many creative insights appeared while their creators were walking.

○ *Spend time in natural light.* Sunlight (and bright light that imitates sunlight) stimulates an upswing in positive mood that may manifest in creative solutions to your ideas.

○ *Carry a notepad or digital recorder.* When inspiration strikes, it may dissipate very quickly (as did Coleridge's experience with *Kubla Khan*). You want to make sure you have a way to remember your insights!

Once an insight arrives, you might want to jump into the *connect* brainset and evoke as many ideas as you can before the state of disinhibition resolves itself. Remember that ideas that arrive via insight (the "aha!" effect) often feel almost like religious experiences. Because of this, you may have a tendency to cling to an insight that isn't as helpful as it initially seems. All ideas, even those insights that seem as if they were sent by destiny, should be subjected to scrutiny in the *evaluate* brainset.

The Evaluation and Elaboration Stages

Although you should judge your ideas in the *evaluate* brainset rather than the *absorb* brainset, make sure you don't jump into the evaluation prematurely. Try to enter the *envision* brainset and play out any creative solutions you may have come up with to their probable conclusion. See any potential directions in which you might take each solution before you subject it to evaluation. Remember that when you're judging your ideas you can always toss some of them into the "later" pile so that you don't discard them prematurely. Thomas Edison related that he tried literally hundreds of substances to make the filament of the lightbulb. He had tried tungsten early in the process but had discarded it prematurely. Later, after much time and effort, he came back to it only to find that it did indeed solve his problem.

Once you have evaluated a creative idea and found it worthy, you need to flesh it out and make it a *real thing* instead of just an idea. This will likely take some planning in the *reason* brainset. You can use the Goal-Setting Guidelines in Chapter Eight to help you devise a plan. Finally comes the task of actual creative production. This may mean struggling through 70,000 words of a novel, standing on shaky platforms for three years to paint your masterpiece on a chapel ceiling, fitting bicycle parts and old pipes together to make a prototype running stroller, or sitting in a recording studio for days at your own expense cutting a CD. The elaboration stage of creativity is the 99% perspiration that Edison talked about. This is the time to get yourself into the *stream* brainset; let this brainset keep you motivated and guide you as you meet the challenge of creative production.

The Implementation Stage

If your idea or product is to be considered creative, it not only has to be original, but it also has to be useful or adaptive in some way (remember our definition of creativity from Chapter One), which means it has to be available to at least a certain segment of the population who can either appreciate it or use it. Your creative process isn't finished until you get your work "out there." Although you could make a video of your work—art, music, drama, homemade gadgets, and so forth—and post it on YouTube, many creative people are unwilling to "hawk" their accomplishments in such a clearly self-serving venue. Here are a few tips on getting your work out there from publicist Diane Terman of New York, who has worked with many creative individuals, including Salvador Dali:

- *Increase your visibility in your community.* Contact your local newspaper and let reporters know what you're doing. Local papers are often looking for new human interest stories. Volunteer your services at a local charity or fund-raising event. If you're a musician, offer to play for free at such an event. If you're an artist, offer to donate a poster or sign relevant to the event or do sketches of patrons. If you do something well, offer to give free lessons as a community service. Most communities have community centers, YMCA branches, or nursing homes where any type of free lessons would be welcome. (Again, make sure your local paper knows about it, and bring business cards to distribute!)

- *Create "talking points."* Be able to explain what it is that you do and why it's special in three sentences or less. (Publicists call this "elevator talk," because it needs to be short enough that you can impart the essence of your work in the time it takes an elevator to get from the lobby to the 10th floor.) When you have only a short amount of time to pique someone's interest, you don't want to be scrounging for the right words. Have answers prepared ahead of time to questions people are likely to ask about your creative work. Rehearse talking points before a mirror until they seem natural and "off the cuff." Don't be afraid to throw in a little humor.

- *"Brand" yourself.* Develop a special logo that's associated with your work (make it unique, tied to what you do, and creative). Then splash that logo everywhere. Have it on your business cards, stationery or note cards, and your Web page. Develop a name or slogan that identifies your work. This should be short and pithy.

◦ ***Finally, develop a Web presence.*** From Facebook to Twitter to your own Web page, the Internet is the place to see and be seen today.[5]

Take a moment to reflect on your understanding of the creative process now versus when we first explored it in Chapter Four—does it make more sense now? Are you feeling more confident in your abilities to think creatively? If the answer is "yes," you are now ready to put your creative brain into gear and get out there and innovate!

If you're using the token economy incentive, now is the time to add up the tokens you've earned so far. The Token Economy Totals chart is located in Appendix Two. Be sure to reward yourself with an item from the Rewards List you compiled (see Appendix Two). You have truly earned the reward! Even if you have not been using the token economy incentive, you should congratulate yourself. You have engaged in time well spent by learning more about the capabilities of your fabulous brain . . . and it's a reward that will continue to pay dividends for the future. Your creative brain is now equipped with the tools it needs not just to live in the twenty-first century but to help shape it!

On the personal level, your creative efforts will enhance your own life and the lives of those close to you. Looking at the world creatively will increase the beauty and novelty that you find in everyday things. The creative environment you implement will improve your home and workplace and will inspire your loved ones and associates. Engaging in new creative skills, such as playing a musical instrument, painting, writing, or learning a new language, will bring you hours of enjoyment and satisfaction. Your creative efforts will help you add ingenuity to solving everyday problems, whether finding new ways to use old objects or concepts or finding that new objects or concepts can solve old problems. You'll see things from novel and creative perspectives that will augment your appreciation for the complexity and richness of the world.

Your present and future creativity will not only improve your own life, but it will also perform a service to your community and to society at large. Take a moment to think of how the creativity of others has affected your life—from symphonies to poetry to architecture to medical advancements. From the ceiling of the Sistine Chapel to the artwork in your local gallery, from Shakespeare to Stephen King, from Mozart to John Lennon, how much happiness, how much intuitive understanding of the human condition, how much pure pleasure have you derived from the creative work of others? Perhaps others whose names you may never even know will derive pleasure from your own work some day.

Your creativity is needed to improve our chances for survival in an ever-changing and uncertain world. Creativity is the only thing that has allowed us to survive as a species. Who knows what challenges we may face in the future? It may fall to our generation and our

"What wonders yet lie within
the creative brain?"

cumulative creativity to ensure the survival of not only ourselves but our entire planet.

You are now fluent in seven different brainsets, and you are an expert at moving flexibly among them. Go out and light up the world with the unique and innovative ideas that only *your* creative brain can produce!

❋ APPENDIX 1

How to Score the CREATES Brainsets Assessment

THE ASSESSMENT TO DETERMINE WHICH OF THE CREATES BRAINSETS comprise your mental comfort zone contains two parts or clusters of responses.

Scoring Cluster One Questions

Circle your response for each question as well as the numbers in line with your response on the following grid (note that some answers may not have any numbers in line with them). Then total the number of circled responses in each column and add the totals for each page together at the end of the grid.

Question	If You Picked	C	R	En	A	T	Ev	St	D	Sp
1	answer a		1						1	
	answer b									
2	answer a						1		1	
	answer b									
3	answer a	1								1
	answer b		1						1	
4	answer a		1						1	
	answer b			1	1	1		1		1
5	answer a	1		1	1					1
	answer b						1		1	
6	answer a		1				1		1	
	answer b									
7	answer a		1					1	1	
	answer b			1	1					1
8	answer a	1		1	1					1
	answer b		1				1		1	
9	answer a		1						1	
	answer b									
10	answer a	1			1					1
	answer b									
11	answer a		1				1		1	
	answer b			1						1
12	answer a		1						1	
	answer b			1						1
13	answer a		1							
	answer b			1						
14	answer a				1					1
	answer b		1				1		1	
	Subtotal 1–14									

Question	If You Picked	C	R	En	A	T	Ev	St	D	Sp
15	answer a			1						1
	answer b	1	1							
16	answer a		1						1	
	answer b				1					1
17	answer a						1		1	
	answer b				1					1
18	answer a		1						1	
	answer b									
	answer c					1				
19	answer a			1	1	1				1
	answer b		1						1	
20	answer a						1		1	
	answer b									
21	answer a						1		1	
	answer b									
22	answer a	1								
	answer b									
23	answer a		1				1		1	
	answer b	1		1	1					1
24	answer a			1						1
	answer b		1						1	
	answer c									
	answer d					1				
25	answer a					1				
	answer b									
26	answer a	1								1
	answer b		1						1	
	Subtotal 15–26									

Question	If You Picked	C	R	En	A	T	Ev	St	D	Sp
27	answer a	1			1					1
	answer b		1						1	
28	answer a	1								
	answer b									
29	answer a									
	answer b	1								1
	answer c						1		1	
30	answer a									
	answer b	1								1
	answer c		1				1		1	
31	answer a									
	answer b					1				
32	answer a	1								
	answer b					1				
	Subtotal 1–14									
	Subtotal 15–26									
	Subtotal 27–32									
	GRAND TOTAL									

Your primary mental comfort zone is the column in which you have the highest number points in one of the first seven columns. Your secondary mental comfort zone is the column in which you have the next highest number of points.

C = *connect* brainset

R = *reason* brainset

En = *envision* brainset

A = *absorb* brainset

T = *transform* brainset

Ev = *evaluate* brainset

St = *stream* brainset

Now look at your point count in the last two columns. This determines your preferred pathway to creative ideas. If you have the highest
number of points in the D column, you prefer the *deliberate* pathway.
If you scored higher in the Sp column, you prefer the *spontaneous*
pathway. You'll learn about the *deliberate* and *spontaneous* pathways
in Chapter Four. If your scores in the D and Sp columns were approximately the same, you are already able to flexibly switch between the
two pathways. You will learn how to do this even more effectively in
Chapter Twelve.

As you read through this book, pay particular attention to brainsets that do not match your favored mental comfort zone. Your goal
is to develop the ability to access (and to tolerate) brainsets that feel
uncomfortable to you now.

Scoring Cluster Two Exercises

Before you score the Cluster Two exercises, take a moment to think
about which of the exercises you enjoyed the most and write down the
number of that exercise. It will be important in the scoring because
you will usually favor an exercise that reflects your mental comfort
zone. You can use the grid that follows the explanation of the Cluster
Two exercises to write your scores.

Exercise #1

This exercise tests your abilities to filter out irrelevant information and
concentrate on a specific task. These skills are facilitated by entering
into the *reason* brainset. You'll learn more about the *reason* brainset
in Chapter Eight.

1. The correct number of words that contain both *s* and *t* is 31. If you
   found 29, 30, or 31 words, give yourself 1 R and 1 Ev point (you
   can use the grid at the end of this Appendix to keep track of your
   Cluster Two points).

2.   Reading speed is partially dependent upon your ability to remain on task and keep your mind from wandering. If you were able to finish reading the passage in the allotted time, give yourself 1 R point.

3.   If you found that you were able to remain focused on the letters, give yourself 1 more R and 1 Ev point. If you found that you became distracted by or interested in the content of the reading passage, give yourself 2 A points. Becoming interested in stimuli around you to the point that you lose track of time and wander off task is a characteristic of the *absorb* brainset. You will be reading more about distraction and the *absorb* brainset in Chapter Five.

4.   If you remembered that the fusiform gyrus (answer c) was the part of the brain that recognizes faces, you were paying attention to the content of the passage rather than on finding the letters *s* and *t*. Give yourself 1 *absorb* point.

Finally, if Exercise #1 was your favorite of the Cluster Two exercises, give yourself 2 R points.

Exercise #2

This exercise is a measure of spatial ability. Specifically, it's a measure of your ability to localize an object in mental space and reproduce it at a later time. This type of mental visualization is a function of activation of the right hemisphere of the brain, which is most active in the *envision* brainset. You'll read more about visualization in Chapter Six.

If you were able to reproduce the dot in this exercise within the 3 cm as calculated by the instructions in Exercise #2 (part 2), give yourself 1 En point. This means you were able to visualize and hold in mind the location of the dot on the page.

If Exercise #2 was your favorite of the Cluster Two exercises, give yourself 1 En point.

Exercise #3

This exercise tests your ability to come up with multiple solutions to an open-ended problem. This is an ability most easily accessed through the *connect* brainset. You'll be learning more about open-ended problems in Chapter Seven. If you came up with nine or more answers about what to do with Ron, give yourself 2 C points.

If Exercise #3 was your favorite of the Cluster Two exercises, give yourself 2 C points.

Exercise #4

This exercise tests your ability to reason a problem out sequentially. This ability is most easily accessible through the *reason* brainset.

1. The correct answer is BAT. If you got the correct answer, give yourself 1 R point.
2. If you got the correct answer in under one minute, give yourself another R point.

If Exercise #4 was your favorite of the Cluster Two exercises, give yourself 2 R points.

Exercise #5

This exercise tests your ability to mentally manipulate 3-D objects. Mental rotation uses a different part of the brain than locating an object in mental space (as you did in Exercise #2). However, mental rotation is still a part of the mental imagery ability that is best accessed in the *envision* brainset.

1. The correct answers are: A for the first rotation and B for the second rotation. If you got them both, right give yourself 1 En point.
2. If you got both answers right in under one minute, give yourself an additional En point.

If Exercise #5 was your favorite of the Cluster Two exercises, give yourself 1 En point.

Exercise #6

This exercise challenges your imagination and ability to become absorbed in a task. Think about how you completed this task:

o   If you stopped writing periodically and actively thought about what would happen next in your story give yourself 1 R point.
o   If the story streamed into your head and you wrote without consciously planning what was going to happen next in your story, give yourself 1 St point and 1 En point.

If Exercise #6 was your favorite of the Cluster Two exercises, give yourself 2 En and 2 St points.

Exercise #7

This exercise is a "projective test" similar to the famous Rorschach inkblot tests used in psychiatric diagnosis (read more about inkblot tests in the Notes to Chapter Two).

The most common responses to this inkblot are to see it as a face or as two people facing each other.

o   If you saw something other than a face or two people facing each other, give yourself 1 En point.
o   If you saw people or objects moving in the inkblot, give yourself 1 En point.
o   If you didn't see anything but a blot of ink, give yourself 1 R point.

If Exercise #7 was your favorite of the Cluster Two exercises, give yourself 2 En points.

Exercise #8

This exercise tests your ability to detect errors. This is best done in the *evaluate* brainset. You'll learn more about this aspect of creativity in Chapter Nine.

1. If you were able to find eight errors on your first reading of this passage, award yourself 2 Ev points.
2. If you found that you paid attention to the content of the passage and forgot to look for errors, award yourself 1 A point.

If you were able to spot the errors without being distracted by the content of the passage award yourself another Ev point.

If Exercise #8 was your favorite of the Cluster Two exercises, give yourself 2 Ev points.

Exercise #9

This exercise is similar to Exercise #3 in that it tests your ability to come up with multiple answers to a prompt. This is best done in the *connect* brainset. However, unlike #3, this exercise asks you to respond with answers of a personal nature.

∘ If you were able to come up with twelve or more small things that give you pleasure, give yourself 1 C point.
∘ If you came up with four or fewer small things that give you pleasure, give yourself one T point.

If Exercise #9 was your favorite of the Cluster Two exercises, give yourself 2 C points.

Exercise #10

This exercise tests your ability to access multiple associational networks and to solve problems using insight. You'll learn more about insight in Chapter Four. The problems in this exercise are called remote association problems; you can learn more about remote associations in the Notes to Chapter Two. In order to solve the problems, you need to keep associational networks related to all three word prompts open. This is best accomplished with the defocused attention of the *absorb* brainset. You'll learn more about defocused attention in Chapter Five.

Here are the answers to the problems:

Luck	Rock	Times	Hard
Stop	Pocket	Tower	Watch
Share	Fish	Money	Market
Horse	Dive	Chair	High
Leaves	Free	Water	Fall

o   If you were able to answer four or five of the problems within the time limit, give yourself 1 C point.

o   If most of the answers came to you suddenly (the "aha!" effect), give yourself 1 A point.

o   If you were able to answer four or five of the problems within the time limit but you consciously reasoned out most of the solutions, give yourself 1 R point.

If Exercise #10 was your favorite of the Cluster Two exercises, give yourself 2 A points.

Exercise	Question	C	R	En	A	T	Ev	St	D	Sp
1	1. If your answer was 29, 30, or 31 words	1					1		1	
	2. Finished the passage	1							1	
	3. answer a: read the content				2					2
	answer b: focused only on finding the letters	1					1		1	
	4. answer c: circled "fusiform gyrus"				1				1	
	If #1 was your favorite Cluster Two exercise		2						2	

Exercise	Question	C	R	En	A	T	Ev	St	D	Sp
2	answer a: within the 3 cm composite range			1						
	answer b: no points									
	If #2 was your favorite Cluster Two exercise			1					1	
3	You wrote 9 or more solutions	2								1
	If #3 was your favorite Cluster Two exercise	2								1
4	1. Correct answer is "BAT"		1						1	
	2. Under 1 minute		1						1	
	If #4 was your favorite Cluster Two exercise		2						2	
5	1. Correct answers were A and B			1						
	2. If you finished in under 1 minute			1						
	If #5 was your favorite Cluster Two exercise			2						
6	If you consciously planned your story		1							
	If your story came to you without effort			1				1		1
	If #6 was your favorite Cluster Two exercise			2				2		2
7	Saw something other than face or two people			1						
	If you saw movement			1						1
	If you saw only an inkblot		1						1	
	If #7 was your favorite Cluster Two exercise			2						1
	Subtotal 1–7									

Exercise	Question	C	R	En	A	T	Ev	St	D	Sp
8	1. If you found 8 or more errors						2		1	
	2. answer a: paid attention to content				1					1
	answer b: not distracted by content						1		1	
	If #8 was your favorite Cluster Two exercise						2		2	
9	If your list includes 12 or more items	1								1
	If your list includes 4 or fewer items				1					
	If #9 was your favorite Cluster Two exercise	2								1
10	Answered 4 or 5 correctly	1								
	Answers came suddenly				1					2
	Able to reason out the answers		1						1	
	If #10 was your favorite Cluster Two exercise				2					
	Subtotal 1–7									
	Subtotal 8–10									
	Total from Cluster One Exercises									
	GRAND TOTAL									

When you finish entering your points into the grid, add the total points from the Cluster One questions and then determine your total score for each brainset and for the *deliberate* and *spontaneous* pathways. Again, your primary mental comfort zone is the brainset in which you have the most points. Your secondary mental comfort zone is the brainset in which you have the next highest number of points.

❋ APPENDIX 2

The Token Economy System

THE TOKEN ECONOMY INCENTIVE HAS BEEN SHOWN TO LEAD TO behavior change in a variety of clinical settings, including drug and alcohol addiction centers and Weight Watchers International. Even though the concept may seem overly simplistic, it is powerful enough to change drug and eating behaviors. It can also help you learn how to access different brainsets.

Creating a Rewards List

Before you begin using the token economy system, you need to establish a list of incentives toward which you can work. You do this by making a list of rewards that you would like to earn. Items on this list should be activities or indulgences that you do not allow yourself on a regular basis (they should be true rewards that you would like to have—things that are not so big that you can't really afford them but not so small that you consider them trivial). Examples that others have used include: a professional massage, a new handbag or pair of shoes, dinner at an upscale restaurant, a new article of clothing, a professional pedicure, an expensive book, a bottle of fine wine, a nice perfume or aftershave, or a new piece of sporting equipment. Your list should include four or five items.

Earning Your Rewards

Copy the chart below. At the end of most chapters in this book, you will find exercises to help you learn to access specific brainsets. In the description of each exercise, the number of tokens you can earn for completing the exercise is listed. Each time you earn a token, color in one box adjacent to the appropriate brainset. Each time you earn twenty tokens, you can exchange them for a reward from your Rewards List. If you make it a personal challenge to earn rewards, you will find that the system will actually improve your ability to enter different brainsets.

																Total
Connect	C	C	C	C	C	C	C	C	C	C	C	C	C	C	C	
Reason	R	R	R	R	R	R	R	R	R	R	R	R	R	R	R	
Envision	E	E	E	E	E	E	E	E	E	E	E	E	E	E	E	
Absorb	A	A	A	A	A	A	A	A	A	A	A	A	A	A	A	
Transform	T	T	T	T	T	T	T	T	T	T	T	T	T	T	T	
Evaluate	V	V	V	V	V	V	V	V	V	V	V	V	V	V	V	
Stream	S	S	S	S	S	S	S	S	S	S	S	S	S	S	S	
Flex	F	F	F	F	F	F	F	F	F	F	F	F	F	F	F	
														Total		

You can earn bonus tokens when you complete exercises in brainsets that are outside of your mental comfort zone (see Chapter Two to determine your mental comfort zone). Award yourself bonus tokens as follows:

- ○ If your mental comfort zone is *Connect,* give yourself double tokens for exercises in *Reason* and *Evaluate.*
- ○ If your mental comfort zone is *Reason,* give yourself double tokens for exercises in *Absorb* and *Connect.*

- ° If your mental comfort zone is *Envision*, give yourself double tokens for exercises in *Reason* and *Evaluate.*
- ° If your mental comfort zone is *Absorb*, give yourself double tokens for exercises in *Reason* and *Evaluate.*
- ° If your mental comfort zone is *Transform*, give yourself double tokens for exercises in *Absorb* and *Stream.*
- ° If your mental comfort zone is *Evaluate*, give yourself double tokens for exercises in *Absorb, Connect,* and *Stream.*
- ° If your mental comfort zone is *Stream*, give yourself double tokens for exercises in *Reason* and *Evaluate.*

Remember that you can print out a Token Economy chart and colorful tokens at http://ShelleyCarson.com.

Good luck with enhancing your creativity using this system!

❋ APPENDIX 3

The Daily Activities Calendar

FILL OUT THE DAILY ACTIVITIES CALENDAR EACH DAY FOR ONE WEEK. Each two-hour block of time should reflect the major (most time-consuming) activity you engaged in during that time. Try to fill in the calendar at approximately the same time each day—either just before you go to bed or on rising in the morning (for use with *Stream* Exercise #3).

Time	Monday	Tuesday	Wednesday	Thursday	Friday	Saturday	Sunday
8 to 10 AM							
10 AM to Noon							
Noon to 2 PM							
2 to 4 PM							
4 to 6 PM							
6 to 8 PM							
8 to 10 PM							
10 PM to Midnight							

※ NOTES

Chapter One   Wanted: *Your* Creative Brain

1. The definition of creativity accepted by most researchers is found in Frank Barron's classic book on creativity: *Creative Person and Creative Process*. See Barron (1969).

2. A set of studies conducted by Colin Martindale at the University of Maine suggested that people who were categorized as highly creative demonstrated different brain activation patterns when solving two different types of problems (divergent versus convergent problems—you'll learn more about these in Chapter Seven), while people who were rated as less creative tended to display the same brain activation patterns when trying to solve both types of problems. These studies indicate that people who use their creative thinking skills change between brain activation patterns more easily than those who have less-developed creative thinking skills. A review of these studies is found in Martindale (1999).

3. For information on creativity and business schools, see Gangemi (2006). Gordon Brown's comments come from a talk given at the Innovation Edge conference in London, on March 10, 2009, sponsored by the National Endowment for Science, Technology and the Arts (NESTA). You can access

the speech at www.nesta.org.uk/assets/external_video/public_services_ innovation_summit__gordon_brown. Information on creative parenting comes from Google and Amazon.com searches conducted on February 5, 2009. For information on the sports conference, see ENAS conference bulletin available at www.enas-sport.net/SysBilder/enas_File/Congress_2009_160609.pdf. For information on sports figures and creative achievers, see Colvin (2008).

4. For more information on the theory of how creativity is a "fitness indicator" and thus makes an individual attractive to potential mates, see Miller (2000) and Miller (2001).

5. For the Buss and Barnes study, see Buss and Barnes (1986). For more information on the evolutionary theory of mate selection, see David Buss's book: Buss (2003). For differences between the sexes in human mate selection, see Buss (1989). Also see Nettle and Clegg (2006).

Chapter Two   Your Mental Comfort Zone

1. The three premises of the CREATES model:

Creatively productive individuals in the arts and sciences are more likely to access states of mental disinhibition (see Chapter Five for a discussion). For empirical and theoretical evidence, see Carson et al. (2003), Carson (2010a), Carson (in press), and Dietrich (2003).

Creatively productive individuals are able to switch brainsets. This is an aspect of cognitive flexibility. Cognitive or mental flexibility appears to be a characteristic of creative thought; highly creative subjects tend to be able to change mental states depending upon the task at hand (see Martindale, 1999). We are currently conducting a cognitive flexibility study in our lab (see Carson and Yong, 2010). Based on the results of about 80 subjects, individuals who scored higher on measures of creativity were able to switch mental sets more effectively than those who scored lower on creativity measures. Learning to enter certain brainsets may actually increase your cognitive flexibility. For an explanation of how reducing levels of certain neurotransmitters through disinhibition may lead to increased cognitive flexibility, see Heilman (2005).

You can learn to enter different brainsets through training practice. A number of studies have demonstrated that it is possible to modulate brain activation patterns through practice. For an example of brain activation modulation through neurofeedback, see Kaiser and Othmer (2000). For a review of how it is possible to change brain activation through cognitive behavioral therapy (the principles of which guide many of the exercises in this book), see Porto et al. (2009). Finally, note that the popular Six Hats program (de Bono, 1992) successfully trains business teams to switch thinking modes during the creative process.

2. See Csikszentmihalyi (1996).

3. This exercise is from David Perkins's informative and entertaining book on creativity: *Archimedes' Bathtub* (see Perkins, 2000). Perkins's book has other interesting puzzles . . . but don't read them until you finish this assessment!

4. The mental rotation figures are adapted from the Vandenberg and Kuse Mental Rotation Test. See Vandenberg and Kuse (1978).

5. This inkblot is patterned after the famous Rorschach Inkblot test. The Rorschach is called a "projective" test because individuals project their own personalities and concerns onto the pictures (which are after all only inkblots). The test was created by Swiss psychologist Hermann Rorschach in 1921 to detect underlying thought disorder in patients who were unwilling or unable to talk about their symptoms openly. Though the test yields interesting information, many psychologists consider the inkblot test to lack reliability and validity (see Lilienfeld et al., 2001). It is used in this assessment as a measure of imagination rather than of personality or mental disorder.

6. The types of problems in this exercise are called "remote association" problems. Similar problems were developed by Sarnoff Mednick to test the ability to activate multiple associational networks in the brain simultaneously. Mednick believes that creativity is predicated on the ability to combine and recombine items or concepts in novel ways—the more remotely related the items are to begin with, the more original and creative the resulting combination will be. See Mednick (1962).

Chapter Three   Tour Your Creative Brain

1. The associationist theory of creativity was first elaborated by Sarnoff Mednick. See Mednick (1962).

2. For information on connections between dispersed areas of the brain and creative thinking, see Fink et al. (2009); Razumnikova (2007).

3. *Ten billion neurons.* Many researchers place the number of neurons at 10 billion (see Andreasen, 2005). However, estimates have ranged from 10 billion all the way up to one trillion neurons. The reason for the debate is our uncertainty about the number of neurons located in the cerebellum or so-called "little brain," located in the back of the skull just below the occipital lobe. See Williams and Herrup (1988).

4. Read more about how memories are stored and retrieved in Schacter (1996).

5. For a good review of the split-brain studies, see Schiffer (1998).

6. The basic neuroscience in this chapter can be found in a variety of text-books. I recommend Kandel et al. (2000) and Kolb and Wishaw (2008).

7. See Sporns et al. (2004).

8. See Charron and Koechlin (2010); Ridderinkhof et al. (2004).

9. See Baddeley (1986).

10. For research on the areas of the brain and the "me" center, see Craik et al. (1999); Fossati et al. (2003); Northoff et al. (2006).

11. See Buckner et al. (2008).

12. While there are likely additional areas involved in judgment and deci-sion making, the role of frontal areas including the executive centers, OFC, and parts of the ACC have been replicated. See Longe et al. (2010); Walton et al. (2004).

13. The original description of the Phineas Gage incident is in Harlow (1868), republished in Macmillan (2000).

14. For a review of disinhibition syndrome, see Cummings (1993).

15. For a review of the role of nucleus accumbens in the reward circuit, see Ikemoto and Panksepp (1999).

16. The original study of rats and the reward or pleasure center was acciden-tally conducted by James Olds and Peter Milner of McGill University in the 1950s. They had inserted electrodes into the brains of rats at a location in the limbic system that they thought would stimulate fear. Fortunately, their aim was slightly off and the reward circuit of the brain was discovered! See Olds and Milner (1954).

17. Teresa Amabile (Harvard Business School) has conducted extensive research on motivation and creativity. Her findings indicate that people who engage in creative acts are highly motivated by intrinsic rewards (see Amabile, 1996). The reward circuit is mediated by the neurotransmitter dopamine. When you do something that is intrinsically rewarding, dopamine is released in the reward center of the brain, producing pleasure and increasing your motivation to repeat the rewarding behavior.

18. The pioneering work on the fear circuit and the amygdala was conducted by Joseph LeDoux at NYU. See his review: LeDoux (2000).

19. For a discussion of emotional hijacking, see Chapter Ten. Also see Goleman (1995).

20. See Kolb and Wishaw (2008).

21. For information on the association centers and metaphors, see Ramachandran and Hubbard (2001); and Ramachandran and Hubbard (2003).

22. For information on Einstein's brain, see Witelson et al. (1999).

Chapter Four   Brainsets and the Creative Process

1. The LaughLab Web site is www.laughlab.co.uk/.

2. The *deliberate* and *spontaneous* pathways to creativity are described in Dietrich (2004a).

3. Researchers Janet Metcalfe (Indiana University) and David Wiebe (University of British Columbia) conducted a study in which participants either solved insight or noninsight problems. Those who answered problems with a moment of insight ("aha!" or *spontaneous* solutions) reported having no inkling that they were getting close to an answer until the solution was upon them, whereas participants who did not have an insight moment reported getting "warmer" as they neared a solution. See Metcalfe and Wiebe (1987).

4. For a discussion of the deliberate nature of the composition of the Brandenburg Concertos, see Siddharthan (1999).

5. The Mozart letter is cited in Ghiselin (1952), p. 34.

6. For a discussion of the validity of the Mozart letter and examples of other Romantic composers' creative process, see Solomon (1980).

7. Information on Jay Greenberg is from a segment of *60 Minutes*, which aired Nov. 28, 2004, "Prodigy, 12, Compared to Mozart: Scott Pelley Talks to Boy Who Has Written Five Full Symphonies," by Rebecca Leung, www .cbsnews.com/stories/2004/11/24/60minutes/main657713.shtml. Additional information on Greenberg is available at www.cbsnews.com/stories/2006/11/ 22/60minutes/main2205521.shtml.

8. The description of Schumann's beliefs about his compositions was reported by Lombroso (1891/1976) in his book *The Man of Genius*. Confirmation of Schumann's psychotic beliefs is also reported by Eric Frederick Jensen in his biography of Schumann (see Jensen, 2001).

9. The John Forbes Nash quotation is found in Nasar (1998), p. 11.

10. See Jung-Beeman et al. (2004); Kounios et al. (2008).

11. See Christoff et al. (2010).

12. See Buckner et al. (2008).

13. See Dietrich (2004a).

14. The first account of the story of Archimedes and the bathtub is found in the writings of the Roman writer and engineer Marcus Vitruvius Pollio in his work *De Architectura*, written in the 1 B.C., some two centuries after Archimedes' discovery. *De Architectura* contains 10 books on the architecture of ancient Greece and Rome. The Archimedes story appears in Book IX. An English translation of the 10 books can be found at http://penelope .uchicago.edu/Thayer/E/Roman/Texts/Vitruvius/home.html.

15. See Ghiselin (1952) for other examples of creative luminaries describing the creative process.

16. Graham Wallas's model of the creative process is found in Wallas (1926). Wallas built his model on testimonial accounts of highly creative individuals, including mathematician Henri Poincaré and experimental physiologist Hermann von Helmholtz. Wallas's model is widely accepted (with some occasional modifications) by both researchers in the field of creativity and by creative luminaries themselves. See Ghiselin (1952) for some firsthand accounts.

17. Pasteur is cited in Harnad (1990).

18. For more information on the incubation stage, see Smith and Dodds (1999).

19. For an example of the effectiveness of token economies in clinical settings, see Higgins and Silverman (1999).

Chapter Five   Opening the Mind: Accessing the *Absorb* Brainset

1. The William James quotation is found in James (1890/1905), p. 110.

2. The Joe Lawson quotations come from Erin Schulte, "The Evolution of the Postmodern Caveman," *Esquire*, March 22, 2007.

3. From a taped interview with S.W. for my research on creative achievers on March 4, 1999.

4. I have combined several areas of research to form what I call the *absorb* brainset, including research on mindfulness and the personality trait of openness to experience, as well as the brain research on response to novelty and disinhibition. All of these concepts have been shown to be correlated, and the mindfulness research has demonstrated that this state is amenable to purposeful manipulation and training. It, therefore, seems valuable to conceptualize this constellation of attributes as a brain state (the *absorb* brainset) rather than as a personality trait. For more information on openness to experience, see McCrae and Costa (1987); McCrae (1994); McCrae and John (1992). For information on mindfulness and how it can be cultivated, see Langer (1989), and Carson and Langer (2006). For the relationship between openness and disinhibition, see Peterson and Carson (2000). For evidence that openness is responsive to training, see Federman (2010). Openness is related to a number of neuropsychological factors. See DeYoung et al. (2005).

5. The Blake quotation is from Blake et al. (1982), p. 35. The lines are from "The Marriage of Heaven and Hell," which was composed sometime between 1790 and 1793.

6. The Newton-and-the-apple story is from Stukeley (1936).

7. The Vincent van Gogh quotation is from Stone (1937), p. 424.

8. This version of the story of the discovery of penicillin is found in Perkins (2000).

9. The concept of the "willing suspension of disbelief" as we think of it today is credited to Samuel Taylor Coleridge's *Biographica Literaria*, published in 1817. It is available through Project Gutenberg at www.gutenberg .org/etext/6081.

10. Talking trash cans information comes from CNN.com Technology section, "Talking trash cans keep Berlin clean," posted on September 28, 2005, http://edition.cnn.com/2005/TECH/09/27/spark.rubbish/index.html.

11. For a primer on the cognitive theory of mindfulness and how it can be learned, see Langer (1989), and Langer (1997).

12. For a discussion of a specific type of cognitive disinhibition and how it relates to creativity, see Carson (2010a).

13. See Dagenbach and Carr (1994).

14. Kenneth Heilman (Heilman, 2005) has suggested that modulation of norepinephrine in the prefrontal lobes may be the key to states of mind that allow information into conscious awareness that would ordinarily be blocked. Norepinephrine is associated with high levels of arousal (such as anxiety and excitement). Thus, lower levels of this chemical may be associated with the receptive state I call the *absorb* brainset. Other research suggests that levels of acetylcholine may remain high in the prefrontal lobe during states such as "quiet-waking" (as opposed to "active-waking;" the *absorb* brainset would be a state of quiet-waking, while *deliberate* thinking—see Chapter Four—would be active-waking), while other neurochemicals (including perhaps dopamine and norepinephrine may fluctuate during these altered states of consciousness. See Faw (2006).

15. See Dietrich (2004a) for a full description of TOP.

16. See Kounios (2008).

17. See Martindale (1999) for a review of the studies of alpha activity and creativity.

18. See Martindale (1999).

19. See Peterson and Carson (2000); and Peterson et al. (2002).

20. See Gray et al. (1995).

21. Horace is quoted in Goodwin (1992), p. 425.

22. Styron (1990), p. 40.

23. See Norlander and Gustafson (1996, 1998).

24. See Gray et al (1992) for an example of how amphetamine reduces latent inhibition.

25. See Dardis (1989).

26. See Bardo et al. (1996).

27. See Arias-Carrión and Pöppel (2007).

28. See Ikemoto and Panksepp (1999).

29. See Schacter (1996) for more information on encoding information in long-term memory.

30. The "antechambers of consciousness" is a reference to Sir Francis Galton's description of how he found solutions to problems via what we're calling (after Dietrich, 2004a) the *spontaneous* pathway. See Galton (1911), p. 146.

31. See Ivanovski and Malhi (2007) for information on how meditation can affect brain state.

32. See Kounios et al. (2008).

33. See Kounios et al. (2008).

34. See Jang et al. (1996).

35. See Kubitz and Pothakos (1997); Schneider et al. (2009). Note that at least 10 studies have also found an increase in creativity per se after aerobic activity (see Steinberg et al., 1997).

36. See Horan (2009).

37. See Hobson et al. (2000); and Walker et al. (2002).

Chapter Six   Imagining the Possibilities: Accessing the *Envision* Brainset

1. The Einstein quotation is found in "What Life Means to Einstein: An Interview by George Sylvester Viereck" in *The Saturday Evening Post*, Vol. 202 (26 October 1929), p. 117.

2. For information on how remembering the past and envisioning the future employ similar brain regions, see Addis et al. (2007); Szpunar (2010); Szpunar and McDermott (2009); Szpunar et al. (2006).

3. See Addis et al. (2007).

4. For Salthouse's research on the early onset of cognitive decline, see Salthouse (2009). However, Salthouse's claim that cognitive aging begins in the twenties has been challenged by researchers that criticize his use of cross-sectional rather than longitudinal data. Critics also believe that animal research and other sources of knowledge about the brain may contradict Salthouse's findings; see Schaie (2009) and Nilsson et al. (2009).

5. See Rakic (2002) and Doidge (2007).

6. See Buckner (2010).

7. Personal anecdotes (e.g., Einstein's quotation at the beginning of Chapter Six), as well as empirical evidence, indicate that visualization (mental imagery) skills and imagination are both important components of creative thought. I have brought together what we know about the brain and these two areas of research to define the *envision* brainset. Brain research on imagination (see Buckner, 2010) indicates that there are both *deliberate* and *spontaneous* elements to the imagination process. For empirical evidence on the importance of mental imagery in creative thought, see Daniels-McGhee and Davis (1994).

8. The essence of identity is having a continuous sense of self across time and events. This continuous self is accomplished through the weaving together of episodic or autobiographical memories with images of the ideal self and the self as reflected back to you by others. This weaving together of memories to construct a self appears to use the same brain circuits described by Buckner (2010) that unite memory and imagination. For some interesting reading on developing a sense of self, see Fivush and Haden (2003).

9. For research on mental imagery and healing, see Donaldson (2000); and Warner and McNeill (1988).

10. For research on mental imagery and golf, see Brouziyne and Molinaro (2005); Taylor and Shaw (2002); Woolfolk et al. (2005). For research on mental imagery and basketball, see Clark (1960); Wrisberg and Anshel (1989).

11. For examples of musicians, surgeons, and linemen using mental imagery, see Kosslyn and Moulton (2009).

12. Semihallucinatory experiences are a characteristic of schizotypal personality. A number of studies have indicated that people who are involved in creative professions or hobbies score higher on measures of schizotypal personality than control groups who are not involved in creative professions. See Nettle (2006); Rawlings and Locarnini (2006).

13. Scientists and visualization: According to British researchers Nicholas LeBoutillier and David Marks, here is a list of scientists who have used visualization in their work: Bohr, Cannon, Crick, Descartes, Edison, Einstein, Faraday, Freud, Galton, Hadamard, Helmholtz, Herschel, Kant, Kekulé, Leibniz, Loewi, Maxwell, Neitszche, Poincaré, Snyder, Tesla, Watson, and Watt. See LeBoutillier and Marks (2003).

In the 1992 release of a video based on his best-seller *A Brief History of Time*, eminent Cambridge physicist Stephen Hawking revealed, "I tended to think in pictures and diagrams I could visualize in my head." See Hawking (1992); and *A Brief History of Time* (video) by Gordon Freeman Productions.

14. For examples of improved visualization with training, see Lohman and Nichols (1990); Yates (1986).

15. See Kosslyn et al. (2006).

16. See Lohman and Nichols (1990).

17. The practice of tracing an image in the air to enhance visualization was described by Sir Francis Galton. See Galton (1907).

18. Vision processing in primates and humans is divided into two streams in the brain. The dorsal stream (the "where" stream) projects from the occipital cortex in the back of the brain to the posterior parietal lobe and processes the location of an object in space. The ventral stream (the "what" stream) projects from the occipital cortex to the lower part of the temporal lobe and processes the description of an object (color and shape). See Kosslyn et al. (2006) for more detail.

19. The Einstein quotation is from Ghiselin, 1952, p. 32.

20. The Dickens incident is related in Shaw (2000). The quotation from Tesla is in Tesla and Johnston (1919/1982), p. 64.

21. For information on the brain during sleep, see Hobson and Pace-Schott (2002).

22. See Cai et al. (2009).

23. Information on lucid dreaming is found in Voss et al. (2009).

24. There is growing evidence that this modulation of executive center activation is the result of fluctuations in the neurochemicals norepinephrine and acetylcholine. See Cai et al. (2009) and Heilman (2005) for more information.

25. See D'Esposito et al. (1997).

26. See Kowatari et al. (2009).

Chapter Seven   Thinking Divergently: Accessing the *Connect* Brainset

1. The Poincaré quotation is found in Ghiselin (1952), p. 25.

2. The *connect* brainset is based on research on the brain activation pattern associated with divergent thinking. Because activation of the reward circuits are associated with increased verbal fluency and divergent thinking, I have also included information on the activation of reward circuitry (including some of the research on addiction, which is heavily dependent upon these circuits). In addition, divergent thinking activates associational areas that are involved in the condition of synaesthesia. An examination of the synaesthesia research also contributes to the construct of this brainset. Examples of the relevant literature include the following: For divergent thinking and reward, see Ashby et al. (1999). For reward and addiction, see National Institute on Drug Abuse (2009), *The neurobiology of drug addiction*, www.drugabuse.gov/pubs/Teaching/Teaching2/Teaching.html. For creativity and synaesthesia, see Ramachandran and Hubbard (2003).

3. In my research on creativity and divergent thinking, I've administered divergent thinking tasks to over 1,000 participants. At the end of the tasks, I ask them to record whether the tasks energized or exhausted them. According to data on 326 participants, those who are less divergent report being significantly more exhausted, while participants who score high on these tasks report being energized. There appears to be a correlation between how much you access divergent thinking brain patterns and how energized you become. Further, repeated practice on divergent thinking tasks improves divergent thinking scores and also self-reported energizing feelings (Carson, 2010b).

4. For the connection between divergent thinking and disinhibition, see Peterson and Carson (2000). For the connection between creative thinking and reward, see Ashby et al. (1999); and Isen et al. (1987). For the connection between divergent thinking and nonjudgmental, see McCrae (1987); divergent thinking is highly correlated with openness to experience, the nonjudgmental personality variable related to the *absorb* brainset.

5. For a discussion of how widely divergent thinking is used as a measure of creativity in research and why its use may give us a skewed view of creativity, see Dietrich (2007). I agree with this argument; divergent thinking is only one aspect of creative thought. This is why we need to consider the other brainsets of the CREATES model when we discuss human creativity.

6. For a description of convergent thinking and the differences between convergent and divergent thinking, see Runco (2007).

7. The problem is from the SAT I Reasoning Test (dated May 1997), College Board.

8. See Runco (1999).

9. This personal communication is from a very creative student who took my creativity course at Harvard in response to why it took him three times as long as most other students to complete 10 convergent thinking questions.

10. In the continuing education version of my course *Creativity: Madmen, Geniuses, and Harvard Students*, all students—many of whom are accomplished members of the Boston arts community—take a set of divergent thinking tests, as well as a variety of personality questionnaires. Students who answer "yes" to the "square peg in a round hole" question have displayed significantly higher divergent thinking scores over the years. The "octagonal peg" response was scrawled next to this question on the test booklet of a screenwriter who took the course. (There are other examples of student and study participant responses in this book. Of ethical necessity, all participants and student names will remain anonymous.)

11. This percentage is based on the percentage of 326 participants who found divergent thinking tasks exhausting rather than energizing (see Note #3).

12. These problem types are described in David Perkins's informative and entertaining book on creativity (see Perkins, 2000).

13. The Einstein quotation is cited in Holton (1973), p. 357.

14. Based on a sample of participants who have taken both the Cluster One quiz in Chapter Two and divergent thinking tasks. Individuals who preferred the *reason* brainset had lower divergent thinking scores than those who preferred the *connect* or *absorb* brainset.

15. See Simonton (1997).

16. What follows is a selection of divergent answers for "uses for a soup can," but don't peek until you have completed *Connect* Exercise #1! Additional uses for a soup can that do not involve the "container" description include: string telephone, paperweight, doorstop, weapon, shovel/ladle/scoop, drum, hearing aid, cookie cutter, sharp edge, sand castle mold, bookend, scrap metal, lamp base, hammer, rain gauge, birdhouse, building block, noisemaker, portable stove, advertising space, hockey puck, periscope, goat food, mousetrap, bowling pin, drink holder in car, tie on wedding car, rolling pin, freeze for cold pack.

17. Both this response and the following "divergent" response are from students in my course *Creativity: Madmen, Geniuses, and Harvard Students*.

18. See Osborn (1963).

19. See Roozenburg and Eekels (1995).

20. This Einstein quotation is found in Einstein and Infeld (1938), p. 83.

21. Word association tests have been used for over forty years as a measure of the spread of associational networks. See Mednick et al. (1964).

22. In 1996, when I was doing some early research for my dissertation, I ran a number of subjects through word association tests, divergent thinking tasks, and creative personality tests. This particular subject stood out, not only because of her high scores on the creativity tests, but also because of her unusual responses to the "leaf" prompt. (For example, one of her first responses was the word *Viking*.) I sat with her after testing and diagrammed her responses. Sure enough, once I saw them on paper, I was able to understand the spreading of associations, and the responses that had seemed so bizarre during testing began to make sense.

23. Neuroscientist Jaak Panksepp has been a major influence in spreading the word that play is important for the development of certain neural circuits associated with prosocial behavior and reward. He sees play as a precursor to innovative thought and creativity. See Panksepp (2004).

Photographs of the creative and playful workplaces at PIXAR and other companies are available on Smashing Magazine, www.smashingmagazine .com/2007/12/10/monday-inspiration-creative-workplaces/.

Recent books by Daniel Pink and Joseph Brown have also increased awareness of the value of adult playfulness. See Brown and Vaughan (2009); Pink (2005).

24. See Panksepp (2004).

25. For a review of Alice Isen's work on creativity and mood, see Ashby (1999).

26. See Baas et al. (2008) for the meta-analysis of mood and creativity.

27. See Pronin and Wegner (2006).

28. See Oettingen and Gollwitzer (2002).

29. See Schwarz and Bohner (1996).

30. See Carson and Flaherty (2010). Alice Flaherty has also written an extraordinary book on creative drive called *The Midnight Disease: The Drive to Write, Writer's Block, and the Creative Brain.* See Flaherty (2004).

31. See Biederman and Vessel (2006).

32. For the effect of drugs, see Farah et al. (2009); Swartwood et al. (2003). For dose-dependent effects of amphetamine, see Gray et al. (1992). For the debate over Ritalin and creativity, see Zaslow (2005), p. D1.

33. For caffeine use in artists versus controls, see Kerr et al. (1991). For the dose-dependent effects of caffeine on cognition, see Kaplan et al. (1997).

34. Evidence for increased alpha activity in the prefrontal lobes during effective divergent thinking can be found in Martindale (1999); Fink et al. (2006); Fink et al. (2009); Jung et al. (2010).

35. However, not all researchers agree as to the meaning of this alpha activity: For instance, an Austrian group, including Andreas Fink from the University of Graz, interprets increased alpha activity in the frontal lobes as an indicator of the brain deliberately shutting out information from the outside world via the five senses so that the mind can concentrate on internally generated stimuli. Both this and the deactivation/defocusing explanations make sense theoretically. (Support for the defocusing explanation jibes with findings from neurochemical changes in the brain as well as many of the personal

reports we've heard from the likes of Mozart, Nash, and Poincaré. However, the shutting-out-external-stimuli account makes sense as well, as you can increase alpha activity to some extent just by closing your eyes.) Of course, there's also the possibility that alpha activity is indicative of both explanations. Perhaps we are simultaneously increasing our focus on our inner world *and* broadening our focus by allowing more of the stimuli from that inner world into our conscious awareness when we increase alpha activity in the frontal regions.

36. See Christoff et al. (2010).

37. See Fink et al. (2009). Because increased activation has been found in both the prefrontal areas (roughly equivalent to the dorsolateral prefrontal cortex DLPFC) and the association areas of the temporal and parietal lobes, there is new interest in a theory that emphasizes the activation of a specific prefrontal/parietal network as being important for creative thinking.

38. Evidence for a relative increase in ratio of right-to-left prefrontal hemisphere activation in effective divergent thinking is found in Bechtereva et al. (2004); Carlsson et al. (2000); Howard-Jones et al. (2005); Razoumnikova (2000).

39. The Daniel Pink quotation is from the subtitle of his best seller. See Pink (2005).

Note that increased right-to-left prefrontal activation can be caused by a decrease in left prefrontal activation as well as an increase in right activation. For example. cases of frontotemporal dementia (FTD) in which increased creative activity has been noted tend to have lesions in the left hemisphere (leading to deactivation of that area). See Miller et al. (2000).

40. Evidence for activation of the parietal association cortex in divergent thinking is found in Bechtereva et al. (2004); Razumnikova (2000); Starchenko et al. (2003).

41. See Seeley et al. (2008).

42. See Miller et al. (2000).

43. For information on creativity and synaesthesia, see Ramachandran and Hubbard (2001; 2003).

44. See Mednick (1962).

45. For information on Tommy McHugh's condition, see Lythgoe et al. (2005).

46. For Tommy's quotation to reporter Jim Giles, see Giles (2004).

47. Divergent thinking training programs use exercises similar to those described in this chapter. These have been shown to be effective at increasing divergent thinking skills. See Scott et al. (2004).

Chapter Eight   Shaping the Creative Idea: Accessing the *Reason* Brainset

1. Ayn Rand quotation is from Rand (1943/1993).

2. I have defined the *reason* brainset as the brain activation pattern associated with logical, sequential, and realistic (cause-and-effect) thinking. It is modeled on research that has investigated reasoning skills, including rational problem solving, convergent thinking, setting and maintaining goals, intentional thought, and abstract reasoning.

3. For Edison, Bach, and other examples of creative work done via the *deliberate* pathway (and thus the *reason* mode), see Dietrich (2004a). For information on art in the *Trompe l'Oeil* style, see Ebert-Schifferer et al. (2002).

4. For accounts of Coleridge and the writing of *Kubla Khan*, see Skeat (1963–1964).

5. For criticism of *Kubla Khan* as a *spontaneous* vision, see Weisberg (1993).

6. The Clancy quotation is found in Clancy (2005), p. 33. For a theory of how delusions (such as the alien abduction syndrome) are formed using rational thinking processes, see Maher (1988).

7. Decartes' famous one-liner first appeared in the Latin in *The Principles of Philosophy* (IX), published in 1644. However the phrase appeared earlier in French ("Je pense donc je suis."), in *Discourse on Method (Discourse on the Method of Rightly Conducting the Reason, and Seeking Truth in the Sciences)*, published in 1637. Translations of both books are available online through Project Gutenberg at www.gutenberg.org.

8. For information on Alex the parrot, see Pepperberg (1999) and Pepperberg (2008).

9. See Banaji and Kihlstrom (1996).

10. For information on talking trash cans around the world, see Talking trash, www.talkingtrash.fi/.

11. See Tolkien (1954–55/2005).

12. For information on serial or sequential processing versus parallel processing, see Gazzaniga et al. (1998).

13. For information on the sequential nature of "multitasking" see Parasuraman (1998); Hahn et. al. (2008).

14. For more information on the functions of the prefrontal lobes, see Kolb and Wishaw (2008).

15. For information on goal setting, see Moskowitz and Grant (2009).

16. For more on left hemisphere activation with verbal thought, see Logie et al (2003).

17. For recruitment of right hemisphere prefrontal regions when dealing with complexity, see Charron and Koechlin (2010); Howard-Jones et al. (2005); Beeman and Chiarello (1998).

18. Beta frequency tends to predominate during states of high arousal, alertness, and active concentration. Alpha frequency tends to predominate in restful waking states. Beta is associated with more focused attention, while alpha is associated with more diffuse attention. See Parasuraman et al. (1998).

19. See Tomporowski (2003).

20. For research on the Mozart Effect, see Schellenberg (2003); Roth and Smith (2008).

21. For a good description of secondary and primary process, see Ochse (1990).

22. See Kris (1952).

23. See Dietrich (2003).

24. For articles on neuro-psychoanalysis, see Kaplan-Solms and Solms (2000); Solms and Turnbull (2002).

25. Thought stopping is a cognitive-behavioral technique that has been used extensively in clinical settings to help control anger, depressive rumination, and

OCD obsessions. Though it has shown limited value for the treatment of obsessions, research indicates it is effective as a tool in anger management and prevention of depression. See Peden et al. (2001).

26. The problem-solving exercise is adapted from my work on the Department of Defense program *afterdeployment.org*. One of the programs housed within this site is an online Resilience program designed to help build resilience for troops serving in Iraq and Afghanistan and their families. There are workshops on resilience-building skills, including steps for effective problem solving. The site is free and available to anyone.

27. The goal-setting exercise is adapted from my work on the Department of Defense program *afterdeployment.org*. For the value and effectiveness of setting goals, see Tubs (1986).

Chapter Nine   Recognizing Useful Ideas: Accessing the *Evaluate* Brainset

1. See Ambady and Rosenthal (1993).

2. I patterned the *evaluate* brainset on psychological and neuroscientific research that describes judgment and the propensity to judge (a judgmental attitude). There is an advantage of conceptualizing evaluation as a brainset rather than as a stage of the creative process. My work with creative professionals has shown me that people have to get into a certain highly focused state in order to evaluate their work with accuracy. If they remain in the defocused state associated with *absorb, envision,* or *connect,* they often make vague or indecisive stabs at evaluation that are not effective or helpful to their creative work.

3. Type I and II errors. (These are statistical terms that help determine whether a statistical result differs from the null hypothesis.) Checking for these errors can be useful in everyday judgments and decision making as well. Type I error, also known as an "error of the first kind" or a "false positive," occurs when we judge something to be true or appropriate that is not in fact true or appropriate. For example, if a pregnancy test indicates you are pregnant when you are not, that would be a Type I error. Type I errors are sometimes referred to as errors of excessive credulity or acceptance. The Type II error, also known as an "error of the second kind" or a "false negative," occurs

when we judge something as not being true or appropriate when, in fact, it is. For example, if a pregnancy test indicates that you are not pregnant when you actually are, that would be a Type II error. These are sometimes referred to as errors of excessive skepticism. In our parlance of brainsets, the person whose comfort zone is the *absorb* or the *envision* brainset is more likely to make Type I errors by pursuing ideas and creative products that ultimately have little value, while the person who prefers the *evaluate* brainset is more likely to make Type II errors by judging ideas or products as inferior when they are, in fact, worthwhile.

4. Because categorization of stimuli into "friend" or "foe" and "dangerous" or "safe" are related to our survival, it seems appropriate that a system of internal reward for making such categorizations should have evolved. In fact, there is some evidence for such a system. There is also some evidence that we can automatically adjust categorization boundaries when faced with an item that may not fit into a narrow category (category uncertainty). See Grinband et al. (2006).

5. For information on hoarders, see Frost and Steketee (1998).

6. See Frost and Steketee (1998).

7. The Pauling quotation is found in Csikszentmihalyi (1996), p. 116.

8. See Simonton (1999).

9. This version of Edison's quotation is cited in Fraser (1991), p. 76.

10. The procedure of monitoring your self-talk and treating it as a hypothesis, then seeking evidence to support or refute the hypothesis, and finally replacing unfounded hypotheses with more positive and realistic self-talk was first described by Aaron Beck in his groundbreaking cognitive theory of depression. See Beck et al. (1979). If you're finding that negative self-talk is interfering with your creative work, I recommend the book *Unlock Your Creative Genius* by clinical psychologist Bernard Golden (see Golden, 2006). I also recommend Ellen Langer's book *On Becoming an Artist* (see Langer, 2005).

11. See Vogels et al. (2002) for more on activation of DLPFC (especially in the left hemisphere) and orbitofrontal cortex during evaluation.

12. Speculation about the modulation of norepinephrine during states of focused attention is found in Heilman et al. (2003); Heilman (2005).

13. See Sanfey et al. (2006).

Chapter Ten   Using Emotion Creatively: Accessing the *Transform* Brainset

1. The Einstein quotation is from Einstein, A., Religion and science, *New York Times Magazine*, November 9, 1930, pp. SM1–4. The quotation is on page SM1.

2. I've based the *transform* brainset primarily on research that examines the relationship of creativity and psychopathology, as well research that addresses the clinical states of dysthymia and depression. Certain states of mental distress have been shown to be an impetus for creative and innovative activity. Although I will discuss this at length throughout the chapter, a major archival study of over 1,000 eminent luminaries conducted by Arnold Ludwig (who was then at the University of Kentucky) found that "psychological unease" was one of the strongest predictors of creativity within this group. See Ludwig (1995).

3. Stream of affect is described in Watson and Clark (1994).

4. For differences between moods and emotions, see Plutchik (2003). Note that clinical mood states differ from the typical ups and downs of mood in daily life by the degree of their duration and frequency. A mood disorder must also cause distress and a certain degree of dysfunction in one's life. See American Psychiatric Association (2004). For a review of evidence-based psychotherapies for depression, see Gallagher (2005).

5. For more information on the components of emotion, see Scherer (1984).

6. For more about emotional hijacking, see Goleman (1995).

7. Early versions of the *Diagnostic and Statistical Manual of Mental Disorders (DSM)* classified disorders as "neurotic" (including what we would now call anxiety and mood disorders) or "psychotic." The term *neurotic* is no longer used clinically, but is still used frequently in vernacular speech and is a favorite descriptor of Woody Allen movie characters!

8. Psychologists have long recognized that individuals who are depressed have an exaggerated self-referential focus. They spend more time ruminating about their own distress, and they are deemed less socially competent by themselves and others, partly because of their focus on the self during conversation. See Lewinsohn (1980).

9. Aaron Beck, the pioneer of the cognitive theory of depression, believed that a negative view of self (combined with a negative view of the world and the future) was at the heart of depression. See Clark and Beck (1999).

10. Although there are very few accounts throughout history of people actually *liking* negative mood states, it may be the case that we have become, as a society, much less willing and able to tolerate them in recent times. For instance, depression rates have increased for people born after 1940 and for every generation born thereafter (see Lewinsohn et al., 1993)—yet these generations did not live through the hardships of the Great Depression and were for the most part too young to remember the deprivations that accompanied World War II. In addition, prescriptions for antidepressant/antianxiety medications have increased substantially even though many of those prescribed the medications don't actually suffer from depression (see Ulene, 2009), suggesting that many people are taking medications rather than finding ways of coping with negative moods.

11. For the Emily Dickinson poem, see Dickinson and Johnson (1976). Edvard Munch painted several versions of *The Scream*. The oldest was painted in 1893 and resides in the National Gallery of Norway. For a discussion of the blues, see Davis (1995). Note that not all blues music is melancholy. For *Long Day's Journey into Night*, see O'Neill (1956). Horowitz's quotation about Tchaikovsky is found in the article "Pacific Symphony paints 'Tchaikovsky Portrait' this week" by Timothy Mangen in *The Orange County Register* on December 24, 2009. For *The Catcher in the Rye*, see Salinger (1951).

12. See Ludwig (1995) and his description of psychological unease.

13. For information on the increase in depression, see World Health Organization (2001); Twenge et al. (2010).

14. Graham Greene's quotation is from Greene (1980). It was also cited in the Books section of the *New York Times* on April 4, 1991, "Graham Greene, 86, Dies; Novelist of the Soul," www.nytimes.com/books/00/02/20/specials/greene-obit.html.

15. For information on sublimation as a defense mechanism, see Vaillant (1977). Creative therapies are generally used as an adjunct therapy rather than a primary therapy. For evidence of effectiveness, see Gussak (2009); Lyshak-Stelzer et al. (2007); Monti et al. (2006).

16. For more on Isaac Newton, see Westfall (1994).

17. Plato discussed four different types of madness in *The Phaedrus* (c. 370 B.C.). The Aristotle quotation is from Aristotle, *Problems II or XVI: Books XXII–XXXVIII*, translated by W. S. Hett (1936), pp. 155–157. Cambridge: Harvard University Press.

18. See Lombroso (1891/1976).

19. Mood disorders: see Jamison (1993); alcoholism: see Dardis (1989); psychotic behavior: see Prentky (1989).

20. William Blake: see Shaw (2000). Tesla: see Pickover (1998). Dickens and Beethoven: see Shaw (2000).

21. See Jamison (1989).

22. See Carson (in press); Dietrich (2003).

23. See Carson et al (2003); Norlander and Gustafson (1996; 1998).

24. See Jamison (1993) for a discussion of how hypomania can enhance creativity.

25. See Carson (in press) for a discussion of how psychosis proneness and hyperconnectivity can both enhance creativity.

26. Richards et al. (1988) did a study of bipolar individuals, their first-degree relatives, cyclothymes (people who have a mild version of bipolar disorder), and control subjects. They found that cyclothymes and first-degree relatives of those with full-blown bipolar disorder were more creative than the other two groups. This finding lends support to the idea that a small amount of psychopathology may be beneficial to creativity, but full-blown mental illness is detrimental. They later repeated this study looking at people who were psychosis prone (see Kinney et al., 2000–2001).

27. See Raichle (2001).

28. See Way et al. (2010).

29. See Gray (1990).

30. One of the main components of cognitive-behavioral treatment for depression is behavioral activation. Getting clients up, moving, and reengaged with the environment has therapeutic benefits. See Craske (2010); Gawrysiak et al. (2009).

31. The Core Strengths exercise is adapted from my work with the afterde-
ployment.org project. Recognizing your strengths is a resilience skill. Please
visit afterdeployment.org for more information on resilience skills.

32. For a review of the Pennebaker studies on expressive writing, see
Pennebaker and Chung (2007).

Chapter Eleven   Performing Creatively: Accessing the *Stream* Brainset

1. The Emerson quote is found in Emerson (1856), p. 7.

2. Information about Flight 1549 was retrieved from CNN.com on
November 18, 2009, www.cnn.com/2009/OPINION/11/18/langewiesche
.miracle.hudson.flight/index.html#cnnSTCText.

3. For more about the experience of flow, see Csikszentmihalyi (1996) and
Csikszentmihalyi (2008).

4. The *stream* brainset is the component of the CREATES model that is
defined as a state of automatic performance. In this state, actions seem to
stream in a meaningful manner without the sensation of having consciously
guided them. This brainset is patterned on research in the field of improvisation, and upon Csikszentmihalyi's concept of flow (see Csikszentmihalyi,
1996). For the *stream* component of the CREATES model, I owe much to
Csikszentmihalyi's groundbreaking work. The difference between flow and
the *stream* brainset is that flow is conceived as a state of optimal experience (see Csikszentmihalyi, 2008) while the *stream* brainset is conceived as
a brain activation pattern that facilitates creative performance in a variety of
domains.

5. See Bengtsson et al. (2007).

6. Sullenberger's "surreal" quotation is from the article "Pilot Says Hudson
River Landing Was 'Surreal.'" *The New York Times*, February 3, 2009.
Retrieved from *The New York Times* online: www.nytimes.com/2009/02/03/
nyregion/03pilot.htmlTopofForm.

7. See Csikszentmihalyi (1996).

8. For additional information on flow, see Csikszentmihalyi's talk on TED
.com: www.ted.com/talks/lang/eng/mihaly_csikszentmihalyi_on_flow.html.

9. For a discussion of implicit and explicit memory, see Schacter (1996).

10. See Dietrich (2004b).

11. For the "10-Year Rule," see Chase and Simon (1973); Simon and Chase (1973). For the application of the rule to Bobby Fischer, see Ericsson et al. (1993).

12. See Colvin (2008); Ericsson et al. (1993).

13. See Gardner (1993).

14. See Csikszentmihalyi (1996).

15. See Csikszentmihalyi (1996).

16. For a review of Amabile's work on intrinsic motivation, see Amabile (1996) and Amabile (1998). For Bill Breen's interview with Amabile, see Breen (2004).

17. See Hennessey and Amabile (1988); Csikszentmihalyi (1996).

18. This definition of impulsivity is found in glossary of the American Association for the Advancement of Science at www.aaas.org/spp/bgenes/glossary.

19. See APA (2004). Public speaking is feared by somewhere between 20 and 50% of the population, depending upon the criteria used to measure fear.

20. Tetris is a trademark owned by Tetris Holding and licensed to The Tetris Company. The game was designed by Alexey Pajitnov. This information was retrieved from www.tetris.com. For an interesting article on flow and video games, see LeMay (2007).

21. See Bengtsson et al. (2007); Limb and Braun (2008).

22. See Bengtsson et al. (2007); Limb and Braun (2008).

23. See Dietrich (2003).

24. See Cowan (2005).

25. Internal rewards (mediated by dopamine at the nucleus accumbens site) can be so subtle that the individual is not aware of feeling good. However, the subtle release of dopamine may be sufficient to influence future behavior (we are more likely to repeat behavior that is rewarded). See Berridge and Robinson (2003) for a discussion of the psychological components of the Reward system.

26. See Csikszentmihalyi (1996).

27. The Doing What You Love exercise is based on a cognitive-behavioral technique for the treatment of depression in which the individual gradually increases the number of calendar slots that contain positively reinforcing activities. See Craske (2010) for more information on cognitive-behavioral techniques.

Chapter Twelve   Flexing Your Creative Brain

1. See Herrera (1983).

2. See Freeman and Golden (1997).

3. See Moore (2009).

4. The discovery of penicillin is recounted in Perkins (2000).

5. The Grisham quotation is found in Moore (2009).

6. For information about implicit filtering of social codes, see Cacioppo et al. (2005).

7. See Dietrich (2003); Dietrich (2004a).

8. A number of confluence theories of creative achievement have been described. See Amabile (1996); Eysenck (1995); and Ludwig (1995).

9. See Heilman (2005).

10. See Linden (2006); Paquette et al. (2003).

11. Although there are no studies that look specifically at brain changes due to token economy interventions, there are studies that show that contingency training (of which token economy is one type) *can* help subjects to voluntarily influence brain states. See Weiskopf et al. (2004) for a review.

12. See Heilman (2005).

13. Norepinephrine is released from brain stem nuclei as part of the brain's global alarm system. See Tsigos and Chrousos (2002).

14. See Carson (in press).

15. As the field of molecular biology matures, there is increasing evidence that genes turn on and off due to environmental factors. See Munafò et al. (2009) for an example and review.

16. The tendency is for attention to broaden with an increase in positive affect. See Ashby et al. (1999); Isen et al. (1987).

17. In one ongoing task, I have asked subjects to write down a memory from childhood, and it is coded for global (big picture) versus local statements. Thus far, subjects who score high in openness and in divergent thinking have shown greater global scores whereas those who score higher on convergent tasks show more detail statements. This data is based on a small sample, but the results are in the predicted direction.

18. See Heilman (2005) for the effects of norepinephrine. Dopamine deficits in frontal regions of the brain have been associated with inability to maintain focused attention (a symptom of ADHD). See Coccaro et al. (2007) for recent research.

19. Please note that you will not *cause* conditions such as attention deficit disorder or psychosis proneness by purposefully entering a state of disinhibition. (Mental disorders are characterized by rigid patterns of activation, and we are aiming for cognitive flexibility here.) What I am emphasizing is that a disinhibited state may make some daily tasks (including keeping track of time) more difficult.

20. See Carson and Yong (2010).

21. There is a growing body of research that indicates you can increase your ability to flexibly shift attentional states by *practicing* shifting attentional states. See White and Shah (2006) for examples.

22. For more on polymaths, see Andreasen (2005).

23. See Silver (2010).

24. See Simonton (1999).

25. The Internet not only opens up venues to enhance your individual learning but also opens opportunities for social creativity endeavors. See Fischer and Giaccardi (2007).

Chapter Thirteen   Applying the Brainsets to Real-World Creativity

1. The FDR quotation is from his first inaugural address, delivered on March 4, 1933.

2. See Wallas (1926).

3. See Dietrich (2004a).

4. A good example of his kind of problem finding is described by Phil Baechler, inventor of the Baby Jogger. Phil wanted to combine spending time with his infant son along with his favorite pastime—jogging. However, ordinary baby strollers wouldn't stand up to the rigors of running on grass or sand. Baechler recognized this as a creative problem and used it to invent a product and launch a new career. His story is found in the June 11, 1984, issue of *People* magazine and online at www.people.com/people/archive/article/0,,20088037,00.html.

5. The suggestions provided by publicist Diane Terman were included in a guest lecture she gave at Harvard. See Terman (2008).

✳ REFERENCES

Addis, D. R., Wong, A. T., & Schacter, D. L. (2007). Remembering the past and imagining the future: Common and distinct neural substrates during event construction and elaboration. *Neuropsychologia, 45,* 1378–1385.

Amabile, T. M. (1998). How to kill creativity. *Harvard Business Review, 76*(5), 76–87.

Amabile, T. M. (1996) *Creativity in context.* Boulder, CO: Westview Press.

Ambady, A., & Rosenthal, R. (1993). Half a minute: Predicting teacher evaluations from thin slices of nonverbal behavior and physical attractiveness. *Journal of Personality and Social Psychology, 64,* 431–441.

American Psychiatric Association (2004). *Diagnostic and statistical manual of mental disorders (4th ed.—text revision).* Washington, DC: American Psychiatric Association.

Andreasen, N. C. (2005). *The creating brain: The neuroscience of genius.* New York: Dana Press.

Arias-Carrión, O., & Pöppel, E. (2007). Dopamine, learning and reward-seeking behavior. *Acta Neurobiologiae Experimentalis, 67*(4), 481–488.

Ashby, F. G., Isen, A. M., & Turken, A. U. (1999). A neuropsychological theory of positive affect and its influence on cognition. *Psychological Review, 106*(3), 529–550.

Baas, M., De Dreu, C.K.W., & Nijstad, B. A. (2008). A meta-analysis of 25 years of mood–creativity research: Hedonic tone, activation, or regulatory focus? *Psychological Bulletin, 134*(6), 779–806.

Baddeley, A. (1986). *Working memory.* Oxford: Clarendon Press.

Banaji, M. R., & Kihlstrom, J. F. (1996). The ordinary nature of alien abduction memories. *Psychological Inquiry, 7,* 132–135.

Bardo, M. T., Donohew, R. L., & Harrington, N. G. (1996). Psychobiology of novelty-seeking and drug-seeking behavior. *Behavioral Brain Research, 77,* 23–43.

Barron, F. (1969). *Creative person and creative process.* New York: Holt, Rinehart, and Winston.

Bechtereva, N. P., Korotkov, A. D., Pakhomov, S. V., Roudas, M. S., Starchenko, M. G., & Medvedev, S. V. (2004). PET study of brain maintenance of verbal creative activity. *International Journal of Psychophysiology, 53,* 11–20.

Beck, A. T., Rush, A. J., Shaw, B. F., & Emery, G. (1979). *Cognitive therapy of depression.* New York: Guilford Press.

Beeman, M., & Chiarello, C. (1998). *Right hemisphere language comprehension: Perspectives from cognitive neuroscience.* Mahwah, NJ: Erlbaum.

Bengtsson, S. L., Csikszentmihalyi, M., & Ullen, F. (2007). Cortical regions involved in the generation of musical structures during improvisation in pianists. *Journal of Cognitive Neuroscience, 19*(5), 830–842.

Berridge, K. C., & Robinson, T. E. (2003). Parsing reward. *Trends in Neurosciences, 26,* 507–513.

Biederman, I., & Vessel, E. A. (2006). Perceptual pleasure and the brain. *American Scientist, 94,* 247–253.

Blake, W., Erdman, D. V., & Bloom, H. (1982). *The complete poetry and prose of William Blake (newly revised ed.).* New York: Random House.

Breen, B. (2004). The 6 myths of creativity. *Fast Company,* December 1, 2004. Retrieved from www.fastcompany.com/magazine/89/creativity.html.

Brouziyne, M., & Molinaro, C. (2005). Mental imagery combined with physical practice of approach shots for golf beginners. *Perceptual and Motor Skills, 101*(1), 203–211.

Brown, S., & Vaughan, C. (2009). *Play: How it shapes the brain, opens the imagination, and invigorates the soul.* New York: Avery.

Buckner, R. L. (2010). The role of the hippocampus in prediction and imagination. *Annual Review of Psychology, 6,* 27–48.

Buckner, R. L., Andrews-Hanna, J. R., & Schacter, D. L. (2008). The brain's default network anatomy, function, and relevance to disease. *Annals of the New York Academy of Sciences, 1124,* 1–38.

Buss, D. (1989). Sex differences in human mate selection: Evolutionary hypotheses tested in 37 cultures. *Behavioral and Brain Sciences, 12*(1), 1–49.

Buss, D. (Ed). (2003). *The evolution of desire: Strategies of human mating.* (4th ed.). New York: Perseus.

Buss, D., & Barnes, M. (1986). Preferences in human mate selection. *Journal of Personality and Social Psychology, 50*(3), 559–570.

Cacioppo, J. T., Visser, P. S., & Pickett, C. L. (Eds). (2005). *Social neuroscience: People thinking about thinking people.* Cambridge, MA: MIT Press.

Cai, D. J., Mednick, S. A., Harrison, E. M., Kanady, J. C., & Mednick, S. C. (2009). REM, not incubation, improves creativity by priming associative networks. *Proceedings of the National Academy of Sciences (PNAS), 106*(25), 10130–10134.

Carlsson, I., Wendt, P. E., & Risberg, J. (2000). On the neurobiology of creativity: Differences in frontal activity between high and low creative subjects. *Neuropsychologia, 38,* 873–885.

Carson, S. H. (in press). Creativity and psychopathology: A genetic shared-vulnerability model. *Canadian Journal of Psychiatry.*

Carson, S. H. (2010a). Creativity and latent inhibition. In B. Lubow & I. Weiner (Eds.), *Latent inhibition: Data, theories, and applications to schizophrenia.* Cambridge, UK: Cambridge University Press.

Carson, S. H. (2010b). [Divergent thinking and self-reported increases in energy]. Unpublished raw data.

Carson, S. H., & Flaherty, A. (2010). Light therapy improves creativity (and productivity) independent of mood in subjects free of mood disorder. Manuscript submitted for publication.

Carson, S. H., & Langer, E. J. (2006). Mindfulness and self-acceptance. *Journal of Rational Emotive Behavioral Therapy, 24*(1), 29–43.

Carson, S. H., Peterson, J. B., & Higgins, D. M. (2003). Decreased latent inhibition is associated with increased creative achievement in high-functioning individuals. *Journal of Personality and Social Psychology, 85*(3), 499–506.

Carson, S. H., & Yong, E. (2010). [Creativity and mental shifting: Flexible movement between brain states]. Unpublished raw data.

Chambers, R., Lo, B.C.Y., & Allen, N. B. (2008). The impact of intensive mindfulness training on attentional control, cognitive style, and affect. *Cognitive Therapy and Research, 32*(3), 303–322.

Charron, S., & Koechlin, E. (2010). Divided representation of concurrent goals in the human frontal lobes. *Science, 328*(5976), 360–363.

Chase, W. G., & Simon, H. A. (1973). Perception in chess. *Cognitive Psychology, 4,* 55–81.

Christoff, K., Gordon, A., & Smith, R. (2010). The role of spontaneous thought in human cognition. In O. Vartanian & Dr. Mandel (Eds.), *Neuroscience of decision-making: Contemporary approaches to cognitive neuroscience.* New York: Psychology Press.

Clancy, S. (2005). *Abducted: How people come to believe they were kidnapped by aliens.* Cambridge: Harvard University Press.

Clark, D. A., & Beck, A. T. (1999). *Scientific foundations of cognitive theory and therapy of depression.* New York: Wiley.

Clark, L. V. (1960). Effect of mental practice on the development of a certain motor skill. *Research Quarterly of the American Association for Health, Physical Education, and Recreation, 31,* 560–569.

Coccaro, E. F., Hirsch, S. L., & Stein, M. A. (2007). Plasma homovanillic acid correlates inversely with history of learning problems in healthy volunteer and personality disordered subjects. *Psychiatry Research, 149*(1–3), 297–302.

Colvin, G. (2008). *Talent is overrated: What* really *separates world-class performers from everybody else.* New York: Penguin.

Cowan, N. (2005). *Working memory capacity.* New York: Psychology Press.

Craik, F.I.M., Moroz, T. M., & Moscovitch, M., et al. (1999). In search of the self: A positron emission tomography study. *Psychological Science, 10,* 26–34.

Craske, M. (2010). *Cognitive-behavioral therapy.* Washington, DC: American Psychological Association.

Csikszentmihalyi, M. (2008). *Flow: The psychology of optimal experience (P.S.).* New York: Harper Perennial Modern Classics.

Csikszentmihalyi, M. (1996). *Creativity: Flow and the psychology of discovery and invention.* New York: HarperCollins.

Csikszentmihalyi, M. Talk given on TED.com: www.ted.com/talks/lang/eng/ mihaly_csikszentmihalyi_on_flow.html.

Cummings, J. L. (1993). Frontal-subcortical circuits and human behavior. *Archives of Neurology, 50*(8), 873–880.

Dagenbach, D., & Carr, T. H. (Eds.). (1994). *Inhibitory processes in attention, memory and language.* New York: Academic Press.

Daniels-McGhee, S., & Davis, G. A. (1994). The imagery-creativity connection. *Journal of Creative Behavior, 28*(3), 150–176.

Dardis, T. (1989). *The thirsty muse: Alcohol and the American writer.* New York: Tichnor & Fields.

Davis, Francis. (1995). *The history of the blues.* New York: Hyperion.

de Bono, E. (1992). *Serious creativity: Using the power of lateral thinking to create new ideas.* New York: Harper.

D'Esposito, M., Detre, J. A., & Aguirre, G. K., et al. (1997). A functional MRI study of mental image generation. *Neuropsychologia, 35*(5), 725–730.

DeYoung, C. G., Peterson, J. B., & Higgins, D. M. (2005). Sources of openness/intellect: cognitive and neuropsychological correlates of the fifth factor of personality. *Journal of Personality, 73*(4), 825–858.

Dickinson, E., & Johnson, T. H. (1976). *The complete poems of Emily Dickinson.* New York: Back Bay Books.

Dietrich, A. (2007). The wavicle of creativity. *Methods, 42,* 1–2.

Dietrich, A. (2004a). The cognitive neuroscience of creativity. *Psychonomic Bulletin and Review, 11*(6), 1011–1026.

Dietrich, A. (2004b). Neurocognitive mechanisms underlying the experience of flow. *Consciousness and Cognition, 13,* 746–761.

Dietrich, A. (2003). Functional neuroanatomy of altered states of consciousness: The transient hypofrontality hypothesis. *Consciousness and Cognition, 12,* 231–256.

Doidge, N. (2007). *The brain that changes itself: Stories of personal triumph from the frontiers of brain science.* New York: Penguin.

Donaldson, V. W. (2000). A clinical study of visualization on depressed white blood cell count in medical patients. *Applied Psychophysiology and Biofeedback, 25*(2), 117–128.

Ebert-Schifferer, S., Singer, W., Staiti, P., Veca, A., & Wheelock, A. K. (2002). *Deceptions and illusions: Five centuries of trompe l'oeil painting.* Washington, DC: National Gallery of Art.

Einstein, A., & Infeld, L. (1938). *The evolution of physics.* New York: Simon & Schuster.

Emerson, R. W. (1856). The poet. In *Essays: Second series* (2nd ed.). Boston: Phillips, Sampson.

Ericsson, K. A., Krampe, R. T., & Tesch-Romer, C. (1993). The role of deliberate practice in the acquisition of expert performance. *Psychological Review, 100*(3), 363–406.

Eysenck, H. J. (1995). *Genius: The natural history of creativity.* Cambridge, UK: Cambridge University Press.

Farah, M. J. (1987). The neural basis of mental imagery. *Trends in Neurosciences, 12*(10), 395–399.

Farah, M. J., Haimm, C., Sankoorikal, C., & Chatterjee, A. (2009). When we enhance cognition with Adderall, do we sacrifice creativity? A preliminary study. *Psychopharmacology, 202,* 541–547.

Faw, B. (2006). Latest findings in the mechanisms of cortical "arousal": "Enabling" neural correlates for all consciousness. *Electroneurobiología, 14*(2), 199–210.

Federman, D. J. (2010). The co-joint change in kinaesthetic ability and *openness to experience* in the professional development of DMT trainees. *The Arts in Psychotherapy, 37*(1), 27–34.

Fink, A., Grabner, R. H., & Benedek, M., et al. (2009). The creative brain: Investigation of brain activity during creative problem solving by means of EEG and fMRI. *Human Brain Mapping, 30,* 734–748.

Fink, A., Grabner, R. H., Benedek, M., & Neubauer, A. C. (2006). Divergent thinking training is related to frontal electroencephalogram alpha synchronization. *European Journal of Neuroscience, 23,* 2241–2246.

Fischer, G., & Giaccardi, E. (2007) Sustaining social creativity. *Communications of the ACM, 50*(12), 28–29.

Fivush, R., & Haden, C. A. (Eds.). (2003). *Autobiographical memory and the construction of a narrative self: Developmental and cultural perspectives.* Mahwah, NJ: Erlbaum.

Flaherty, A.W. (2004). *The midnight disease.* Boston: Houghton Mifflin.

Fossati, P., Hevenor, S. J., & Graham, S. J., et al. (2003). In search of the emotional self: An FMRI study using positive and negative emotional words. *American Journal of Psychiatry, 160,* 1938–1945.

Fraser, H. W. (1991). Thomas Alva Edison. *World book encyclopedia, volume 6.* Chicago: World Book.

Freeman, A., & Golden, B. (1997). *Why didn't I think of that: Bizarre origins of ingenious inventions we couldn't live without.* New York: Wiley.

Frost, R. O., & Steketee, G. S. (1998). Hoarding: Clinical aspects and treatment strategies. In M. A. Jenike, L. Baer, & W. E. Minichiello (Eds.), *Obsessive-compulsive disorders: Practical management* (3rd ed.). St. Louis: Mosby Publishing.

Gallagher, R. (2005). Evidence-based psychotherapies for depressed adolescents: A review and clinical guidelines. *Primary Psychiatry, 12*(9), 33–39.

Galton, F. (1911). *Inquiries into human faculty and its development* (2nd ed.). New York: Dutton.

Gangemi, J. (2006). Creativity comes to B-School. *Business Week,* March 26, 2006. www.businessweek.com/print/bschools/content/mar2006/bs20060326_8436_bs001.htm?chan=bs.

Gardner, H. (1993). *Creating minds: An anatomy of creativity as seen through the lives of Freud, Einstein, Picasso, Stravinsky, Eliot, Graham and Gandhi.* New York: Basic Books.

Gawrysiak, M., Nicholas, C., & Hopko, D. R. (2009). Behavioral activation for moderately depressed university students: Randomized controlled trial. *Journal of Counseling Psychology, 56*(3), 468–475.

Gazzaniga, S. M., Ivry, R. B., & Mangun, G. R. (1998). *Cognitive neuroscience.* New York: Norton.

Ghiselin, B. (1952). *The creative process.* Berkeley: University of California Press.

Giles, J. (2004). Change of mind. *Nature, 430*(14), 14.

Golden, B. (2006). *Unlock your creative genius.* Amherst, NY: Prometheus.

Goleman, D. (1995). *Emotional intelligence: Why it can matter more than IQ.* New York: Bantam Books.

Goodwin, D. W. (1992). Alcohol as muse. *American Journal of Psychotherapy, 46*(3), 422–433.

Gray, J. A. (1990). Brain systems that mediate both emotion and cognition. *Cognition and Emotion, 4*(3), 269–288.

Gray, J. A., Joseph, M. H., & Hemsley, D. R., et al. (1995). The role of meso-limbic dopaminergic and retohippocampal afferents to the nucleus accumbens in latent inhibition: Implications for schizophrenia. *Behavioural Brain Research, 71*, 19–31.

Gray, N. S., Pickering, A. D., Hemsley, D. R., Dawling, S., & Gray, J. A. (1992). Abolition of latent inhibition by a single 5 mg dose of *d*-amphetamine in man. *Psychopharmacology, 107*, 425–430.

Greene, G. (1980). *Ways of escape.* New York: Simon & Schuster.

Grinband, J., Hirsch, J., & Ferrera, V. P. (2006). A neural representation of categorization uncertainty in the human brain. *Neuron, 49*, 757–763.

Gussak, D. (2009). The effects of art therapy on male and female inmates: Advancing the research base. *The Arts in Psychotherapy, 36*(10), 5–12.

Hahn, B., Wolkenberg, F. A., & Ross, T. J., et al. (2008). Divided versus selective attention: Evidence for common processing mechanisms. *Brain Research, 1215*, 137–146.

Harlow, J. M. (1868). Recovery from the passage of an iron bar through the head. *Publications of the Massachusetts Medical Society, 2*, 327–347. Republished in M. Macmillan (2000). *An odd kind of fame: Stories of Phineas Gage.* Cambridge, MA: MIT Press.

Harnad, S. (1990). Creativity: Method or magic? http://cogprints.org/1627/1/harnad.creativity.htm.

Heilman, K. M. (2005). *Creativity and the brain.* New York: Psychology Press.

Heilman, K. M., Nadeau, S. E., & Beversdorf, D. O. (2003). Creative innovation: Possible brain mechanisms. *Neurocase, 9*(5), 369–379.

Hennessey, B. A., & Amabile, T. M. (1988). The conditions of creativity. In R. J. Sternberg (Ed.), *The nature of creativity*. Cambridge, UK: Cambridge University Press.

Herrera, H. (1983). *A biography of Frida Kahlo*. New York: HarperCollins.

Higgins, S. T., & Silverman, K. (1999). *Motivating change among illicit drug abusers: Research on contingency management interventions*. Washington, DC: American Psychological Association.

Hobson, J. A., & Pace-Schott, E. F. (2002). The cognitive neuroscience of sleep: Neuronal systems, consciousness and learning. *Nature Neuroscience, 3*, 679–693.

Hobson, J. A., Pace-Schott, E. F., & Stickgold, R. (2000). Dreaming and the brain: Toward a cognitive neuroscience of conscious states. *Behavioral and Brain Sciences, 23*, 793–842.

Holton, G. (1973). *Thematic origins of scientific thought: Kepler to Einstein*. Cambridge, MA: Harvard University Press.

Horan, R. (2009). The neuropsychological connection between creativity and meditation. *Creativity Research Journal, 21*(2–3), 199–222.

Howard-Jones, P. A., Blakemore, S. J., Samuel, E. A., Summers, I. R., & Claxton, G. (2005). Semantic divergence and creative story generation: An fMRI investigation. *Cognitive Brain Research, 25*, 240–250.

Ikemoto, S., & Panksepp, J. (1999). The role of nucleus accumbens dopamine in motivated behavior: A unifying interpretation with special reference to reward-seeking. *Brain Research Reviews, 31*(1), 6–41.

Isen, A. M., Daubman, K. A., & Nowicki, G. P. (1987). Positive affect facilitates creative problem solving, *Journal of Personality and Social Psychology, 52*, 1122–1131.

Ivanovski, B., & Malhi, G. S. (2007). The psychological and neurophysiological concomitants of mindfulness forms of meditation. *Acta Neuropsychiatrica, 19*, 76–91.

James, W. (1890/1905). *The principles of psychology*. New York: Henry Holt.

Jamison, K. (1993). *Touched with fire*. New York: Free Press.

Jamison, K. (1989). Mood disorders and patterns of creativity in British writers and artists. *Psychiatry, 52*, 125–134.

Jang, K. L., Livesley, W. J., & Vernon, P. A. (1996). Heritability of the Big Five personality dimensions and their facets: A twin study. *Journal of Personality, 64*(3), 577–591.

Jensen, E. F. (2001). *Schumann*. New York: Oxford University Press.

Jung, R. E., Segall, J. M., & Bockholt, H. J., et al. (2010). Neuroanatomy of creativity. *Human Brain Mapping, 31*, 398–409.

Jung-Beeman, M., Bowden, E. M., Haberman, J., Frymiare, J. L., Arambel-Liu, S., & Greenblatt, R., et al. (2004). Neural activity when people solve verbal problems with insight. *PLoS Biology, 2,* 500–510.

Kaiser, D. A., & Othmer, C. (2000). Effect of neurofeedback on variables of attention in a large multi-center trial. *Journal of Neurotherapy, 4*(1), 5–15.

Kandel, E., Schwartz, J. H., & Jessell, T. M. (2000). *Principles of neural science.* New York: McGraw-Hill.

Kaplan, G. B., Greenblatt, D. J., & Ehrenberg, B. L., et al. (1997). Dose-dependent pharmacokinetics and psychomotor effects of caffeine in humans. *Journal of Clinical Pharmacology, 37*(8), 693–703.

Kaplan-Solms, K., & Solms, M. (2000). *Clinical studies in neuro-psychoanalysis: Introduction to a depth neuropsychology.* London: Karnac Books.

Kerr, B., Shaffer, J., Chambers, C., & Hallowell, K. (1991). Substance use of creatively talented adults. *Journal of Creative Behavior, 25,* 145–153.

Kinney, D. K., Richards, R., & Lowing, P. A., et al. (2000–2001). Creativity in offspring of schizophrenic and control parents: An adoption study. *Creativity Research Journal, 13*(1), 17–25.

Kolb, B., & Wishaw, I. Q. (2008). *Fundamentals of human neuropsychology* (6th ed.). New York: Worth.

Kosslyn, S. M., & Moulton, S. T. (2009). Mental imagery and implicit memory. In K. D. Markman, W.M.P. Klein, & J. A. Suhr (Eds.), *Handbook of imagination and mental simulation.* New York: Psychology Press.

Kosslyn, S. M., Thompson, W. L., & Ganis, G. (2006). *The case for mental imagery.* New York: Oxford University Press.

Kounios, J., Fleck, J. I., Green, D. L., Payne, L., Stevenson, J. L., Bowden, M., & Jung-Beeman, M. (2008). The origins of insight in resting state brain activity. *Neuropsychologia, 46,* 281–291.

Kowatari, Y., Lee, S. H., Yamamura, H., Nagamori, Y., Levy, P., Yamane, S., & Yamamoto, M. (2009). Neural networks involved in artistic creativity. *Human Brain Mapping, 30*(5), 1678–1690.

Kris, E. (1952). *Psychoanalytic explorations in art.* Madison, CT: International Universities Press.

Kubitz, K. A., and Pothakos, K. (1997). Does aerobic exercise decrease brain activation? *Journal of Sport and Exercise Psychology, 19,* 291–301.

Langer, E. J. (2005). *On becoming an artist.* New York: Ballantine.

Langer, E. J. (1997). *The power of mindful learning.* Reading, MA: Addison-Wesley.

Langer, E. J. (1989). *Mindfulness.* Reading, MA: Addison-Wesley.

LeBoutillier, N., & Marks, D. F. (2003). Mental imagery and creativity: A meta-analytic review study. *British Journal of Psychology, 94,* 29–44.

LeDoux, J. E. (2000). Emotion circuits in the brain. *Annual Review of Neuroscience, 23,* 155–184.

LeMay, P. (2007). Developing a pattern language for flow experiences in video games. *Situated Play, Proceedings of DiGRA 2007 Conference,* 449–455. Retrieved from www.digra.org/dl/db/07311.53582.pdf.

Lewinsohn, P. M., Mischef, W., Chapion, W., & Barton, R. (1980). Social competence and depression: The role of illusory self-perceptions. *Journal of Abnormal Psychology, 89,* 203–212.

Lewinsohn, P. M., Rohde, P., Seeley, J. R., & Fischer, S. A. (1993). Age-cohort changes in the lifetime occurrence of depression and other mental disorders. *Journal of Abnormal Psychology, 102*(1), 110–120.

Lilienfeld, S. O., Wood, J. M., & Garb, H. N (2001). What's wrong with this picture? *Scientific American, 284*(5), 80–87.

Limb, C. J., & Braun, A. R. (2008). Neural substrates of spontaneous musical performance: An fMRI study of jazz improvisation. *PLoS One, 3*(2), e1679.

Linden, D. E. (2006). How psychotherapy changes the brain—the contribution of functional neuroimaging. *Molecular Psychiatry, 11,* 528–538.

Logie, R. H., Venneri, A., Sala, S. D., Redpath, T. W., & Marshall, I. (2003). Brain activation and the phonological loop: The impact of rehearsal. *Brain and Cognition, 53*(2), 293–296.

Lohman, D. F., & Nichols, P. D. (1990). Training spatial abilities: Effects of practice on rotation and synthesis tasks. *Learning and Individual Differences, 2*(1), 67–93.

Lombroso, C. (1891/1976). *The man of genius.* London: Walter Scott.

Longe, O., Maratos, F. A., & Gilbert, P., et al. (2010). Having a word with yourself: Neural correlates of self-criticism and self-reassurance. *NeuroImage, 49*(2), 1849–1856.

Ludwig, A. (1995). *The price of greatness: Resolving the creativity and madness controversy.* New York: Guilford Press.

Lyshak-Stelzer, F., Singer, P., St. John, P., & Chemtob, C. M. (2007). Art therapy for adolescents with posttraumatic stress disorder symptoms: A pilot study. *Art Therapy, 24*(4), 163–169.

Lythgoe, M.F.X., Pollak, T. A., Kalmus, M., deHaan, M., & Chong, W. K. (2005). Obsessive, prolific artistic output following subarachnoid hemorrhage. *Neurology, 64,* 397–398.

Maher, B. A. (1988). Anomalous experience and delusional thinking: The logic of explanations. In T. F. Oltmanss & B. A. Maher (Eds.), *Delusional beliefs* (pp. 15–33). New York: Wiley-Interscience.

Martindale, C. (1999). Biological basis of creativity. In R. J. Sternberg (Ed.), *Handbook of creativity*. Cambridge, UK: Cambridge University Press.

McCrae, R. R. (1994). Openness to experience: Expanding the boundaries of Factor V. *European Journal of Personality, 8,* 251–272.

McCrae, R. R. (1987). Creativity, divergent thinking, and openness to experience. *Journal of Personality and Social Psychology, 52*(6), 1258–1263.

McCrae, R. R., & Costa, P. T., Jr. (1987). Validation of the five-factor model of personality across instruments and observers. *Journal of Personality and Social Psychology, 52,* 81–90.

McCrae, R. R., & John, O. P. (1992). An introduction to the Five-Factor Model and its applications. *Journal of Personality, 60*(2), 175–215.

Mednick, M. T., Mednick, S. A., & Jung, C. C. (1964). Continual association and function of level of creativity and type of verbal stimulus. *Journal of Abnormal and Social Psychology, 69,* 511–515.

Mednick, S. (1962). The associative basis of the creative process. *Psychological Review, 69,* 220–232.

Metcalfe, J., & Wiebe, D. (1987). Intuition in insight and noninsight problem solving. *Memory & Cognition, 15*(3), 238–246.

Miller, B. D., & Cummings, J. L. (2006). *The human frontal lobe: Functions and disorders* (2nd ed.). New York: Guilford Press.

Miller, B. L., Boone, K., Cummings, J., Read, S. L., & Mishkin, F. (2000). Functional correlates of musical and visual talent in frontotemporal dementia. *British Journal of Psychiatry, 176,* 458–463.

Miller, G. (2000). Sexual selection for indicators of intelligence. In G. Bock, J. Goode, & K. Webb (Eds.), *The nature of intelligence*. Novartis Foundation Symposium 233. Chichester, West Sussex, UK: Wiley.

Miller, G. F. (2001). Aesthetic fitness: how sexual selection shaped artistic virtuosity as a fitness indicator and aesthetic preference as mate choice criteria. *Bulletin of Psychology and the Arts, 2,* 20–25.

Monti, D. A., Peterson, C., & Kunkel, E. J., et al. (2006). A randomized, controlled trial of mindfulness-based art therapy (MBAT) for women with cancer. *Psycho-Oncology, 15*(5), 363–373.

Moore, D. (2009). John Grisham marks 20th anniversary of "A Time to Kill." *USA Today,* updated June 22, 2009. Retrieved online at www.usatoday.com/life/books/news/2009-06-21-john-grisham-a-time-to-kill_N.htm.

Moskowitz, G., & Grant, H., (Eds.). (2009). *The psychology of goals*. New York: Guilford Press.

Munafò, M., Durant, C., Lewis, G., & Flint, J. (2009). Gene x environment interactions at the serotonin transporter locus. *Biological Psychiatry, 65,* 211–219.

Nasar, S. (1998). *A beautiful mind: The life of mathematical genius and Nobel laureate John Nash*. New York: Simon & Schuster.

National Institute on Drug Abuse. (2009). The neurobiology of drug addiction. www.drugabuse.gov/pubs/Teaching/Teaching2/Teaching.html.

Nettle, D. (2006). Schizotypy and mental health amongst poets, visual artists, and mathematicians. *Journal of Research in Personality, 40,* 876–890.

Nettle, D., & Clegg, H. (2006). Schizotypy, creativity and mating success in humans. *Proceedings of the Royal Society, B. Biological Sciences, 273*(1586), 611–615.

Nilsson, L. G., Sternang, O., Ronnlund, M., & Nyburg, L. (2009). Challenging the notion of an early-onset of cognitive decline. *Neurobiology of Aging, 30,* 521–524.

Norlander, T., & Gustafson, R. (1998). Effects of alcohol on a divergent figural fluency test during the illumination phase of the creative process. *Creativity Research Journal, 11,* 265–274.

Norlander, T., & Gustafson, R. (1996). Effects of alcohol on scientific thought during the incubation phase of the creative process. *Journal of Creative Behavior, 30(4),* 231–248.

Northoff, G., Heinzel, A., de Greck, M., Bermpohl, F., Dobrowolny, H., & Panksepp, J. (2006). Self-referential processing in our brain: A meta-analysis of imaging studies on the self. *NeuroImage, 31,* 440–457.

Ochse, R. (1990). *Before the gates of excellence: The determinants of creative genius*. New York: Cambridge University Press.

Oettingen, G., & Gollwitzer, P. M. (2002). Self-regulation of goal pursuit: Turning hope thoughts into behavior. *Psychological Inquiry, 13,* 304–307.

Olds, J., & Milner, P. (1954). Positive reinforcement produced by electrical stimulation of the septal area and other regions of rat brain. *Journal of Comparative and Physiological Psychology, 47,* 419–427.

O'Neill, E. (1956). *Long day's journey into night*. First performed on February 2, 1956, at the Royal Dramatic Theater in Stockholm, Sweden.

Osborn, A. F. (1963). *Applied imagination: Principles and procedures of creative problem solving* (3rd ed.). New York: Scribner.

Panksepp, J. (2004). *Affective neuroscience: The foundations of human and animal emotions*. New York: Oxford University Press.

Paquette, V., Levesque, J., & Mensour, B., et al. (2003). Change the mind and you change the brain: Effects of cognitive-behavioral therapy on the neural correlates of spider phobia. *NeuroImage 18*, 401– 409.

Parasuraman, R. (1998). The attentive brain: Issues and prospects. In R. Parasuraman (Ed.), *The attentive brain* (pp. 3–15). Cambridge, MA: MIT Press.

Parasuraman, R., Warm, J. S., & See, J. E. (1998). Brain systems of vigilance. In R. Parasuraman (Ed.), *The attentive brain* (pp. 221–256). Cambridge, MA: MIT Press.

Peden, A. R., Rayens, M. K., Hall, L. A., & Beebe, L. H. (2001). Preventing depression in high-risk college women: A report of an 18-month follow-up. *Journal of American College Health, 49*(6), 299–306.

Pennebaker, J. W. (1997). Writing about emotional experiences as a therapeutic process. *Psychological Science, 8*(3), 162–166.

Pennebaker, J. W., & Chung, C. K. (2007). Expressive writing, emotional upheavals, and health. In H. S. Friedman & R. C. Silver (Eds.), *Foundations of health psychology*. New York: Oxford University Press.

Pepperberg, I. M. (2008). *Alex & me: How a scientist and a parrot uncovered a hidden world of animal intelligence—and formed a deep bond in the process.* New York: HarperCollins.

Pepperberg, I. M. (1999). *The Alex studies: Cognitive and communicative abilities of grey parrots.* Cambridge, MA: Harvard University Press.

Perkins, D. (2000). *Archimedes' bathtub: The art and logic of breakthrough thinking.* New York: Norton.

Peterson, J. B., & Carson, S. (2000). Latent inhibition and openness to experience in a high-achieving student population. *Personality and Individual Differences, 28*(2), 323–332.

Peterson, J. B., Smith, K., & Carson, S. (2002). Openness and extraversion are associated with reduced latent inhibition: Replication and commentary. *Personality and Individual Differences, 33*, 1137–1147.

Pickover, C. A. (1998). *Strange brains and genius.* New York: Plenum Press.

Pink, D. H. (2005). *A whole new mind: Why right-brainers will rule the future.* New York: Riverhead Books.

Plutchik, R. (2003). *Emotions and life: Perspectives from psychology, biology, and evolution.* Washington, DC: American Psychological Association.

Porto, P. R., Oliveira, L., & Mari, J., et al. (2009). Does cognitive behavioral therapy change the brain? A systematic review of neuroimaging in anxiety disorders. *Journal of Neuropsychiatry and Clinical Neurosciences, 21*, 114–125.

Prentky, R. (1989). Creativity and psychopathology: Gamboling at the seat of madness. In J. A. Glover, R. R. Ronning, & C. R. Reynolds (Eds.), *Handbook of creativity*. New York: Plenum Press.

Pronin, E., & Wegner, D. M. (2006). Manic thinking: Independent effects of thought speed and thought content on mood. *Psychological Science, 17*(9), 807–813.

Rakic, P. (2002). Neurogenesis in adult primate neocortex: An evaluation of the evidence. *Nature Reviews Neuroscience, 3*, 65–71.

Ramachandran, V. S., & Hubbard, E. M. (May, 2003). Hearing colors, tasting shapes. *Scientific American, 289*(5), 53–59.

Ramachandran, V. S., & Hubbard, E. M. (2001). Synaesthesia—A window into perception, thought and language. *Journal of Consciousness Studies, 8*, 3–34.

Rand, A. (1943/1993). *The fountainhead.* New York: Plume Books.

Rawlings, D., & Locarnini, A. (2006). Dimensional schizotypy, autism, and unusual word associations in artists and scientists. *Journal of Research in Personality, 42*(2), 465–471.

Razumnikova, O. M. (2007). Creativity related cortex activity in the remote associates task. *Brain Research Bulletin, 73*(1–3), 96–102.

Razumnikova, O. M. (2000). Functional organization of different brain areas during convergent and divergent thinking: An EEG investigation. *Cognitive Brain Research, 10*, 11–18.

Raichle, M. E., MacLeod, A. M., Snyder, A. Z., Powers, W. J., Gusnard, D. A., & Shulman, G. L. (2001). A default mode of brain function. *Proceedings of the National Academy of Sciences USA, 98*(2), 676–682.

Richards, R., Kinney, D. K., & Lunde, I., et al. (1988). Creativity in manic-depressives, cyclothymes, their normal relatives, and control subjects. *Journal of Abnormal Psychology, 97*, 281–288.

Ridderinkhof, K. R., Ullsperger, M., Crone, E. A., & Nieuwenhuis, N. (2004). The role of the medial frontal cortex in cognitive control. *Science, 306*(5695), 443–447.

Roozenburg, N.F.M., & Eekels. J. (1995). *Product design: Fundamentals and methods.* Chichester, West Sussex, UK: Wiley.

Roth, E. A., & Smith, K. H. (2008). The *Mozart effect*: Evidence for the arousal hypothesis. *Perceptual and Motor Skills, 107*(2), 396–402.

Runco, M. A. (2007). *Creativity: Theories and themes: Research, development, and practice.* Burlington, MA: Elsevier Academic Press.

Runco, M. A. (1999). Divergent thinking. In M. A. Runco and S. R. Pritzker (Eds.), *Encyclopedia of creativity.* (Vol. 2, pp. 103–108). San Diego: Academic Press.

Salinger, J. D. (1951). *The catcher in the rye.* New York: Little, Brown.

Salthouse, T. (2009). When does age-related cognitive decline begin? *Neuro-biology of Aging, 30*(4), 507–514.

Sanfey, A. G., Loewenstein, G., McClure, S. M., & Cohen, J. D. (2006). Neuro-economics: Cross-currents in research on decision-making. *Trends in Cognitive Sciences, 10*(3), 108–116.

Schacter, D. L. (1996). *Searching for memory: The brain, the mind, and the past.* New York: Basic Books.

Schaie, K. W. (2009). "When does age-related cognitive decline begin?" Salthouse again reifies the "cross-sectional fallacy." *Neurobiology of Aging, 30,* 528–529.

Schellenberg, E. G. (2003). Does exposure to music have beneficial side effects? In I. Peretz & R. Zatorre (Eds.), *The cognitive neuroscience of music* (pp. 430–448). New York: Oxford University Press.

Scherer, K. R. (1984). On the nature and function of emotion: A component process approach. In K. R. Scherer & P. Ekman (Eds.), *Approaches to emotion* (pp. 293–317). Hillsdale, NJ: Erlbaum.

Schiffer, F. (1998). *Of two minds: The revolutionary science of dual-brain psychology.* New York: Free Press.

Schneider, S., Brümmer, V., Abel, T., Askew, C. D., & Strüder, H. K. (2009). Changes in brain cortical activity measured by EEG are related to individual exercise preferences. *Physiology & Behavior, 98,* 447–452.

Schwarz, N., & Bohner, G. (1996). Feelings and their motivational implications: Moods and the action sequence. In P. M. Gollwitzer & J. A. Bargh (Eds.), *The psychology of action: Linking cognition and motivation to behavior* (pp. 119–145). New York: Guilford.

Scott, G., Leritz, L. E., & Mumford, M. D. (2004). The effectiveness of creativity training: A quantitative review. *Creativity Research Journal, 16*(4), 361–388.

Seifert, C. M., Meyer, D. E., Davidson, N., Patalano, A. L., & Yaniv, I. (1995). Demystification of cognitive insight: Opportunistic assimilation and the prepared-mind perspective. In R. J. Sternberg & J. E. Davidson (Eds.), *The nature of insight* (pp. 65–124). Cambridge, MA: MIT Press.

Seeley, W. W., Matthews, B. R., & Crawford, R. K., et al. (2008). Unravelling Bolero: progressive aphasia, transmodal creativity and the right posterior neocortex. *Brain, 131,* 39–49.

Shaw, K. (2000). *The mammoth book of oddballs and eccentrics.* New York: Carroll & Graf.

Siddharthan, R. (1999). Music, mathematics and Bach. *Resonance, 4*(5), 61–70.

Silver, J. (2010). Publishing books, memoirs, and other creative non-fiction. Retrieved from www.harvardwriters.com.

Simon, H. A., & Chase, W. G. (1973). Skill in chess. *American Scientist, 61,* 364–403.

Simonton, D. K. (1999). *Origins of genius: Darwinian perspectives on creativity.* New York: Oxford University Press.

Simonton, D. K. (1997). Creative productivity: A predictive and explanatory model of career trajectories and landmarks. *Psychological Review, 104,* 66–89.

Skeat, T. C. (1963–64). Kubla Khan. *British Museum Quarterly, 26*(3–4), 77–83.

Smith, S. A., & Dodds, R. A. (1999). Incubation. In M. A. Runco and S. R. Pritzker (Eds.), *Encyclopedia of creativity* (vol. 2, pp. 39–43). San Diego: Academic Press.

Solms, M., & Turnbull, O. (2002). *The brain and the inner world: An introduction to the neuroscience of subjective experience.* New York: Other Press.

Solomon, M. (1980). On Beethoven's creative process: A two-part invention. *Music and Letters, 61,* 272–283.

Sporns, O., Chialvo, D. R., Kaiser, M., Hilgetag, C. C. (2004). Organization, development and function of complex brain networks. *Trends in Cognitive Sciences, 8*(9), 418–425.

Starchenko, M. G., Bechtereva, N. P., Pakhomov, S. V., & Medvedev, S. V. (2003). Study of the brain organization of creative thinking. *Human Physiology, 29,* 151–152.

Steinberg, H., Sykes, E. A., & Moss, T., et al. (1997). Exercise enhances creativity independently of mood. *British Journal of Sports Medicine, 31*(3), 240–245.

Stone, I. (Ed.). (1937). *Dear Theo: The autobiography of Vincent Van Gogh.* New York: Signet.

Stukeley, W. (1936). *Memoirs of Sir Isaac Newton's life.* London: Taylor and Francis (edited by A. H. White; originally published in 1752).

Styron, W. (1990). *Darkness visible: A memoir of madness.* New York: Random House.

Swartwood, M. O., Swartwood, J. N., & Farrell, J. (2003). Stimulant treatment of ADHD: Effects on creativity and flexibility in problem solving. *Creativity Research Journal, 15*(4), 417–419.

Szpunar, K. K. (2010). Episodic future thought: An emerging concept. *Perspectives in Psychological Science, 5,* 142–162.

Szpunar, K. K., & McDermott, K. B. (2009). Episodic future thought: Remembering the past to imagine the future. In K. D. Markman, W.M.P. Klein, & J. A. Suhr (Eds.), *Handbook of imagination and mental simulation.* New York: Psychology Press.

Szpunar, K. K., Watson, J. M., & McDermott, K. B. (2006). Neural substrates of envisioning the future. *Proceedings of the National Academy of Sciences (PNAS), 104*(2), 642–647.

Taylor, J. A., & Shaw, D. F. (2002). The effects of outcome imagery on golf-putting performance. *Journal of Sports Sciences, 20*(8), 607–613.

Terman, D. (2008). Marketing your creativity. Talk given for Psy E-1240 on April 22, 2008, Harvard University.

Tesla, N., & Johnston, B. (1919/1982). *My inventions: The autobiography of Nikola Tesla.* Austin, TX: Hart Bros.

Tolkien, J.R.R. (1954–55/2005). *The lord of the rings (50th anniversary ed.).* Boston: Houghton Mifflin Harcourt.

Tomporowski, P. D. (2003). Effects of acute bouts of exercise on cognition. *Acta Psychologica Amsterdam, 112*(3), 297–324.

Tsigos, C., & Chrousos, G. P. (2002). Hypothalamic-pituitary-adrenal axis, neuroendocrine factors, and stress. *Journal of Psychosomatic Research, 53,* 865–871.

Tubs, M. E. (1986). Goal setting: A meta-analytic examination of the empirical evidence. *Journal of Applied Psychology, 71*(3), 474–483.

Twenge, J., Gentile, B., DeWall, C. N., Ma, D., Lacefield, K., & Schurtz, D. R. (2010). Birth cohort increases in psychopathology among young Americans, 1938–2007: A cross-temporal meta-analysis of the MMPI. *Clinical Psychology Review, 30*(2), 145–154.

Ulene, V. (2009). Antidepressants: The right people aren't always getting them. *Los Angeles Times,* May 1, 2009. Retrieved from http://articles .latimes.com/2009/may/11/health/he-themd11.

Vaillant, G. E. (1977). *Adaptation to life.* Boston: Little, Brown.

Vandenberg, S. G., & Kuse, A. R. (1978). Mental rotations, a group test of three-dimensional spatial visualization. *Perceptual and Motor Skills, 47,* 599–601.

Vogels, R., Sary, G., Dupont, P., & Orban, G. A. (2002). Human brain regions involved in visual categorization. *NeuroImage, 16,* 401–414.

Vorderman, C. (2007). *Super brain: 101 easy ways to a more agile mind.* New York: Gotham Books.

Voss, U., Holzmann, R., Tuin, I., & Hobson, J. A. (2009). Lucid dreaming: A state of consciousness with features of both waking and non-lucid dreaming. *Sleep, 32*(9), 1191–1200.

Walker, M. P., Liston, C., Hobson, J. A., & Stickgold, R. (2002). Cognitive flexibility across the sleep-wake cycle: REM-sleep enhancement of anagram problem solving. *Cognitive Brain Research, 14*(3), 317–324.

Wallas, G. (1926). *The art of thought.* New York: Harcourt Brace.

Walton, M. E., Devlin, J. T., & Rushworth, M.F.S. (2004). Interactions between decision making and performance monitoring within prefrontal cortex. *Nature Neuroscience, 7,* 1259–1265.

Warner, L., & McNeill, M. E. (1988). Mental imagery and its potential for physical therapy. *Physical Therapy, 68*(4), 516–521.

Watson, D., & Clark, L. A. (1994). Emotions, moods, traits and temperament: conceptual distinctions and empirical findings. In P. Ekman & R. J. Davidson (Eds.), *The nature of emotions: Fundamental questions.* New York: Oxford University Press.

Way, B. M., Creswell, J. D., Eisenberger, N. I., & Lieberman, M. D. (2010). Dispositional mindfulness and depressive symptomatology: Correlations with limbic and self-referential neural activity during rest. *Emotion, 10*(1), 12–24.

Weisberg, R. (1993). *Creativity: Beyond the myth of genius.* New York: Freeman.

Weiskopf, N., Scharnowski, F., Veit, R., Goebel, R., Birbaumer, N., & Mathiak, K. (2004). Self-regulation of local brain activity using real-time functional magnetic resonance imaging (fMRI). *Journal of Physiology (Paris), 98,* 357–373.

Westfall, R. (1994). *The life of Isaac Newton.* Cambridge, UK: Cambridge University Press.

White, H. A., & Shah, P. (2006). Training attention-switching ability in adults with ADHD. *Journal of Attention Disorders, 10,* 44–53.

Williams, R. W., & Herrup, K. (1988). The control of neuron number. *Annual Review of Neuroscience, 11,* 423–453.

Witelson, S. F., Kigar, D. L., & Harvey, T. (1999). The exceptional brain of Albert Einstein. *The Lancet, 353,* 2149–2153.

Woolfolk, R. L., Parrish, M. W., & Murphy, S. M. (1985). The effects of positive and negative imagery on motor skill performance. *Cognitive Therapy and Research, 9,* 335–341.

World Health Organization. (2001). *Mental health: New understanding, new hope.* Geneva: World Health Organization.

Wrisberg, C. A., & Anshel, M. H. (1989). The effect of cognitive strategies on the free throw shooting performance of young athletes. *The Sport Psychologist, 3*(2), 95–104.

Yanagisawa, H., Ippeita, D., & Tsuzuki, D., et al. (2010). Acute moderate exercise elicits increased dorsolateral prefrontal activation and improves cognitive performance with stroop test. *NeuroImage, 50*(4), 1702–1710.

Yates, L. G. (1986). Effect of visualization training on spatial ability test scores. *Journal of Mental Imagery, 10*(1), 81–91.

Zaslow, J. (2005). What if Einstein took Ritalin? ADHD's impact on creativity. *Wall Street Journal,* February 3, 2005, p. D1.

✳ ABOUT THE AUTHOR

Shelley Carson received her PhD in psychology from Harvard University, where she continues to teach, conduct research, and publish on the topics of creativity, psychopathology, and resilience. Her work has been featured on the Discovery Channel, CNN, and NPR, and she has won multiple teaching awards for her popular course "Creativity: Madmen, Geniuses, and Harvard Students." She also writes the Life as Art blog for *Psychology Today*, and discusses current findings in creativity research on her Web site http://ShelleyCarson.com.

✳ ABOUT HARVARD MEDICAL SCHOOL

Since 1782 Harvard Medical School has been an international leader in the effort to improve healthcare and decrease human suffering from disease. Today there are more than 10,000 faculty members who practice in 17 affiliated hospitals and research institutions. Harvard Health Publications is the consumer health publishing division of Harvard Medical School and draws on the expertise of faculty members to translate the latest research in order to help individuals improve their health and quality of life.

For more information on Harvard Health Publications, go to health.harvard.edu.

✳ INDEX